THE CITIZEN'S
Constitution

AN ANNOTATED GUIDE

SETH LIPSKY

BASIC BOOKS

A Member of the Perseus Books Group
New York

Hardcover edition was first published in 2009 by Basic Books,
A Member of the Perseus Books Group
Paperback edition was first published in 2011 by Basic Books

Designed by Jeff Williams

Library of Congress Cataloging-in-Publication Data
Lipsky, Seth.
  The citizen's constitution / Seth Lipsky
    p. cm.
  Includes bibliographical references and index.
  Hardcover ISBN 978-0-465-01858-1 (alk. paper)
    1. United States—Popular works. 2. Constitutional law—United States—Popular works.
  I. Title.

KF4550.Z9L57 2009
342.7302—DC22
                                                                      2009023043

Paperback ISBN: 978–0–465–02124–6
E-book ISBN: 978-0-465-02430-8

10 9 8 7 6 5 4 3 2 1

THE CITIZEN'S
Constitution

Contents

IN MEMORY OF MY FATHER

KARL LIPSKY

PREFACE

The enthusiasm that has greeted *The Citizen's Constitution* is no doubt related to the fact that our country is in what might be called a constitutional moment. Almost every week a new story bursts into the headlines. Nearly half the states in the union are challenging the constitutionality of a new national health care plan. Gyrating world currency markets are igniting a debate over the constitutional meaning of money. Arizona is precipitating a showdown with the federal government over who controls immigration. Our courts—and our newspaper columns—are crackling with the question of habeas corpus. The states are wrestling with whether to permit the laws of marriage to comprise same-sex unions. Technology is making it possible for our privacy to be invaded in ways undreamed of in the past. The Supreme Court's decision to vouchsafe the rights of a conservative group to air a film critical of a Senate candidate during the election season is triggering a bitter debate over whether corporations and organizations should guaranteed free speech. Every one of these issues, and countless more, will be worked out with reference to a parchment of fewer than eight thousand words, written, for the most part, ten generations ago.

Yet the excitement of the moment was not what originally inspired the present volume. It grew slowly during my forty years as newspaper editor, a career in which I presided at thousands of daily editorial meetings, hardly one of which passed without at least a reference to some provision of the document that has established our system of checks and balances. It is a career that has left me astonished at the scale and range of problems that can be, and so often are, reasoned out against the clauses of our national law—whether it be a boat owner in Pennsylvania seeking the right to oysters in the beds of New Jersey, a foreign diplomat in Ohio trying to prevent his

American wife from winning a divorce, or a retired security guard wanting to keep a pistol at his home—to name but a few of the situations in which ordinary individuals sought to solve a problem by turning to a law written by giants long before they were born.

The need for a layman's edition of the Constitution struck me one day when I pulled out the pocket edition that had been published by the commission the government established for the 200th anniversary of the signing.[1] The topic on the table was the right to privacy—we'd been talking about abortion—and I needed a quick reference. I had the government's little edition handy; it's small enough to tuck into a wallet. But I discovered that neither the Constitution nor the government pamphlet contains the word "privacy" per se, even though it is central to one of the most controversial cases in American history.[2] Nor did the pocket edition contain any reference to case law, to the intentions of the founders, or to the actions of Congress that might illuminate the point about privacy that had come under dispute.

At the time I could have consulted the edition of the Constitution containing an analysis, interpretation, and annotation of cases prepared by the Congressional Research Service of the Library of Congress and issued by the Government Printing Office.[3] But that volume, which runs to some two thousand pages, wasn't handy; even had it been, I'd have found that, like Edward Corwin's classic edition, what it contains is more helpful to a legal scholar than to a layman. Another magnificent compendium, *The Founders' Constitution*, compiled by Professors Kurland and Lerner of the University of Chicago, runs to five volumes, though it has become more accessible in recent years in a paperback edition from the Liberty Fund. It would have been difficult to have these volumes at hand when, a year or so later, I was trying to ex-

---

1. September 17, 1987.

2. *Roe v. Wade.*

3. Established pursuant to the requirement of the founding fathers that each house of Congress publish a regular journal of its proceedings.

plain to a European friend the reason that gun control is not such an easy question in America.[4]

Another conversation that left me in need of this book concerned the gold standard, which has been back in the news in the midst of a global financial crisis that has heard a number of leaders call for the establishment of a new world currency. It was easy to discover that the word "gold" occurs once in the Constitution[5] it was less easy to discover what kind of intent lay behind, and what kind of experience lay in front of, the famous phrasing concerning the obligations of the states. In the course of answering that riddle I found myself consulting half a dozen books when I would have preferred to rely on only one. And what did the authors of the Constitution mean by the word "dollars," which is used twice in the document? These are the sorts of questions a newspaper editor can encounter.

So I set out to produce the present volume. It differs from other annotations in that it is a citizen's guide—a view of the Constitution by an editor who hews to what might be called the plain language school of the law. It distills into notes a reading of the standard texts surrounding the Constitution. These include the several records kept of the Convention held at Philadelphia that sweltering summer of 1787, among them James Madison's notes, Justice Yates's "Secret Proceedings," and Luther Martin's marvelous memo to the legislature of Maryland, "The Genuine Information." These also include the letters and journalism hammered out during the referenda held in the thirteen states of the young Confederation on whether to ratify the document. Of this material, the *Federalist Papers*, written under the pen name "Publius," are the most famous, but there are myriad others, all illuminating intent. Experience is reported and ruled upon in the opinions of the high court. These form the Himalayas of legal precedent in whose foothills we hoe the vines of liberty.

This volume leavens these weighty references with a career's worth of reading and reporting the news at home and abroad—a

---

4. The Second Amendment.
5. Article I, Section 10.

marbling of the constitutional cake, so to speak, with a newspaper-man's batter. It does not always focus on the definitive decisions of the Supreme Court, though an effort has been made to touch on the main ones. Sometimes interest was piqued by the newsworthiness or the irony or the humor of a case. It was not surprising to discover the relevance of the arguments of the partisans of the Constitution to what we are talking about today. What was surprising was the relevance of the arguments put forward by the opponents of the Constitution, the so-called Anti-Federalists. We tend to think of the newspaper columns written to win the toughest ratification fight[6] as works of surpassing wisdom. It turns out that James Madison, Alexander Hamilton, John Jay, and the boys—meaning the Federalists—could be slippery characters, offering with regard to the rights of the states reassurances that look, two centuries later, almost disingenuous. The Constitutional Convention itself was held in such secrecy that George Washington upbraided his fellow delegates when one of them dropped a scrap of paper on the floor.

To a surprising degree the matters that were disputed then are still being fought over today. Some say that the openness of the Constitution to interpretation is its greatest feature. They thrill to it as a living document. Life is constantly breathed into it anew, and not only by judges and lawyers and congressmen and presidents. Yet others say that the Constitution's greatest strength is its immutability—the notion that it sets a standard against which our laws can be measured. Certainly both sides agree that much constitutional work remains to be done. The Bill of Rights, when ratified, applied only to the Congress. It did not apply to the states. It was not until the Fourteenth Amendment that the process of incorporating its protections to the states was permitted—a process that for more than a century has been taking place in scores of cases in scores of courtrooms and is far from completed.

---

6. New York. Although Rhode Island was the last to ratify, New York's fight was the most glorious.

Whether one prefers the so-called living Constitution of, say, Justices Brennan or Breyer or the so-called dead Constitution of Justice Scalia, the fact is that not all matters can be solved by the Constitution. America's greatest failure, slavery, was one of them. The founders shrank from confronting it, choosing compromise in exchange for a nation. Slavery confounded the courts at nearly every turn, culminating in the catastrophe of *Dred Scott*, in which the Supreme Court itself proved inadequate and told a black man who had lived on free soil that he could never be an American. The whole country seemed to understand that the next stop was civil war and, it turned out, a rewriting of our fundamental law in an effort to expiate our nation's original sin.

All the more inspiring is the fact that ordinary Americans continue to turn to the Constitution, loyalty to which more than anything else—race, religion, national origin, language—defines what it means to be an American. This has led me to the view that the real heroes of constitutional law are the citizens themselves, the litigants who put their faith in the courts and the Constitution and often devote their life savings to the contest. One of my favorite stories is that of the vagrant who was thrown into the dock on charges of breaking into a poolroom at Panama City, Florida. He swore he was innocent, and throughout his trial he kept insisting the Supreme Court said he had the right to a lawyer. He pressed his case long after he was sent to prison, where he retreated to the library and, by hand, wrote his own appeals.

One of the appeals he scrawled—called a pauper's petition—was noticed at the Supreme Court, which assigned one of the greatest legal minds in the country[7] to argue his case. The prisoner was famously wrong about what he said at his own trial—that the Supreme Court said he had a right to counsel. It hadn't said so— yet. But the prisoner, the Court decided, turned out to be right about the Constitution. It established the right to a lawyer for all

---

7. Abe Fortas was eventually named an associate justice of the Supreme Court.

accused of crimes in America. The Supreme Court ordered a new trial, but the prisoner refused the high-powered lawyers assigned to handle his case. He insisted on using a local lawyer from the town where the crime was committed. The local lawyer was able to elicit testimony that cleared the prisoner, whose name—Clarence Earl Gideon[8]—will be remembered as long as there is an America. I have thought about *Gideon v. Wainright*[9] hundreds of times over the years. What I keep marveling at is the astounding thing this vagrant accomplished by dint of having at some point either read the Constitution or heard some mortal's idea of the fantastic things it says.

SETH LIPSKY
New York City

---

8. The great telling of this story is Anthony Lewis, *Gideon's Trumpet* (New York: Vintage, 1989).

9. Louie L. Wainwright was director of the Florida Division of Corrections.

The Constitution
of the United States

∞

PREAMBLE

We the People[1] of the United States,[2] in Order to form a more perfect[3] Union, establish Justice, insure domestic Tranquility,[4] provide for the common defence,[5] promote the general Welfare, and secure the Blessings of Liberty to ourselves and our Posterity,[6] do ordain and establish[7] this Constitution for the United States of America.[8]

---

1. As opposed to the states. Said Samuel Adams: "I confess, as I enter the Building I stumble at the Threshold. I meet with a National Government, instead of a Federal Union of Sovereign States." Arguing against ratification in Virginia, Patrick Henry demanded: "Who authorized them to speak the language of, We, the people, instead of, We, the states? States are the characteristics and the soul of a confederation."

One delegate to the Constitutional Convention who emerged among the Anti-Federalists, Luther Martin, recommended to Maryland that it reject the Constitution: "We appeared totally to have forgot the business for which we were sent . . . we adopted principles which would be right and proper, only on the supposition that there were no State governments at all, but that all the inhabitants of this extensive continent were in their individual capacity, without government, and in a state of nature."

The Federalists would have none of it. At the Pennsylvania ratifying convention, James Wilson declared: "I know very well all the common-place rant of State sovereignties, and that government is founded in original compact." But he insisted that the Preamble "is not an unmeaning flourish. The expressions declare, in a practical manner, the principle of this constitution. It is ordained and established by the people themselves; and we, who give our votes for it, are merely the proxies of our constituents. We sign it as their attorneys, and as to ourselves, we agree to it as individuals."

2. Connecticut, Delaware, Georgia, Maryland, Massachusetts, New Hampshire, New Jersey, New York, North Carolina, Pennsylvania, South Carolina, and Virginia attended the Constitutional Convention in Philadelphia; Rhode Island, which was in the grip of a paper money faction that opposed the Federalists, refused. About Rhode Island, James Madison wrote: "Nothing can exceed the wickedness and folly which continue to rule there. All sense of character, as well as of right is obliterated. Paper money is still their idol, though it is debased to eight for one."

3. Among the imperfections in the union formed under the Articles of Confederation were the absence of an executive and the weakness of the federal Congress. The legislature couldn't levy taxes, impose uniform tariffs, raise an army, or make land grants. State legislatures were straining the patience of the founders. "We have, probably, had too good an opinion of human nature in forming our confederation," Washington wrote to John Jay the summer before the Constitutional Convention. One of the advocates of a strong federal government, Alexander Hamilton, in 15 *Federalist* on the "Insufficiency of the Present Confederation to Preserve the Union," wrote: "We may indeed with propriety be said to have reached almost the last stage of national humiliation."

4. The rebellion in Massachusetts, where Captain Daniel Shays and his men had only recently been defeated, raised fundamental is-

sues. Shays led farmers and debtors in a campaign to block foreclosures carried out for the purpose of collecting taxes levied to pay debts of the Revolution; the rebels wanted Massachusetts to finance these levies by issuing paper money, then rarely used. Shays' rebels appeared in arms against the courts, and in September 1776 they forced the Massachusetts Supreme Court at Springfield to adjourn. Shays' Rebellion gained the enactment of relief for debtors in Massachusetts and, coming as it did on the eve of the Constitutional Convention, put the questions not only of taxation and monetary authority but contracts into sharp relief at Philadelphia.

5. As the delegates gathered at Philadelphia, the new nation was surrounded by enemies, Spain having closed New Orleans and Britain the West Indies; France was imposing trade sanctions.

6. At the time of the Convention, $60 million in Revolutionary War debt was owed by the federal and state governments.

7. Hamilton singled out this phrase in 84 *Federalist*: "Here, in strictness, the people surrender nothing, and as they retain every thing, they have no need of particular reservations." It is typical of the Federalists' sly evasions.

8. The name of the new nation was given in the first of the Articles of Confederation.

ARTICLE I.

SECTION I. All legislative Powers herein granted[9] shall be vested in a Congress[10] of the United States, which shall consist of a Senate and House of Representatives.[11]

---

9. Congress is limited to powers "herein granted." The Constitution sketches the separate powers of the three branches of government generally, but only in the case of the Congress does it actually enumerate them. During the Rehnquist years, the Supreme Court made a particular project of demarcating the outer limit of the legislative

powers of Congress. In any event, the phrase about powers "herein granted" is absent from the Articles that establish the presidency and the Supreme Court.

10. The unicameral legislature provided for under the Articles of Confederation was also known as Congress; each state had one vote.

11. A sudden change in the weather in Philadelphia in the summer of 1787 may have had an impact on this simple but celebrated clause, Max Farrand speculates in *Fathers of the Constitution*. During the first weeks of the Federal Convention, it had been insufferably hot, bringing a sense of lethargy to the proceedings. Abruptly in mid-July, the weather turned cool and pleasant, and on July 16 the framers struck what Max Farrand calls "the great compromise." There was, he writes, "no other that compared with it in importance. Its most significant features were that in the upper house each State should have an equal vote and that in the lower house representation should be apportioned on the basis of population." The compromise, as Farrand puts it, provided that "direct taxation should follow the same proportion" of the population, that "money bills should originate in the lower house," and that they "should not be amended in the upper house." The restriction on amendments was subsequently dropped.

Absent a bicameral legislature, ratification would have failed. The inclusion of a Senate addressed the concerns of small states, which feared that a Congress apportioned solely on population would leave them at a disadvantage. If the House of Representatives speaks for the people, the Senate protects the interests of the states as sovereign political entities. "This body alone forecast the continued existence of the states," wrote one historian, as senators were to be chosen by the state legislatures and each state, regardless of its size, had two senators, in contrast to the more democratic House; accordingly, the Anti-Federalists favored the existence of a Senate and opposed a unicameral legislature, which existed in several states at the time of the Constitutional Convention.

SECTION 2. The House of Representatives shall be composed of Members chosen every second Year by the People[12] of the several States,[13] and the Electors[14] in each State shall have the Qualifications requisite for Electors of the most numerous Branch of the State Legislature.[15]

———————

12. As opposed to the legislatures of the states.

13. The practice of electing representatives by districts is not suggested in the Constitution. The authority to set congressional districts has been drawn from Section 4 of Article I. Here, at this word "states," will be centered the debate over the District of Columbia Voting Rights Act, which has been advancing in the 111th Congress and would give the federal district voting representation in the House.

14. "Who are to be the electors of the federal representatives?" asks Madison in 57 *Federalist*. His answer: "Not the rich more than the poor; not the learned more than the ignorant; not the haughty heirs of distinguished names, more than the humble sons of obscure and unpropitious fortune. The electors are to be the great body of the people of the United States. They are to be the same who exercise the right in every State of electing the correspondent branch of the Legislature of the State."

15. The requirements—such as minimum property holdings, if any, or minimum age—that voters must satisfy are to be determined by the state. There is nothing overtly sexist or racist in the Constitution's description of qualifications. Yet at the time of the founding, in no state save for New Jersey were women permitted to vote, nor were slaves, and in only some cases were free black citizens permitted to vote. Requirements such as poll taxes, literacy tests, and understanding clauses were applied differently to black voters and white voters. The Fifteenth, Nineteenth, Twenty-fourth, and Twenty-sixth Amendments prohibit states from setting certain restrictions on who may vote. The Fourteenth Amendment's equal protection clause also prevents states from setting certain voter requirements.

No Person shall be a Representative who shall not have attained to the Age of twenty five Years, and been seven Years a Citizen of the United States, and who shall not, when elected, be an Inhabitant of that State in which he shall be chosen.[16]

---

16. Whether states may impose additional requirements lay unresolved for two centuries, until Bobbie Hill and the League of Women Voters went to court against Governor William J. Clinton of Arkansas and the state legislature over term limits. Arkansas had amended its constitution to prevent Arkansans who had served in the House for three or more terms, or in the Senate for two or more terms, from having their names placed on the ballot for reelection. The matter reached the high court in the mid-1990s, by which time twenty-three states had enacted term limits for U.S. senators and representatives. In 1995 the Supreme Court, in a 5 to 4 decision in *U.S. Term Limits v. Thornton*, struck down the Arkansas restrictions, ruling that no qualification can be imposed beyond those enumerated in the Constitution. In a dissent, Justice Thomas wrote: "Where the Constitution is silent about the exercise of a particular power—that is, where the Constitution does not speak either expressly or by necessary implication—the Federal Government lacks that power and the states enjoy it." The Articles of Confederation had provided term limits; delegates to Congress could serve no more than three out of every six years. Although neither the states nor Congress may pass laws creating additional requirements, both the House and the Senate retain the power to expel any member who does not meet any of the standards that either chamber might establish. (Please see p. 27.)

Representatives and direct Taxes shall be apportioned among the
several States which may be included within this Union, according
to their respective Numbers, which shall be determined by adding to
the whole Number of free Persons, including those bound to Service
for a Term of Years, and excluding Indians not taxed,[17] three fifths
of all other Persons.[18]

---

17. Census enumerators began to include Indians who had re-
nounced their tribes in 1860. The instructions provided for the 1880
census said "Indians not taxed" meant "Indians living on reservations
under the care of Government agents, or roaming individually, or in
bands, over unsettled tracts of country." In 1940 the government did
away with the category "Indians not taxed."

18. Slaves. This is one of the most infamous clauses in the Constitution, because not only did it countenance slavery but it was seen
as doubly demeaning to the men and women held in bondage that
they were each counted as but three-fifths of a person. The political
dynamic behind this clause, however, is full of ironies. It was the
North that opposed counting a slave as a whole person. It was the
South that wanted slaves to be so counted. The three-fifths compromise meant that the ill-gotten gains of slavery were no longer solely
financial but that slaveholders were to receive political gains as
well—the more slaves a state had, the more representatives it would
have in the Congress.

The idea of counting a slave as a fraction of a freeman dates back
to 1776 and the Continental Congress. In his autobiography
Thomas Jefferson records the question as what formula the Continental Congress would use to requisition money from each state.
Should each state be taxed according to the number of white inhabitants? Or the number of inhabitants of any color or condition? John
Adams said, "The numbers of people were taken by this article as an
index of the wealth of the state." Benjamin Harrison, a member of
Congress from Virginia, "proposed as a compromise that two slaves
should be counted as one freeman."

Under the Articles, in which each state had the same representation, there was no incentive to show a large population, and states faced the threat of a population-based tax. So they had an incentive to understate their true population. The Constitution changed the equation. Suddenly representation in Congress was no longer equal for each state but was based on population. So states now had reason to bolster their population. The issue was an existential one for the country. William Davie of North Carolina is recorded in *The Records of the Federal Convention* as saying that he "saw that it was meant by some gentlemen to deprive the Southern States of any share of Representation for their blacks. He was sure that N. Carola. would never confederate on any terms that did not rate them at least as 3/5. If the Eastern States meant therefore to exclude them altogether the business was at an end."

Of the three-fifths clause, Gouverneur Morris, the Pennsylvania delegate, said this to the Convention: "The admission of slaves into the Representation when fairly explained comes to this: that the inhabitant of Georgia and S.C. who goes to the Coast of Africa, and in defiance of the most sacred laws of humanity tears away his fellow creatures from their dearest connections & damns them to the most cruel bondages, shall have more votes in a Govt. instituted for protection of the rights of mankind, than the Citizen of Pa or N. Jersey who views with a laudable horror, so nefarious a practice." The three-fifths clause, Luther Martin declared in *The Genuine Information*, involved "the absurdity of increasing the power of a State in making laws for free men in proportion as that State violated the rights of freedom."

The actual Enumeration shall be made within three Years after the first Meeting of the Congress of the United States, and within every subsequent Term of ten Years,[19] **in such Manner as they shall by Law direct.**[20]

---

19. The discovery in the 1920 census of the movement of people to cities from farms precipitated a crisis. Congress refused to accept

the census's finding and reapportion House seats. The less populated states argued, among other things, that many of their inhabitants had been dislocated temporarily by World War I.

20. A dispute over the manner of enumeration reached the Supreme Court in 2002, when Utah sued the commerce secretary, Donald Evans, over "hot deck imputation," which census officials use when they are unable to get information about occupancy from a specific address and, instead, impute the number of residents, or the absence of them, by extrapolating the information from the nearest building of the same type. Hot deck imputation increased the 2000 census count by some 1.2 million persons nationally, or 0.4 percent, but Utah's count by only 0.2 percent. Justice Breyer, in the opinion of the Court in *Utah v. Evans,* noted this constitutional language, saying it suggested "the breadth of congressional methodological authority, rather than its limitation." Justice Thomas dissented: "Despite their awareness that estimation techniques could be used to supplement data, the Framers chose instead to require an 'actual Enumeration' or 'counting of whole persons.'"

Whether the Census Bureau can do more than simply enumerate has been a lively topic since the founding. Madison and others pressed for gathering as much information as possible. Census questionnaires inquire about, to mention a few matters, race, ethnicity, physical disabilities, employment. The Court long ago gave a green light to Congress to ask all sorts of questions. In an aside in an unrelated case testing Congress's power to issue paper money, the Court noted that Congress's census-gathering effort extended a bit further than the Constitution provided for. The Court stated that while the Constitution calls for only states' free persons to be counted, "Congress has repeatedly directed an enumeration not only of free persons in the States but of free persons in the Territories, and not only an enumeration of persons but the collection of statistics respecting age, sex, and production. Who questions the power to do this?"

The Number of Representatives shall not exceed one for every thirty Thousand,[21] but each State shall have at Least one Representative; and until such enumeration shall be made, the State of New Hampshire shall be entitled to chuse three, Massachusetts eight, Rhode Island and Providence Plantations one, Connecticut five, New York six, New Jersey four, Pennsylvania eight, Delaware one, Maryland six, Virginia ten, North Carolina five, South Carolina five, and Georgia[22] three.[23]

---

21. The first presidential veto involved this figure of 30,000. President Washington exercised it to block the First Congress from allowing some states to have representatives whose constituencies comprised fewer than 30,000 people. The process of allocating congressional seats among the states has been contentious ever since. After the 1990 census, Montana sued, claiming that rounding downward the number of seats it would allocate violated the Constitution's provision that states be represented in the House "according to their respective Numbers." The Supreme Court disagreed, saying Congress had "a measure of discretion."

Based on the count in 2000 of America's population, 9,380 is the number of representatives Congress would be permitted to create. The apportionment following the 2000 census left each House member representing an average of 646,952 people. The current size of the House, 435 seats, dates to a 1911 law that authorized 433 representatives, with room for two more when Arizona and New Mexico were admitted as states. The House eventually swelled to 437 seats with the additions of Alaska and Hawaii but was adjusted back to 435.

22. One founder, George Reed of Delaware, argued that these numbers gave more weight to Georgia than its population deserved. He claimed that Georgia's "number of inhabitants had stood below that of Delaware." Gouverneur Morris responded that rapid migration was even then occurring within the country. "Such is the rapid-

ity of the population of that State, that before the plan takes effect, it will probably be entitled to 2 Representatives," Morris said. By the end of negotiations Delaware was given three.

23. The first House of Representatives was to include as many as sixty-five members. Madison urged that the number be doubled, as it "was too small a number to represent the whole inhabitants of the U. States; They would not possess enough of the confidence of the people, and wd. be too sparsely taken from the people, to bring with them all the local information which would be frequently wanted." Others called for fewer members, with Roger Sherman of Connecticut urging fifty on the grounds that "the great distance they will have to travel will render their attendance precarious and will make it difficult to prevail on a sufficient number of fit men to undertake the service." After the first apportionment, which followed the 1790 census, the House was expanded to 105 seats, with each seat representing about 33,000 inhabitants as counted for apportionment purposes.

When vacancies happen in the Representation from any State, the Executive Authority thereof shall issue Writs of Election to fill such Vacancies.[24]

---

24. The terrorist attacks of September 11, 2001, and the subsequent mailings of anthrax to the Capitol ignited worries that this was inadequate and that a quicker method for filling House vacancies was needed to ensure that Congress would be able to function should a large number of its members be lost in an attack or other catastrophe. Elections, with their primaries and absentee balloting, take many months. Concern that the House could be left unfilled has led to hearings and a number of proposals to amend the Constitution to provide for a speedier replacement of deceased or incapacitated representatives. Under one proposal, each incoming representative and senator would provide a list of three possible designees to take his or

her place in the event of death, incapacitation, or disappearance. Under another, each representative would run for office along with an alternate who would step in to fill any vacancy.

The House of Representatives shall chuse their Speaker[25] **and other Officers; and shall have the sole Power of Impeachment.**[26]

————

25. Although all speakers have been members of Congress, there is no requirement that the Speaker actually be a member of the House, according to a lecture delivered in 1911 by a member of Congress from Massachusetts, Samuel McCall.

26. While the House is empowered to impeach members of the other two branches, neither representatives nor senators can be impeached. This is less a constitutional prohibition than a precedent, set in 1797 when the House impeached a signer of the Constitution, Senator William Blount of Tennessee, for plotting to help the British gain control of Spanish Florida and Louisiana. After voting to expel Blount, the Senate dropped a move for an impeachment trial. The authority of the Senate and the House to expel their members is granted at Article I, Section 5.

SECTION 3. The Senate of the United States shall be composed of two Senators from each State,[27] **chosen by the Legislature thereof,**[28] **for six Years;**[29] **and each Senator shall have one Vote.**

————

27. The creation of a Senate in which each state had equal representation failed to satisfy those Anti-Federalists who believed that the whole legislative branch ought to put every state on an equal footing, as under the Articles of Confederation. The compromise—which set a House whose representation would be based on population alongside a Senate in which each state would be represented

equally—so angered Maryland's Luther Martin that he refused to sign the Constitution. The proposal, he stated, "was only consenting, after they had struggled to put *both their feet on our necks,* to take *one of them off,* provided we would consent to let them *keep the other on,* when they knew at the same time, that they could not put *one foot on our necks,* unless *we would consent to it,* and that by being permitted to keep on that one foot, they should *afterwards be able to place the other foot on whenever they pleased."*

28. This selection scheme—eventually undone by the Seventeenth Amendment—was, while it lasted, a pillar of federalism in that it preserved a balance of power to the states in the face of the federal government. Yet it was also a potential self-destruct clause. A number of states could basically shutter the federal government by refusing to elect senators. Chief Justice Marshall, in an 1821 ruling in a case involving the sale of lottery tickets, *Cohens v. Virginia,* observed, en passant: "It is true, that if all the States, or a majority of them, refuse to elect Senators, the legislative powers of the Union will be suspended."

29. A six-year term worried the Anti-Federalists, who feared what today is called a "Beltway mentality" well before there was a Beltway. Luther Martin warned the Maryland House of Delegates in 1787 that a six-year term would lure a senator away from his state: "If he has a family, he will take his family with him to the place where the government shall be fixed; that will become his home, and there is every reason to expect, that his future views and prospects will centre in the favors and emoluments of the general government, or of the government of that State where the seat of empire is established. In either case, he is lost to his own State."

Immediately after they shall be assembled in Consequence of the first Election, they shall be divided as equally as may be into three Classes. The Seats of the Senators of the first Class shall be vacated at the Expiration of the second Year, of the second Class at the Expiration of the fourth Year, and of the third Class at the Expiration of the sixth Year, so that one third may be chosen every second Year;[30] and if Vacancies happen by Resignation, or otherwise, during the Recess of the Legislature of any State, the Executive thereof may make temporary Appointments until the next Meeting of the Legislature, which shall then fill such Vacancies.[31]

---

30. "A very effectual *check* upon the power of the Senate" is the way the staggering of terms was characterized by one founder, Fisher Ames, in the Massachusetts ratifying convention. He reasoned: "If one third new members are introduced, who feel the sentiments of their states, they will awe that third whose term will be near expiring." Anti-Federalists argued that under the Articles of Confederation states appointed delegates annually and possessed the authority to recall them at any moment. When Hawaii was admitted to the Union in 1959, the two new senators drew numbers from a wooden box to see which of two Senate classes each would join; Hiram Fong drew the longer term, Oren Long the shorter.

31. This differs from the House, where vacancies are filled by an election. Senators, however, represent not the people but the states, already have authority to act quickly to fill vacancies; please see footnote 304, page 271.

No Person shall be a Senator who shall not have attained to the Age of thirty Years,[32] and been nine Years a Citizen of the United States,[33] and who shall not, when elected, be an Inhabitant of that State for which he shall be chosen.[34]

---

32. This age requirement mimics that of the Roman senate, a point marked by two of the early annotators, jurists Joseph Story and James Kent.

33. The danger of dual loyalty, various notes of the Constitutional Convention record, worried the founders and undergirded this requirement for the body that had the power to ratify treaties. Gouverneur Morris, noting that a seven-year apprenticeship was required for a shoemaker, had wanted a fourteen-year requirement for senators, according to Rufus King's notes. Others, such as Benjamin Franklin, warned of the danger of placing obstacles in the way of immigrants. George Mason, according to James McHenry's entry of August 9, said he "could not think of excluding those foreigners who had taken a part and borne with the country the dangers and burdenths of the war." Oliver Ellsworth opposed a fourteen-year citizenship requirement on the grounds that it would discourage "meritorious aliens from emigrating to this Country." The nine-year period ended the brief Senate career of Geneva-born Albert Gallatin, who went on to become one of the most powerful members of the House of Representatives, the nation's longest-serving Treasury secretary, an envoy to Europe, a student of Native American languages, and a founder of New York University.

34. The Constitutional Convention rejected proposals that only property owners be eligible to serve as senators.

The Vice President of the United States shall be President of the Senate,[35] but shall have no Vote, unless they be equally divided.

---

35. The power accrued by Vice President Richard Cheney led to much discussion of the placement of this assignment, the only delegation of duties to the vice president, within the Article of the Constitution establishing the legislative branch. The vice presidency, however, was a source of unease from the beginning. Madison's notes show that Elbridge Gerry of Massachusetts "was agst. having any vice President." Gerry, according to Madison's notes, said: "We might as well put the President himself at the head of the Legislature. The close intimacy that must subsist between the President & vice-president makes it absolutely improper." Madison also noted: "Col: Mason, thought the office of vice-President an encroachment on the rights of the Senate; and that it mixed too much the Legislative & Executive, which as well as the Judiciary departments, ought to be kept as separate as possible." Roger Sherman defended putting the vice president at the head of the Senate. He said, according to Madison, that if "the vice-President were not to be President of the Senate, he would be without employment."

Cheney himself cited Article I in arguing that the vice president isn't subject to certain regulations intended for the executive branch. At issue were rules related to classified material. Other questions that have sent government lawyers scurrying for a definition of the vice presidency have, over the years, involved more mundane matters, such as how the vice president's staff is to be treated under the tax laws of the District of Columbia. Barton Gellman, writing in *Slate*, reported on conflicting memoranda within the Justice Department. He quoted Nicholas Katzenbach, who served as attorney general, as writing in 1961, when he was an assistant attorney general: "Perhaps the best thing that can be said is that the vice president belongs neither to the Executive nor to the Legislative Branch but is attached by the Constitution to the latter." Governor Sarah Palin, pressed on the matter during the 2008 vice presidential debate, defended "our Founding Fathers" as "very wise" in "allowing through the Constitution much flexibility" in the office of the vice president.

The Senate shall chuse their other Officers,[36] and also a President pro tempore,[37] in the Absence of the Vice President, or when he shall exercise the Office of President of the United States.

---

36. These include the sergeant at arms and doorkeeper, the chaplain, the secretary of the Senate, and party secretaries. The sergeant at arms/doorkeeper was originally known as just the doorkeeper; his duties included buying firewood and tending to the Senate's horses. Mark Twain, in a humorous fictional sketch from 1867, describes being made Senate doorkeeper and charging each senator fifty cents for admission to the chamber.

37. By custom, this is the most senior senator from the majority party. The position has bounced in and out of the presidential line of succession. For nearly a century, beginning in 1792, it was in line, after the vice president. It was out of the line of succession between 1886 and 1947. Since then, the president pro tempore has been back in the line, but lower, after the vice president and the Speaker of the House. The president pro tempore owes a fair amount of what parliamentary role he occupies to Richard Nixon. Until Nixon's accession under President Eisenhower, the vice president mostly occupied himself by presiding over the Senate. Nixon preferred the executive branch to Congress, moving his main office out of the Capitol and leaving more of the parliamentary procedure in the Senate to the president pro tempore.

The Senate shall have the sole Power to try[38] all Impeachments.[39] When sitting for that Purpose, they shall be on Oath[40] or Affirmation.[41]

―――――――――――

38. The Senate acts as the petit jury in that it decides the verdict. The House serves as the grand jury in that it votes on whether to bring charges.

39. Eighteen persons have been impeached since America's founding: Senator William Blount of Tennessee (the Senate expelled him and subsequently dropped the impeachment charges, 1799); Judge John Pickering of U.S. District Court in New Hampshire (convicted, 1804); Justice Samuel Chase (acquitted, 1805); Judge James Peck of U.S. District Court in Missouri (acquitted, 1831); Judge West Humphreys of U.S. District Court in Tennessee (convicted, 1862); President Andrew Johnson (acquitted, 1868); Secretary of War William Belknap (acquitted, 1876); Judge Charles Swayne of U.S. District Court in Florida (acquitted, 1905); Judge Robert Archbald of Circuit of the U.S. Commerce Court (convicted, 1913); Judge George English of U.S. District Court in Illinois (resigned before his trial, 1926); Judge Harold Louderback of U.S. District Court in California (acquitted, 1933); Judge Halsted Ritter of U.S. District Court in Florida (convicted, 1936); Judge Harry Claiborne of U.S. District Court in Nevada (convicted, 1986); Judge Alcee Hastings of U.S. District Court in Florida (convicted, 1988; subsequently elected to Congress); Judge Walter Nixon of U.S. District Court in Mississippi (convicted, 1989); President William Clinton (acquitted, 1999); Judge Samuel Kent of U.S. District Court in Texas (resigned before his trial, 2009); and Judge G. Thomas Porteous of U.S. District Court in Louisiana (convicted 2010). Judge Mark Delahay of U.S. District Court in Kansas resigned in 1873 after the House Judiciary Committee recommended his impeachment but before the House voted. President Nixon resigned in 1974 at a similar point in the impeachment proceedings against him.

40. "Do you solemnly swear that in all things appertaining to the trial of the impeachment of William Jefferson Clinton, President of

the United States, now pending, you will do impartial justice according to the Constitution and laws, so help you God?" is the oath under which the senators were put by Chief Justice Rehnquist in the trial of Clinton.

41. Of the option to affirm, Joseph Story writes: "There are known denominations of men, who are conscientiously scrupulous of taking oaths (among which is that pure and distinguished sect of Christians, commonly called Friends, or Quakers) and therefore, to prevent any unjustifiable exclusion from office, the constitution has permitted a solemn affirmation to be made instead of an oath, and as its equivalent."

When the President of the United States is tried,[42] the Chief Justice[43] shall preside:[44] And no Person shall be convicted without the Concurrence of two thirds of the Members present.[45]

42. Both presidents tried in the Senate were acquitted. President Andrew Johnson had the distinction of being tried for violating a law that would later be recognized as unconstitutional—fifty-eight years after the trial. For more on Johnson's impeachment, please see footnote 192 in page 151.

43. Of the United States as opposed to merely the Supreme Court. This is the only reference to the chief justice in the Constitution. The formal title and duties are established in the United States Code, Section 1, which states: "The Supreme Court of the United States shall consist of a Chief Justice of the United States and eight associate justices, any six of whom shall constitute a quorum."

44. The chief justice presides when the president is impeached because the vice president has a personal interest—the presidency.

45. An outcome other than conviction is known as an acquittal. One can be acquitted with less than a majority. This is a deviation from the federal criminal justice system, under which unanimity is required for both convictions and acquittals and a hung jury is called a

mistrial. President Andrew Johnson escaped conviction (i.e., he was acquitted) by a single vote, thirty-five for guilty, nineteen for not guilty.

Judgment in Cases of Impeachment shall not extend further than to removal from Office,[46] and disqualification to hold and enjoy any Office of honor,[47] Trust or Profit under the United States: but the Party convicted shall nevertheless be liable and subject to Indictment, Trial, Judgment and Punishment, according to Law.

---

46. In contrast, the British Parliament could impose a death sentence through a bill of attainder for those impeached and convicted. Or it could forgo impeachment and simply issue a death sentence bill of attainder. Congress cannot send a wrongdoer to prison; only the courts can do that. Nor can Congress impeach an ordinary citizen, a point marked by Luther Martin when defending an associate justice of the Supreme Court, Samuel Chase, against his impeachment for bias toward the Federalists. Said Martin: "Will it be pretended, for I have heard such a suggestion, that the House of Representatives have a right to impeach every citizen indiscriminately? For what shall they impeach them? For any criminal act? Is the House of Representatives, then, to constitute a grand jury to receive information of a criminal nature against all our citizens, and thereby to deprive them of a trial by jury? This was never intended by the Constitution."

47. Impeachment convictions do not necessarily disqualify a person from later holding a seat in Congress, which is arguably not an "office" within the meaning of the word in the Constitution. Alcee Hastings, a federal judge in Florida, was impeached in 1988 for bribery and perjury, convicted by the Senate, and removed from office. But in 1992 he was elected to Congress on the Democratic Party line. Hastings at one point tried to have his impeachment overturned in the courts, but a Supreme Court ruling, in the case of another fallen judge, dashed his hopes. That case involved a federal judge, Walter Nixon, who refused to step down from the bench even

after being convicted in court and jailed for perjury. The House then impeached. A Senate committee heard the evidence, reported it to the Senate, and the full Senate voted to remove Nixon from his judgeship. Nixon went to the Supreme Court with the argument that the evidentiary hearings themselves should have been held by the full Senate. The justices ruled against him, declaring the issue an internal matter of the Senate that was "nonjusticiable." "The Senate's practice," writes one law professor, Michael Gerhardt, "is to vote separately or not at all on whether to disqualify the convicted official from holding future office." Gerhardt notes that in two instances concerning Judges Robert Archbald and West Humphreys, the Senate has disqualified former judges from holding future office under the United States. It similarly disqualified G. Thomas Porteous when he was removed from the federal bench in December 2010.

Section 4. The Times, Places and Manner of holding Elections for Senators and Representatives, shall be prescribed in each State by the Legislature thereof;[48] but the Congress may at any time by Law make or alter such Regulations,[49]

---

48. Justice Scalia cited this clause in 2008 in his concurrence in *Crawford v. Marion County Election Board*, upholding Indiana's requirement that voters must present a valid government photographic identification document in order to vote. Noting that "detailed judicial supervision of the election process would flout the Constitution's express commitment of the task to the States," Scalia wrote: "It is for state legislatures to weigh the costs and benefits of possible changes to their election codes, and their judgment must prevail unless it imposes a severe and unjustified overall burden upon the right to vote, or is intended to disadvantage a particular class."

49. "With uncommon zeal and virulence" is how Joseph Story characterizes the way in which opponents of the Constitution attacked this delegation of authority to make or alter campaign and

election regulations. Wrote Patrick Henry: "Those illumined genii may see that this may not endanger the rights of the people; but in my unenlightened understanding, it appears plain and clear that it will impair the popular weight in the government. Look at the Roman history. They had two ways of voting—the one by tribes, and the other by centuries. By the former, numbers prevailed; in the latter, riches preponderated. According to the mode prescribed, Congress may tell you that they have a right to make the vote of one gentleman go as far as the votes of a hundred poor men." A different view was argued by Hamilton in 59 *Federalist*: "There is intended to be a general election of members once in two years. If the State Legislatures were to be invested with an exclusive power of regulating these elections, every period of making them would be a delicate crisis in the national situation; which might issue in a dissolution of the Union, if the leaders of a few of the most important States should have entered into a previous conspiracy to prevent an election."

It would be hard to imagine either Patrick Henry or Joseph Story—or, for that matter, Alexander Hamilton—anticipating any greater zeal and virulence than has greeted modern efforts to regulate financing of federal election campaigns, culminating in the Federal Election Campaign Act of 1971 and the Bipartisan Campaign Reform Act of 2002. The 1971 act and subsequent amendments had regulated so-called hard money contributions and spending in federal election campaigns and set certain disclosure requirements. The Supreme Court, in 1976, decided a case called *Buckley v. Valeo*, brought by Senator James Buckley against the secretary of the Senate, Francis Valeo, an ex-officio member of the Federal Election Commission. The court concluded that limits could not be placed on the free speech rights of candidates to spend their own money on their own campaigns but could limit a person from spending his own money on someone else's campaign. The 2002 act sought to regulate so-called soft money, including certain preelection advertising by labor unions, corporations, and not-for-profit organizations. Eleven constitutional challenges were filed to the 2002 act, according to a count to which the Supreme Court referred in *McConnell v. Federal Election Commission*, a case whose lead plaintiff was Senator Mitch McConnell of Kentucky. In one of the longest and most complex set of opinions in its history, the Court upheld the bulk of the regulations.

It is, in any event, from this clause, and the corresponding language in Article II, that we get Election Day. Having the entire country vote for federal candidates on the same day—the first Tuesday after the first Monday in the Novembers of years ending in even numbers—dates to 1845, when Congress required that all electors for the president and vice president be chosen on that day. It wasn't until 1842 that Congress required House representatives to be selected by district. Previously some states allowed congressmen to be elected without dividing states into districts. The system ignored regional differences within a state and made it relatively easy for the dominant party in the state to win every congressional seat. And it wasn't until 1872 that Congress extended Election Day to the House; senators were then still chosen by state legislatures (please see p. 271). "Notorious" is the adjective the *New York Times*, in an editorial issued on November 3, 1878, used to describe the "exaggerated and unreasonable influence of the September-voting States upon the October-voting states, and of these in turn upon the November-voting states."

It is here that Congress receives its authority to make it a crime to intimidate voters. In a ruling handed down during Reconstruction, known as *Ex Parte Yarbrough*, the justices cited this clause in upholding the conviction of several members of the Ku Klux Klan who beat a black citizen to prevent him from voting or to punish him for doing so. Said a unanimous court of the government: "If it has not this power, it is left helpless before the two great natural and historical enemies of all republics, open violence and insidious corruption."

except as to the Places of chusing Senators.[50]

---

50. Because senators were originally chosen by state legislatures, this exception guaranteed that Congress wouldn't be able to decide where the legislatures met. Joseph Story writes in his *Commentaries*: "It would not be either necessary, or becoming in congress to prescribe the place, where it should sit." In 1911 the Supreme Court, in *Coyle v. Smith,* chose not to rely on this feature when striking down an act of Congress overruling Oklahoma's voters and requiring the Sooners to keep their capital at Guthrie for several years. Instead, the Supreme Court relied on a constitutional principle that is not found in the Constitution—that states must be admitted on equal footing. The Supreme Court reckoned it wouldn't do for Congress to impose debilitating restrictions on new, incoming states.

The Congress shall assemble at least once in every Year,[51] **and such Meeting shall be on the first Monday in December,**[52] **unless they shall by Law appoint a different Day.**

---

51. "A check on the Executive department" is how, at the Federal Convention, Nathaniel Gorham of Massachusetts characterized the necessity of having "one meeting at least every year." Other delegates questioned whether there would be enough national business to warrant a meeting every year. Rufus King of Massachusetts worried that a frequently assembled Congress would tend to overregulate. "A great vice in our system was that of legislating too much," he remarked, as preserved in *The Records of the Federal Convention.*

52. This schedule, coupled with two other developments, made for mischief and was modified by the Twentieth Amendment. The newly elected Congress wouldn't meet until at least thirteen months after the election, establishing a lengthy lame duck session of Congress every other year. The difficulty arose from the Constitution be-

ing ratified in September 1788, which, as Bruce Ackerman of Yale Law School points out in *The Failure of the Founding Fathers*, didn't give much time for the states to elect senators and representatives before the December start date. The fix, if it can be called that, came when the Continental Congress declared that the regime change empowering the U.S. Congress would occur on March 4, 1789. The two-year term meant that the Congress would expire two Marches hence. This, combined with fall elections and the constitutional mandate that Congress assemble in December, meant that each new Congress waited at least thirteen months after election to convene in December for a long session.

Then, the following December, the same Congress would reconvene for a truncated session ending March 4. The second of these sessions didn't even begin until after the next Congress had been elected. This befuddling legislative schedule was righted in 1933 by the Twentieth Amendment, which set both the beginning and end of congressional terms in early January. Thus each new Congress waited less than two months instead of thirteen. It also shortened the length of lame duck sessions by more than half. Now they might last only from Election Day to January. And while the former schedule, with its mandatory December meeting, required lame duck sessions, the Twentieth Amendment does not.

Section 5. Each House shall be the Judge of the Elections, Returns and Qualifications of its own Members,[53] and a Majority of each shall constitute a Quorum[54] to do Business; but a smaller Number may adjourn from day to day, and may be authorized to compel the Attendance of absent Members,[55] in such Manner, and under such Penalties as each House may provide.

53. In early 2009, as the 2008 vote for senator from Minnesota was being recounted, there was talk of Al Franken attempting to take advantage of Democratic control of the Senate in order to claim

a seat in the upper chamber. The effort was rebuffed not by the Senate but by Minnesota's governor and state secretary, who refused, citing state law, to sign an election certificate during the recount.

54. Must the majority be merely present in the chamber or must the majority be actually voting on the business at hand? For years, it was a common practice for the opposition to break a quorum by refusing to vote. The question came to a head in 1890 in one of those cases where common commerce mixes with high constitutional concepts, namely, a bill directing the Treasury secretary, when computing import duties, to classify worsted as woolen, which carried a higher tariff. When the question was called, the yeas were 138, the nays zero, with 189 not voting. The speaker, Thomas Brackett Reed, instructed the clerk to read him the list of names, and when Reed noticed one of them in the hall, he announced him present. The number present and refusing to vote, 74, together with those recorded as voting, 138, showed a total of 212 members present, constituting the quorum, and the bill was passed. Subsequently an importer of worsted sought to escape the higher tariff by challenging the quorum call by which Reed gained the passage of the law. The Supreme Court would have none of it, bowing, in *United States v. Ballin*, to the constitutional delegation that each house may determine the rules of its proceedings (please see the following page).

55. The sergeant at arms of each chamber can arrest absent members and bring them to the floor of the House or Senate. In the Senate, under Rule 6, all that is needed is for "a majority of the Senators present" to round up absent members. In the House, under Rule 20, a majority of those present, comprising at least fifteen members, can order the sergeant at arms to make arrests. This power is rarely employed. The last instance appears to have come in 1988, when Republicans were by and large staying off the Senate floor in an attempt to prevent a vote on a campaign finance bill. Democrats, led by Senator Robert Byrd, decided to order arrests of senators who weren't on the floor. One Republican, Senator Robert Packwood, described what happened next: "We had a hurried caucus among the Republicans in the cloakroom, and we all scattered." The rest of the story is

perhaps best retold by Senator Arlen Specter, who did so on the floor of the Senate in 2006: "The Sergeant at Arms was a little fellow, Henry Giugni. He started to patrol the halls. He came upon Senator Lowell Weicker. Now, Henry was about 5-foot-4, and Lowell Weicker was 6-foot-4. Lowell was at his fighting weight of about 240 at the time. It was about 3:30 in the morning. Do you know what happens with Senators at 3:30 in the morning? I won't say on the Senate floor. The Sergeant at Arms decided not to arrest Lowell Weicker. He made a very wise judgment. Instead, he went knocking on Senate doors. Senator Robert Packwood made the mistake of answering the door. Senator Packwood compelled them to carry him out of his office. He agreed to walk here, but he insisted on being carried into the Senate Chamber. I don't think Senator Byrd got his quorum, but he got his man, Senator Packwood."

Each House may determine the Rules of its Proceedings,[56] punish its Members for disorderly Behaviour,[57] and, with the Concurrence of two thirds,[58] expel a Member.[59]

56. Hence there are filibusters in the Senate while debate in the House occurs within the confines of strict time limits. As a Congressional Research Service report makes clear, the filibuster is not laid out in any Senate rule. Rather, "possibilities for filibustering exist because Senate Rules deliberately *lack* provisions that would place specific limits on Senators' rights and opportunities in the legislative process. In particular, those Rules establish no generally applicable limits on the length of debate, nor any motions by which a majority could vote to bring a debate to an end." Senate Rule 22, however, lays out the clumsy procedure—cloture—by which a filibuster can be stopped: A minimum of sixty votes is needed, but even with those votes, an additional thirty hours of Senate floor business must occur before the debate can be forced to an end. To amend Rule 22 would, according to the rule itself, take two-thirds of the Senate (even more

than it takes to overcome the filibuster that would surely result were one party to try to amend this rule). On the floor of the House, on the other hand, each topic is generally limited to a single hour of debate.

57. The most famous breach of order was the caning of a leading abolitionist, Senator Charles Sumner of Massachusetts, by Representative Preston Brooks of South Carolina. Brooks was upset at how Sumner, in a speech opposing the extension of slavery to Kansas, had mocked Brooks's relative, Senator Andrew Butler, also of South Carolina, for his fervent support of slavery. Sumner had charged Andrew Butler with taking "a mistress . . . who, though ugly to others, is always lovely to him; though polluted in the sight of the world, is chaste in his sight: I mean the harlot, Slavery." Three days latter, Brooks entered the Senate, found Sumner at his desk, and "slammed his metal-topped cane onto the unsuspecting Sumner's head. As Brooks struck again and again, Sumner rose and lurched blindly about the chamber, futilely attempting to protect himself. After a very long minute, it ended. Bleeding profusely, Sumner was carried away. Brooks walked calmly out of the chamber without being detained by the stunned onlookers." Brooks survived a House censure motion but resigned, only to be reelected. It took Sumner three years to recover and return to the Senate. He served another eighteen years.

58. Only a vote is required, not a trial as in impeachment.

59. This has seldom occurred. Other than during the Civil War, when fourteen senators and three representatives were expelled, only one senator, William Blount in 1797 for treason, and two representatives—Michael "Ozzie" Myers in 1980 and James Traficant in 2002, both for corruption-related matters—have been expelled by a two-thirds vote.

But can Congress refuse to seat an elected—or appointed—member and do so by a simple majority vote? Called exclusion, this practice was used in 1868 to prevent the seating of two representatives-elect and one senator-elect who had aided the Confederacy. In

1900, on a vote of 268 to 50, it refused to seat Brigham H. Roberts, Utah's lone congressman, ostensibly on the grounds that, prior to Utah's statehood, he had had three wives and had been convicted of unlawful cohabitation, though sentiment against him was fanned by an anti-Morman agitator. Roberts, a writer, mounted a defense that included an op-ed piece in the *New York Times* in which he asked: "Does the House of Representatives indorse the individual views of all the men it admits to membership? If Socialists should from some Congressional district elect a Congressman, would his admission to the House say to the world that the American Congress indorsed Socialism?" The *Times* reported that as Roberts left after the vote on his fate, he declared himself a "martyr to a spasm of prejudice."

The Senate spent four years deliberating on whether to admit Reed Smoot of Utah, an apostle in the Mormon Church, before seating him in 1907. The practice of exclusion was halted following a lawsuit filed in 1967 by Adam Clayton Powell, who was being denied his seat in the House pending a congressional inquiry into allegations of corruption. The Supreme Court's decision prevented Congress from using a simple majority vote to avoid the hurdle of a two-thirds majority required for expulsion. Wrote Chief Justice Warren: "Unquestionably, Congress has an interest in preserving its institutional integrity, but, in most cases, that interest can be sufficiently safeguarded by the exercise of its power to punish its members for disorderly behavior and, in extreme cases, to expel a member with the concurrence of two-thirds. In short, both the intention of the framers, to the extent it can be determined, and an examination of the basic principles of our democratic system persuade us that the Constitution does not vest in the Congress a discretionary power to deny membership by a majority vote."

Each House shall keep a Journal of its Proceedings, and from time to time publish the same,[60]

---

60. In 1890 Marshall Field and a number of other merchants sought to avoid duties on certain imported goods on the grounds, among others, that the bill signed by the Speaker of the House and the president of the Senate and enrolled with the secretary of state varied from the record shown in the journal kept by the Congress. Justice John Marshall Harlan wrote for the Court that the clause of the Constitution on which the merchants rested their contentions was the one which declared that each chamber should keep a journal of its proceedings and publish it, and enter the yeas and nays therein. "It was assumed in argument," he wrote, "that the object of this clause was to make the journal the best, if not conclusive, evidence upon the issue as to whether a bill was, in fact, passed by the two houses of congress." But, he added, "the words used do not require such interpretation." Harlan then went on to quote Joseph Story as saying that "the object of the whole clause" was something else, namely, "to insure publicity to the proceedings of the legislature, and a correspondent responsibility of the members to their respective constituents." He quoted Story as asserting: "Intrigue and cabal are thus deprived of some of their main resources, by plotting and devising measures in secrecy." Wrote Harlan: "In regard to certain matters, the constitution expressly requires that they shall be entered on the journal. To what extent the validity of legislative action may be affected by the failure to have those matters entered on the journal we need not inquire."

excepting such Parts as may in their Judgment require Secrecy;[61]

---

61. The founders wrote the Constitution in secret, and the document they produced contains no requirement that Congress debate

before a public audience. The Senate met in private until 1794, when it opened many of its proceedings to the public. The timing was due to public interest in whether the Geneva-born Albert Gallatin would be expelled from the Senate because he'd been a citizen a year less than the constitutionally mandated nine. In a motion to open the Senate to the public, Senator Alexander Martin of North Carolina, who had been a delegate to the Federal Convention of 1787, put forward a resolution on the merits of open government: "While the principles and designs of the individual members are withheld from public view, responsibility is destroyed, which, on the publicity of their deliberations would be restored." The resolution failed.

The resolution that did open the Senate contained no grand statement of principles, but said that "after the end of the present session of Congress, and so soon as suitable galleries shall be provided for the Senate Chamber, the said galleries shall be permitted to be opened every morning, so long as the Senate shall be engaged in their Legislative capacity, unless in such cases as may, in the opinion of the Senate, require secrecy, after which the said galleries shall be closed." Much Senate business continued to be conducted in secret executive sessions, including whether to confirm presidential nominees or ratify treaties. That didn't stop newspapers from learning the details. President Polk, in his diary, vents his frustrations over a reporter, John Nugent, who, in the *New York Herald*, routinely broke news under the pen name Galvienses. He was, in the president's opinion, "an unprincipled newspaper letter writer who was in the daily habit of calumniating and abusing me." When, in 1848, Nugent obtained the treaty that ended the Mexican War as well as Polk's letters to the Senate, the reporter was arrested by the Senate sergeant at arms and jailed for a month—during the day in a Senate committee room and at night at the home of the sergeant at arms. He continued to file stories, under the dateline: "Custody of the Sergeant at Arms."

It wasn't until 1929 that Senate executive sessions were opened to the public. Between that year and May 2007, the full Senate held fifty-four secret sessions, many pertaining to the impeachment of

President Clinton. Other secret meetings included a June 7, 1971, session to discuss the country's involvement in Laos. There have been several secret sessions to discuss antiballistic missile defenses, another to discuss funding for neutron bombs, and a two-day session to discuss the Panama Canal treaties. The Supreme Court has left it to the discretion of each house of Congress to decide which proceedings to keep secret. In 1892, in *Field v. Clark*, it ruled: "It is clear that, in respect to the particular mode in which, or with what fullness, shall be kept the proceedings of either house relating to matters not expressly required to be entered on the journals; whether bills, orders, resolutions, reports, and amendments shall be entered at large on the journal, or only referred to and designated by their titles or by numbers—these and like matters were left to the discretion of the respective houses of congress."

and the Yeas and Nays[62] of the Members of either House on any question shall, at the Desire of one fifth of those Present,[63] be entered on the Journal.

------

62. The prospect of such roll calls, in which each legislator individually enters a recorded vote, irked a number of the founders. The yeas and nays take time. Legislators currently have fifteen minutes to get down to the floor to vote during a roll call vote, and dissenting legislators have taken to calling the roll as a delaying tactic. Madison's notes show that Roger Sherman of Connecticut "had rather strike out the yeas & nays altogether. They never have done any good, and have done much mischief. They are not proper as the reasons governing the voter never appear along with them." Nathaniel Gorham of Massachusetts, a state in which a single member could force the legislature to call yeas and nays, spoke of how the procedure had resulted "in stuffing the journals with them on frivolous occasions."

63. In practice, if a quorum is present, the Senate requires only eleven senators to force a roll call, based on the assumption that a bare minimum of a quorum, or fifty-one senators, is present.

Neither House, during the Session of Congress, shall, without the Consent of the other, adjourn for more than three days, nor to any other Place than that in which the two Houses shall be sitting.[64]

64. The point is that the two houses of Congress are to coordinate their schedules to ensure that each is open for business when needed. The Continental Congress was an itinerant institution, and the new Congress didn't as of yet have a home. Laws could not be passed if one half of this bicameral road show suddenly chose to go home. The matter came under some discussion at the Federal Convention. Rufus King said it was "inconvenient" that this would permit Congress to switch locations easily. According to Madison's notes from August 11, King said the "mutability of place had dishonored the federal Govt. and would require as strong a cure as we could devise." Madison noted that King "thought a law at least should be made necessary to a removal of the Seat of Govt."

But Richard Spaight of North Carolina argued that requiring Congress to pass a law each time it wanted to move gave the president too much oversight of the legislative branch. The president could simply veto the law fixing a new location. Spaight's concerns weren't just about separated powers. They were regional. "This will fix the seat of Govt at N.Y.," he said during the debate. "The present Congress will convene them there in the first instance, and they will never be able to remove; especially if the Presidt. should be Northern Man." When Madison proposed that Congress decide where it would meet, one delegate had a cynic's view of what would follow. "It will serve no purpose to require the two Houses at their first Meeting to fix on a place," John Mercer of Maryland said. "They will never agree."

SECTION 6. The Senators and Representatives shall receive a Compensation for their Services, to be ascertained by Law,[65] and paid out of the Treasury of the United States.[66]

---

65. An amendment that would have prohibited Congress from raising its own pay—that would have allowed a pay raise to become effective only after the next congressional election—was one of two proposed amendments spurned by the states at the time of the ratification of the Bill of Rights. The proposal lay dormant for some two hundred years until it was revived, largely through the efforts of a University of Texas undergraduate, G. D. Watson, who had discovered it in the course of his studies. The measure was approved May 7, 1992, as the Twenty-seventh Amendment, precipitating a constitutional question. The 1989 Ethics Reform Act had provided, among other things, that members of the House and Senate would receive an automatic cost of living adjustment that lagged an employment cost index by half a percentage point. Would the lawmakers have to wait for an intervening election? A federal district judge, Stanley Sporkin, ruled that in providing a methodology for automatic annual adjustments to congressional salaries, the law "meets both the language and the spirit of the 27th amendment" because "a Congressional election has intervened between the passage of the Act and its implementation." For further discussion, please see page 292.

66. Under the Articles of Confederation, the states were required to pay for their delegations to attend sessions of Congress. *Records of the Federal Convention* indicates that Hamilton spoke "strenuous agst. making the National Council dependent on the Legislative rewards of the States. Those who pay are the masters of those who are paid. Payment by the States would be unequal as the distant States would have to pay for the same term of attendance and more days in travelling to & from the seat of the Govt." Gouverneur Morris "remarked that if the members were to be paid by the States it would throw an unequal burden on the distant States, which would be unjust as the Legislature was to be a national Assembly."

They shall in all Cases, except Treason, Felony and Breach of the Peace, be privileged from Arrest[67] during their Attendance at the Session of their respective Houses, and in going to and returning from the same; and for any Speech or Debate in either House, they shall not be questioned in any other Place.[68] No Senator or Representative shall, during the Time for which he was elected, be appointed to any civil Office under the Authority of the United States, which shall have been created, or the Emoluments whereof shall have been encreased during such time;[69] and no Person holding any Office[70] under the United States, shall be a Member of either House during his Continuance in Office.

———

67. Arrests by plaintiffs in private lawsuits were otherwise permitted at the time. The founders wanted to ensure that legislators could travel to Congress from their homes without interference. A professor of law at Yale, Akhil Amar, writes: "Without the privilege, a single private civil litigant, perhaps by design, might undo the voters' verdict by keeping their man off the floor." Jefferson, in his *Manual of Parliamentary Practice*, wrote: "When a Representative is withdrawn from his seat by summons, the 30,000 people whom he represents lose their voice in debate and vote, as they do in his voluntary absence: when a senator is withdrawn by summons, his State loses half its voice in debate and vote, as it does in his voluntary absence. The enormous disparity of evil admits no comparison."

The case that limited immunity from arrest to civil suits came up in 1905, when a member of the House, John Newton Williamson, was indicted in connection with an attempted Oregon land swindle. Williamson argued that if he went to jail he couldn't attend the Congress to which he'd been elected, and that a conspiracy to suborn perjury was neither treason nor felony nor breach of the peace. The Supreme Court examined precedents and authorities going back to fifteenth-century England in concluding that the constitutional language was universally understood as a traditional formula encompassing all crimes: In other words, that parliamentary immunity from arrest had never permitted a member "to withdraw himself from the criminal law of the land." The Library of Congress edition of the Constitution asserts that the clause "is practically obsolete." That didn't stop a senator from Iowa, Roger Jepsen, from claiming that he had immunity from a $35 ticket that he received in Virginia for driving alone in the carpool lane. That happened in 1983.

68. It was from under this clause that the *Chicago Tribune* sprang upon the Treaty of Versailles. Its correspondent at France had acquired the treaty illegally when the text was still a state secret. Confident the *Tribune* could thwart President Wilson's plan to create the League of Nations if only the scheme could be exposed to the light of day, the newspaper's editors needed a way to avoid prosecution. So Senator Borah was assigned by the *Tribune's* proprietor to step onto the Senate floor and read the text of the treaty into the record. He could do so with impunity, because for a speech made in the Senate he could not be questioned in any other place. When he rose to speak, the *Tribune* prepared its presses. When he actually spoke, it let them roll with the text of the treaty, reckoning that as a newspaper it could print anything uttered on the Senate floor. The headline was, "*Tribune* Has Treaty," and the world was spared the League of Nations. Had a legal action been brought, the Supreme Court might not have sustained this scheme. It allowed, in *Gravel v. United States*, a grand jury in 1972 to inquire into the process by which Senator Gravel obtained the classified history of the Vietnam War known as the *Pentagon Papers*.

69. This clause, intended to prevent the president from rewarding pliant members of Congress with better paying, more powerful, or more secure positions in the judiciary or the executive branch, was raised as a potential impediment to President Obama's appointment of Senator Clinton as his secretary of state. At issue was a 2008 executive order by President Bush that raised the pay of the secretary of state some $4,700 a year, to $191,300. Although Congress had no role in the pay raise, and even though Congress subsequently set the secretary of state's salary back to the lower figure, some legal scholars argued that Clinton was ineligible given that the post's salary was, in

fact, "encreased" during her most recent term in the Senate. In rolling back the secretary of state's salary in a bid to help Clinton's cause, Congress performed what is known in Washington circles as the Saxbe fix. The name comes from Senator William Saxbe, whom President Nixon nominated in 1973 to be attorney general. Earlier in Saxbe's term, Congress had raised cabinet salaries to $60,000 from $35,000. Congress rolled back the pay raise for the attorney general and confirmed Saxbe.

The fix failed to convince all skeptics that Saxbe was eligible as attorney general. One was Harvard professor Stephen Breyer, who later became an associate justice of the Supreme Court. Another was Senator Robert Byrd, who said "we should not delude the American people into thinking a way can be found around the constitutional obstacle." Hugo Black's elevation to the Supreme Court from the Senate was opposed by some who argued that the seat Black would be taking was essentially newly created on the Supreme Court. The logic, if there was any, was that the outgoing justice, Willis Van Devanter, had retired with a full pension, and so, the theory went, he still held his seat. Also at issue was that Van Devanter's pension, which Black himself could one day receive, was the creation of legislation from Black's most recent term. The Supreme Court declined to hear a legal challenge to the Black appointment.

70. It has yet to be settled, though the debate has been active for two hundred years, whether a member of Congress can simultaneously serve in the military or hold a military rank or grade. As early as 1803, a New York congressman, John Van Ness, lost his seat after being commissioned a major in the militia of Washington, D.C. Congress found that Van Ness had come into conflict with this clause of the Constitution. He could hold on to his commission, but he had forfeited his seat in Congress. *The History of Congress* indicates that Van Ness said he did not expect his commission to jeopardize his seat in Congress. The House Committee of Elections found otherwise.

In 1847, during the war with Mexico, Representative Edward Baker of Illinois and Representative Archibald Yell of Arkansas took commissions as volunteer officers, leading a House committee to conclude that they had forfeited their seats. Yell died in combat. In 1974 the Supreme Court turned down an opportunity to decide whether this clause prevented members of Congress from holding commissions in the military reserves. While the lower courts held that dual membership in the military reserves and Congress was a violation of this, the Supreme Court reversed on the grounds that the plaintiffs—a group of current and former members of the Armed Forces reserve—lacked standing. More recently, lawyers for an airman facing a conviction for possession of cocaine cited this clause in objecting to the inclusion of Senator Lindsey Graham, a colonel in the Air Force Reserve, on the Air Force court of criminal appeals. The top military appellate court, the U.S. Court of Appeals for the Armed Forces, concluded in 2006 that service "by a Member of Congress performing independent judicial functions runs afoul of the fundamental constitutional principle of separation of powers."

Section 7. All Bills for raising Revenue shall originate in the House of Representatives;[71] but the Senate may propose or concur with Amendments as on other Bills.

---

71. This was a major issue at the Convention. Elbridge Gerry, the Massachusetts delegate, said, "taxation & representation are strongly associated in the minds of the people, and they will not agree that any but their immediate representatives shall meddle with their purses." He said he believed this issue—that is, which house would formulate tax policy—"would be much scrutinized" during the ratification process. Gerry said, "In short the acceptance of the plan will inevitably fail, if the Senate be not restrained from originating Money bills." This check gave comfort to those who worried that small states, with little population, would have an outsize influence in the national government. As Madison put it in 58 *Federalist*: "The house of representatives can not only refuse, but they alone can pro-

pose, the supplies requisite for the support of government. They in a word hold the purse; that powerful instrument by which we behold in the history of the British constitution, an infant and humble representation of the people, gradually enlarging the sphere of its activity and importance, and finally reducing, as far as it seems to have wished, all the overgrown prerogatives of the other branches of the government."

Yet scant protection has been provided by this celebrated clause, with objections being dashed by the Supreme Court, most famously in a lawsuit brought by a taxpayer named Josiah Millard to block legislation initiated in the Senate to build the railroad terminal adjacent to the Capitol known as Union Station. The 1903 act provided three-quarters of a million dollars each to the Baltimore & Ohio Railroad and the Baltimore & Potomac Railroad to build such a station. The money was to be raised through a property tax in the District. The resulting lawsuit, *Millard v. Roberts* (1906), sought to enjoin the U.S. treasurer, Ellis H. Roberts, from paying out money, arguing that the act was void because it originated in the Senate. The court brushed away this claim on the grounds that "whatever taxes are imposed are but means to the purposes provided by the act." In other words, the court held that, despite the tax provision, this was not to be counted as a revenue-raising bill.

More recently, the Supreme Court rejected a claim by German Munoz-Flores, who'd been required, upon being convicted of two misdemeanor counts of aiding aliens to elude immigration officers, to pay $25 on each count to a crime compensation fund that had been established by a law that originated in the Senate. In 1990 the Supreme Court ruled against him on a 9 to 0 vote in an opinion that reckoned, among other points, that the law showed no lack of respect to the House. Justice Story, in his *Commentaries,* writes: "A learned commentator supposes that every bill which indirectly or consequently may raise revenue is, within the sense of the Constitution, a revenue bill. He therefore thinks that the bills for establishing the post-office and the mint, and regulating the value of foreign coin, belong to this class, and ought not to have originated (as in fact they did) in the Senate. But the practical construction of the Constitution has been against his opinion. And, indeed, the history of the origin of the power already suggested abundantly proves that it has been confined to bills to levy taxes in the strict sense of the word, and has not been understood to extend to bills for other purposes, which may incidentally create revenue."

Every Bill which shall have passed the House of Representatives and the Senate, shall, before it become a Law, be presented to the President of the United States; If he approve he shall sign it,[72] but if not he shall return it, with his Objections[73] to that House in which it shall have originated, who shall enter the Objections at large on their Journal, and proceed to reconsider it. If after such Reconsideration two thirds of that House shall agree to pass the Bill, it shall be sent, together with the Objections, to the other House, by which it shall likewise be reconsidered, and if approved by two thirds of that House, it shall become a Law.[74] But in all such Cases the Votes of both Houses shall be determined by yeas and Nays, and the Names of the Persons voting for and against the Bill shall be entered on the Journal of each House respectively.

72. If the president chooses to sign his name, no other notation is necessary. The Supreme Court established this in an 1867 case, *Gardner v. the Collector*, involving a man who objected to paying the Customs House the twenty cents a pound on tea that Congress had legislated in 1861. President Lincoln had signed the bill and added the words "approved" and "December 24." The plaintiff's lawyer argued that because the president hadn't included the year in his signature, the law in effect could never be enforced. "The whole of the very able and ingenious argument of counsel for plaintiff," the Court wrote, "rests on these two propositions, as stated in his own language: 'That the President alone can make the record which is to show the date of his approval; and that if the President's record is de-

fective in respect to the year when it was made, no resort can be had to extrinsic evidence to supply that defect.'" The Court rejected this: "The only duty required of the President by the Constitution in regard to a bill which he approves is, that he shall sign it. Nothing more. . . . Even in the event of his approving the bill, it is not required that he shall write on the bill the word 'approved,' nor that he shall date it."

73. "I have maturely considered the Act passed by the two Houses," is how George Washington began the first veto message, in respect of a bill on apportionment. Karlyn Kohrs Campbell and Kathleen Hall Jamieson reckon Andrew Jackson's veto of the Bank of the United States was his "most famous veto message." They cited its assertion that it is "as much the duty" of the House, the Senate, and the president as it is the Supreme Court "to decide upon the constitutionality of any bill or resolution." President George W. Bush used the veto rarely but was blunt in his messages. "This bill spends too much," he wrote on an appropriations bill in 2007, adding: "This bill has too many earmarks." According to a 2004 Congressional Research Service report titled *Congressional Overrides of Presidential Vetoes,* President Franklin Roosevelt vetoed the most bills, some 372. FDR and President Truman are responsible for more than a third of all vetoes. Truman had 180 of his own. As of spring 2004, there had been 1,484 vetoes.

74. Congress has become more assertive at overriding presidential vetoes, at least over the long run. Before 1969 Congress overrode a veto only about once for every eighteen return vetoes (not counting pocket vetoes). Since then, the rate is about one in five. In the latter part of the twentieth century a dispute arose over whether a president could veto parts of an appropriations bill. The contest between the president and the Congress over the maneuver, known as a line-item veto, resulted in a compromise called the Line-Item Veto Act of 1996. It was short-lived. New York City, feeling the pinch of President Clinton's veto of certain health care–related spending, brought suit. In *Clinton v. City of New York*, the Supreme Court found the line-item veto unconstitutional, making it difficult for the president to minimize earmarks.

If any Bill shall not be returned by the President within ten Days (Sundays excepted)[75] after it shall have been presented to him, the Same shall be a Law, in like Manner as if he had signed it, unless the Congress by their Adjournment prevent its Return, in which Case it shall not be a Law.[76]

---

75. "Gloriously secular" is how one scholar, Sanford Levinson of the University of Texas Law School, describes the Constitution. But, he noted in a review of the first edition of this book, this parenthetical "is a reminder of the expectation that the president would likely observe the Christian Sabbath as a day of rest."

76. Such a veto is called a pocket veto. The need for such a mechanism arises from the schedule of Congress. If both houses pass a bill on its final day before adjournment, and the president decides to sleep on it, to whom is he supposed to return it if all the lawmakers have left the capital? The pocket veto has provoked congressional resentment against presidents as far back as Andrew Jackson and as recently as George W. Bush. Caviled Henry Clay when Jackson vetoed his land bill: "By withholding the bill, the President took upon himself a responsibility beyond the exercise of the veto. He deprived Congress altogether of its constitutional right to act upon the bill, and to pass it, his negative notwithstanding."

Trouble arises when it is unclear whether Congress is in session or adjourned. At the end of 2007, the Senate was holding pro forma sessions, which need last but seconds. Bush, claiming that Congress was adjourned, pocketed a $696 billion military authorization bill because he objected to a provision that would have allowed plaintiffs with legal claims in American courts against Saddam Hussein's regime to press those claims against Iraq's new democracy. Congressional officials argued that he couldn't use a pocket veto in these circumstances. The constitutional issue was sidestepped the following month when Congress passed a revised version incorporating the fix the president wanted.

The wording of this clause had particular significance in the days when presidents crossed the Atlantic by ship. "The fact that the President has ten days from their *presentation* rather than their *passage* within which to sign bills became a matter of great importance when President Wilson went abroad in 1919 to participate in the making of the Treaty of Versailles," Edward Corwin relates. "Indeed, by a curious combination of circumstances plus a little contriving, the late President Roosevelt was enabled on one occasion to sign a bill no less than twenty-three days after the adjournment of Congress."

Every Order, Resolution, or Vote to which the Concurrence of the Senate and House of Representatives may be necessary (except on a question of Adjournment)[77] shall be presented to the President of the United States;[78] and before the Same shall take Effect, shall be approved by him, or being disapproved by him, shall be repassed by two thirds of the Senate and House of Representatives, according to the Rules and Limitations prescribed in the Case of a Bill.

77. To limit the president's control over where and when Congress meets. Wrote President Jefferson in 1790: "The latitude of the general words here used would have subjected the natural right of adjournment of the two houses to the will of the President, which was not intended. They therefore expressly 'except questions of adjournment' out of their operation. They do not here give a right of adjournment, which it was known would exist without their gift, but they defend the existing right against the latitude of their own phrases, in a case where there was no good reason to abridge it. The exception admits they will have the right of adjournment, without pointing out the source from which they will derive it."

The House of Representatives website lists four forms of congressional action—the bill, the joint resolution, the concurrent resolution, and the simple resolution. The bill is the most common. It says "little practical difference between a bill and a joint resolution," which may originate in either house but must be acted on by both. Concurrent resolutions are used for "matters affecting the operations of both Houses" and are not "legislative in character," nor are simple resolutions, which relate to but one of the two houses.

Both houses of Congress must approve a final adjournment, lest one confound the other.

78. Madison's comments at the Constitutional Convention suggest that this phrase merely provides the lawyerly language needed to close any loopholes in the establishment of the presidential veto. Madison commented "that if the negative of the President was confined to *bills*; it would be evaded by acts under the form and name of Resolutions, votes." In other words, without this clause, Madison worried that Congress could try to evade a president's veto through the gimmick of calling a piece of legislation by a name other than a "bill."

Edward Corwin explains that Congress conceives of the "concurrent resolution" as a way to exercise oversight of the president after ceding extraordinary powers to him. In the 1941 Lend Lease Act, which gave the president the unprecedented power to give away Navy ships or any other "defense article" to foreign allies, Congress reserved the right to pass at any future time a concurrent resolution that would force the president to stop giving away America's materiel. Corwin reports that in addition to Lend Lease, other wartime measures, as well as a significant piece of peacetime legislation, the 1939 Reorganization Act, contained provisions by which Congress could use a concurrent resolution to claw back powers given to the president by the legislation.

SECTION 8. The Congress shall have Power[79] To lay and collect Taxes,[80] Duties, Imposts[81] and Excises,[82] to pay the Debts and provide for the common Defence and general Welfare of the United States;[83]

---

79. Here begins the enumeration of the only powers delegated to the Congress. Whether actions were authorized under one of the

enumerated powers was a defining question in the early generations of constitutional government. As more and more governmental action has taken place under implied powers, a modest backlash has begun. In recent years, the Enumerated Powers Act has been introduced in the Congress that would require each act passed to "contain a concise and definite statement of the constitutional authority relied upon for the enactment of each portion of that Act." Congress has so far demurred.

80. This power to tax was denied to the Congress under the Articles of Confederation. Under the Articles, the national government could requisition money from each state, but was at the mercy of the states to actually tax their inhabitants and raise the money. The Constitution casts the states aside, allowing Congress the power to raise revenue directly from the people and commerce.

81. Generally, a tax on an import, although dictionaries differ on whether its meaning is limited to taxes on imports or any tax on a good.

82. One of the wiliest of the founders, Gouverneur Morris, plotted at the Convention in Philadelphia to change this comma to a semicolon. He wanted to alter the meaning of the sentence to create, in the clause following this comma, a separate and unlimited spending power. In the sentence as it currently exists—its original form—the grammar is that the words following the comma are not a general grant of power to spend but a limitation on the taxing power. Had Morris won his semicolon, the spending power would be separate and without limitation. His plot to change the text by adding a dot over the comma was discovered and foiled by the other founders, a point on which Albert Gallatin testified to the House of Representatives in 1798. "Rarely has so much rested on so small a point," is how Philip Hamburger has described this contretemps. In the event, the Supreme Court has, over the decades, essentially permitted the Congress to exercise a general spending power without limitation, despite the grammar.

In 21 *Federalist*, Hamilton described duties, imposts, and excises as taxes "upon articles of consumption." He found them politically preferable to capitation taxes, or those directly levied on wealth. "It is a signal advantage of taxes on articles of consumption, that they contain in their own nature a security against excess." After all, Hamilton notes: "The amount to be contributed by each citizen will in a degree be at his own option, and can be regulated by an attention to his resources. The rich may be extravagant, the poor can be frugal. And private oppression may always be avoided by a judicious selection of objects proper for such impositions."

83. Can this phrase be read as an obstacle to a tax policy undertaken for purposes of wealth redistribution? The Supreme Court, in striking down part of the New Deal legislation, the Agricultural Adjustment Act of 1933, declared: "A tax, in the general understanding of the term, and as used in the Constitution, signifies an exaction for the support of the Government. The word has never been thought to connote the expropriation of money from one group for the benefit of another." In this case, *United States v. Butler*, the group being taxed comprised processors of farm goods (slaughterhouses, cotton spinners, tobacco manufacturers, wheat, rice, and corn millers). The recipients were farmers who were being paid to grow less. The law was challenged by the receivers of a Massachusetts cotton milling company, Hoosac Mills.

Such language might also appear to prevent Congress from setting aside tax revenue and earmarking it for localized spending. Hamilton wrote in his *Report on Manufactures*: "The only qualification of the generality of the phrase in question which seems to be admissible is this: That the object to which an appropriation of money is to be made be general and not local its operation extending, in fact or by possibility, throughout the Union and not being confined to a particular spot."

By 1937 the Supreme Court saw the matter differently. In a pair of opinions that year, the Court cited this phrase as the basis for upholding the unemployment assistance and old age pension programs contained in the Social Security Act of 1935. By the lights of Justice Cardozo, who wrote both opinions, the experience of the Depression redefined just what sorts of expenditures qualified under this clause.

In upholding the unemployment assistance program, which was funded through a tax on employers, Cardozo wrote (*Steward Machine Co. v. Collector*):

> There was need of help from the nation if the people were not to starve. It is too late today for the argument to be heard with tolerance that, in a crisis so extreme, the use of the moneys of the nation to relieve the unemployed and their dependents is a use for any purpose narrower than the promotion of the general welfare.

In upholding the old age pension, Cardozo wrote (*Helvering v. Davis*):

> Congress may spend money in aid of the "general welfare." There have been great statesmen in our history who have stood for other views. We will not resurrect the contest. . . . The line must still be drawn between one welfare and another, between particular and general. Where this shall be placed cannot be known through a formula in advance of the event. There is a middle ground, or certainly a penumbra, in which discretion is at large. The discretion, however, is not confided to the courts. The discretion belongs to Congress, unless the choice is clearly wrong, a display of arbitrary power, not an exercise of judgment.

The meaning of "general welfare"—what expenditures could be made to provide for it—was one of the questions in the early-nineteenth-century debate over whether Congress could pay for internal improvements, such as roads. Madison vetoed the Bonus Bill, President Monroe vetoed the Cumberland Road bill, and Jackson vetoed the Maysville Road bill. The constitutional features that guided this debate were the words about the "general welfare," the commerce clause, and the clause delegating to Congress the power to establish post roads. Said Monroe in his message to Congress: "My idea is that Congress have an unlimited power to raise money, and that in its appropriation they have a discretionary power, restricted only by the duty to appropriate it to purposes of common defense and of general, not local, national, not State, benefit."

but all Duties, Imposts and Excises shall be uniform[84] throughout the United States;

84. Is this a baseless dream? In 1882 Congress passed a law requiring every immigrant arriving by port to pay a head tax of fifty cents, and a New York firm, Funch, Edye & Co., which transported passengers between Holland and America, brought suit. It claimed, among other things, that the tax was not levied uniformly, as it was assessed only in ports and did not apply to overland passengers arriving via Mexico or Canada. The suit became part of what is known as the Head Money Cases and prompted Justice Miller to ask: "Is the tax on tobacco void because, in many of the States, no tobacco is raised or manufactured? Is the tax on distilled spirits void because a few States pay three-fourths of the revenue arising from it?" He continued: "The tax is uniform when it operates with the same force and effect in every place where the subject of it is found. . . . Perfect uniformity and perfect equality of taxation, in all the aspects in which the human mind can view it, is a baseless dream."

A group of oil producers used this clause to protest special exemptions for Alaska contained in the Crude Oil Windfall Profit Tax Act of 1980. They went to court seeking a tax refund on the grounds that the exemption had to apply to their oil as well, as excises had to be uniform throughout the country. Justice Powell, writing for a unanimous court in *United States v. Ptasynski*, said: "The one issue that has been raised repeatedly is whether the requirement of uniformity encompasses some notion of equality. It was settled fairly early that the Clause does not require Congress to devise a tax that falls equally or proportionately on each State. Rather, as the Court stated in the Head Money Cases, a 'tax is uniform when it operates with the same force and effect in every place where the subject of it is found.'" The Court went on to say that it did not think "the language of the Clause or this Court's decisions prohibit all geographically defined classifications. As construed in the Head Money Cases, the Uniformity Clause requires that an excise tax apply, at the same rate, in all portions of the United States where the subject of the tax is found."

To borrow Money[85] on the credit of the United States;[86]

85. The ninth of the Articles of Confederation gave Congress the power "to borrow money, or emit bills on the credit of the United States." At the Federal Convention in Philadelphia, however, the founders pointedly omitted the phrase "or emit bills." This omission is taken by one student of monetary law, Edwin Vieira Jr., as a signal of the founders' intention to deny the Congress the power to issue paper money.

86. No constitutional limits obtain in respect of how much Congress may authorize the government to borrow, a sum that is now more than $11 trillion, which, figuring the American population at 305 million, comes out to more than $36,000 a person. An Anti-Federalist writing under the pseudonym Brutus wrote: "Under this authority, the Congress may mortgage any or all the revenues of the union, as a fund to loan money upon, and it is probably, in this way, they may borrow of foreign nations, a principal sum, the interest of which will be equal to the annual revenues of the country. By this means, they may create a national debt, so large, as to exceed the ability of the country ever to sink. I can scarcely contemplate a greater calamity that could befal this country, than to be loaded with a debt exceeding their ability ever to discharge. If this be a just remark, it is unwise and improvident to vest in the general government a power to borrow at discretion, without any limitation or restriction." Income

from Treasury bills is exempt from local taxes, the Supreme Court
has held.

**To regulate Commerce with foreign Nations, and among the several
States, and with the Indian Tribes;**[87]

87. "The most important of the particular non-military powers of
Congress" is how W. W. Crosskey, in starting his three-volume
study of the Constitution, describes this clause. He calls the power
"one of the plainest in the Constitution" and argues that "once this
single power, in its full scope and plentitude, is correctly understood,
everything else in the Constitution falls into a new perspective." It is
Crosskey's view that the Supreme Court has put restrictions on the
way the Congress may regulate commerce within states that wouldn't
have been countenanced by the founders. In the event, the commerce clause has been a kind of constitutional shuttle on the loom of
our national fabric—flung in one direction by states wanting to regulate matters that are beyond their reach, and in the other direction by
a Congress that wants to regulate matters where it has no authority.

An early chapter in this contest involved a dispute between rival
steamboat companies plying the route between New Jersey and New
York. In 1824 the Supreme Court, in an opinion by Chief Justice
Marshall in *Gibbons v. Ogden*, gave the business to the company with
the federal charter. He took the founders' use of the word "commerce" to connote "the commercial intercourse between nations, and
parts of nations, in all its branches, and is regulated by prescribing
rules for carrying on that intercourse." The instinct to grant supremacy to federal law in the area of commerce held sway well into
the twentieth century. But then the Supreme Court during President
Roosevelt's first term heard the case of a family of kosher butchers in
Brooklyn, New York, the Schechter brothers, who had been put in
the dock for violating regulations promulgated under the National
Industrial Recovery Act.

The charges originated in the Schechters' refusal to bar a customer from picking the individual chicken he wanted to purchase. When one of the poulterers' lawyers, standing before the high bench, tried to convey how a buyer might reach into a cage to select a chicken without looking at it—"What if the chickens are all at one end?" asked Justice Sutherland—the justices began to laugh. The justices, in determining "how far the federal government may go in controlling intrastate transactions upon the ground that they 'affect' interstate commerce," drew a sharp distinction between whether the effects on interstate commerce were direct or indirect. They ruled unanimously that in seeking to regulate the intrastate business practices of the Schechters, Congress had gone too far. The 1935 ruling effectively ended a centerpiece of the New Deal, the National Recovery Act.

FDR's defeat in the Schechter case precipitated his effort, through a bill called the Judiciary Reorganization Act of 1937, to pack the Supreme Court. The effort failed in the Senate. Even without being packed, the Supreme Court began to reverse course. It moved under the commerce clause to expand federal power, notably in upholding, in 1937, the National Labor Relations Act against a challenge from Jones & Laughlin Steel and, in 1942, the Agricultural Adjustment Act against a challenge from a farmer named Roscoe Filburn, who wanted to produce for personal use on his Ohio farm more wheat than the government would allow. The cases are *NLRB v. Jones & Laughlin Steel Corp.* and *Wickard v. Filburn*.

After *Schechter*, it would not be until 1995 that the Court would again strike down an act of Congress under the commerce clause. It came when a high school student, Alfonso Lopez, was arrested in San Antonio, Texas, for bringing a concealed handgun to class and was brought up on charges under a federal law called the Gun-Free School Zones Act of 1990. The Court, though divided, would have none of it: "The possession of a gun in a local school zone is in no sense an economic activity that might, through repetition elsewhere, have such a substantial effect on interstate commerce. . . . To uphold the Government's contention that § 922(q) is justified because firearms possession in a local school zone does indeed substantially affect interstate commerce would require this Court to pile inference upon inference in a manner that would bid fair to convert congressional Commerce Clause authority to a general police power of the sort held only by the States."

The next big test of the commerce clause could be one of the most far-reaching cases in the Court's history, for nearly two dozen states, led by Florida, are challenging the Patient Protection and Affordable Health Care Act, known as Obamacare, on the grounds that, among other things, it exceeds Congress's powers as enumerated here in the commerce clause. The states challenging the law assert that, in requiring persons "to have healthcare coverage or pay a tax penalty," the law "compels persons to perform an affirmative act or incur a penalty, simply on the basis that they exist and reside in the United States."

They argue that refraining from purchasing health care is an "inactivity" that "by its nature cannot be deemed to be in commerce or to have any substantial effect on commerce, whether interstate or otherwise" and, as a result, the law "cannot be upheld under the Commerce Clause."

The assertion is ridiculed in a response filed in federal court by the United States, which rejects the argument that economic decisions to refrain from the purchase of health insurance are "inactivity." Such decisions, the United States asserted, have a "direct and substantial effect on the interstate health care market in which uninsured and insured alike participate" and are "thus subject to federal regulation."

To establish an uniform Rule of Naturalization,[88] and uniform Laws on the subject of Bankruptcies[89] throughout the United States;

88. The first exercise by Congress of this power, the Naturalization Act of 1790, held that one needed to be "a free white person" to be eligible to become a naturalized citizen. Discussion waxed on how long an immigrant must reside in the United States before being eligible

for citizenship. Congress changed the minimum residency requirement no fewer than three times that decade. In the 1790 law, the requirement was two years. In 1795, the minimum was upped to five
years. Then, in 1798, the residency requirement was increased once
again, this time climbing to fourteen years. Federalists, who then
dominated, wanted a lengthy minimum in order to weaken the Republicans, who drew support from immigrants. The requirement was
returned to five years during Jefferson's presidency. The requirements
that the 1795 law imposed—including the five-year residency—
remain mostly in effect today, though immigration law has veered in
myriad directions. National quotas, imposed most prominently in
1924, were ended in 1965. The *Dred Scott* decision foreclosed the
naturalization of persons of African descent until it was reversed by
the Fourteenth Amendment. However, the law continued to exclude
Asian immigrants from achieving citizenship, an exclusion that was
upheld by a subsequent series of federal and Supreme Court decisions. Despite some country-specific exceptions made in the 1940s,
these racial strictures largely survived until the passage of the Immigration and Nationality Act of 1952. In 1984 the idea of open borders was endorsed, at least in principle, by the *Wall Street Journal*,
tribune for a school of thought that sees Americans as defined less by
culture or ethnicity than by their fidelity to the same set of laws—the
Constitution.

89. It was not until 1898 that Congress passed what would be a
long-lasting uniform federal bankruptcy law, known as the Nelson
Act; it modernized the measure in the Bankruptcy Reform Act of
1978.

**To coin Money,[90] regulate the Value thereof, and of foreign Coin,[91]
and fix the Standard of Weights[92] and Measures;[93]**

90. The Coinage Act of 1792 resulted from the first exercise of
this power. It created the U.S. Mint and established the dollar as

"the money of account of the United States." It legislated a dollar to be "the value of a Spanish milled dollar as the same is now current, and to contain three hundred and seventy-one grains and four six-teenth parts of a grain of pure, or four hundred and sixteen grains of standard silver." It set a proportional value of a unit of weight of gold to be fifteen times that of silver. The pain it established for debasing any gold or silver coin struck at the U.S. Mint was death. The act was superseded 173 years later by the Coinage Act of 1965, which wrought changes that President Lyndon Johnson said, when he signed the measure, were "necessary" in the face of a "worldwide shortage of silver" and America's "rapidly growing need for coins." At the signing ceremony, Johnson warned: "If anybody has any idea of hoarding our silver coins, let me say this. Treasury has a lot of sil-ver on hand, and it can be, and it will be used to keep the price of sil-ver in line with its value in our present silver coin." At the time, the price of silver was almost precisely the same as it was in 1792, or $1.29 an ounce. Within fifteen years, it had reached $49 an ounce.

This clause has been interpreted by some to suggest that Congress lacks the power to issue paper money. Daniel Webster cited it in 1836 in a speech on a proposal to permit the Treasury to take pay-ment for land in a form other than gold or silver. Said the silver-tongued senator: "The states are expressly prohibited from making anything but gold and silver a tender in payment of debts, and al-though no such express prohibition is applied to Congress, yet as Congress has no power granted to it in this respect but to coin money and to regulate the value of foreign coins, it clearly has no power to substitute paper or anything else for coin as a tender in pay-ment of debts and in discharge of contracts." Congress did authorize the issuance of paper money, creating, through the Legal Tender Act of 1862, a currency to pay for the Civil War. It was known as the greenback. Its creation was validated by the Supreme Court in a case known as *Knox v. Lee*, involving payment for a flock of 608 sheep once owned by a Mrs. Lee of Pennsylvania but kept in Texas. After being seized by the Confederacy, the sheep were sold to a private buyer named Knox. The court upheld the principle that the greenback could be used at face value in the dispute over the sheep, but based its decision not on this clause but on the "necessary and proper" clause footnoted on page 83.

91. That foreign coins were in general circulation in America was a basic monetary fact. What Congress was being given was the power to regulate their value, or not, in terms of U.S. money—to make them "current" (please see footnote 94). The practice ended in 1857, when Congress passed An Act Relating to Foreign Coins, ending the status of foreign gold or silver coins as legal tender. To one nineteenth-century senator, Thomas Hart "Old Bullion" Benton, taking foreign coins out of general circulation in America was an unconstitutional act. He asserted in his autobiography that it was "the intention and declared meaning of the constitution" that "foreign coins should pass currently as money, and at their full value, within the United States," and that "it was the duty of Congress to promote the circulation of these coins by giving them their full value." The logic of foreign coins, noted in a report in 1877 by the secretary of the U.S. Monetary Commission, included that the "striking of money is expensive, especially of silver money, and it is a useless tax, either upon the Government or individuals, to require that coins issued by mints as reputable and as reliable as our own, should be recoined at our mints." It reckoned the cost at 1.5 percent.

92. The first federal law establishing how much something actually weighed or measured was enacted in 1828, when Congress declared what the U.S. Mint in Philadelphia would use as the official Troy pound—a bulbous-looking brass weight procured from Britain by the American minister in London, Albert Gallatin. The first agency entrusted with the weights and measures, the Office of Standard Weights and Measures, is now known as the National Institute of Standards and Technology. Congress first authorized use of the metric system nationwide in 1866 with a law that forbade any private contract from being invalidated or "liable to objection" because the weights and measures therein used the metric system. In 1975, with the Metric Conversion Act, Congress established that it was "the declared policy of the United States" to "designate the metric system

of measurement as the preferred system of weights and measures for United States trade and commerce." But it refrained from insisting that Americans abandon the foot, the pint, and the pound.

The early days of daylight saving time produced a Supreme Court case on the matter. While Congress established daylight saving time as early as 1918, it repealed the law after the close of World War I, overriding President Wilson's veto. In the subsequent decade, the Supreme Court heard a challenge to Massachusetts' daylight saving time law brought by proponents of standard time. One plaintiff was a man who owned land on the Massachusetts–New Hampshire border, which straddled two different time zones and required him to pay more to hire employees to start at the earlier hour. Another plaintiff claimed that the law put an undue burden on women who have both a husband employed by the railroad, where work was governed by standard time, and children in school, where the schedules were on daylight saving time. These complaints did not impress Justice Holmes, who ruled that Massachusetts was free to advance official time by an hour.

93. The decision to use the same sentence to assign the authority to coin money and regulate its value as well as to fix the standard of weights and measures is one of the most remarkable made by the founders. It suggests that they comprehended money not as a commodity but as a measure of value. The sentence has prompted more than one commentator to remark that rather than inflating the dollar, Congress should reduce the size of the barrel, shorten the length of the mile, or condense time. The Supreme Court, in the Legal Tender Cases known as *Knox v. Lee*, marked this broad point: "We will notice briefly an argument presented in support of the position that the unit of money value must possess intrinsic value. The argument is derived from assimilating the constitutional provision respecting a standard of weights and measures to that conferring the power to coin money and regulate its value. . . . The legal tender acts do not attempt to make paper a standard of value. We do not rest their validity upon the assertion that their emission is coinage, or any

regulation of the value of money; nor do we assert that Congress may make anything which has no value money. What we do assert is, that Congress has power to enact that the government's promises to pay money shall be, for the time being, equivalent in value to the representative of value determined by the coinage acts, or to multiples thereof."

Certainly the powers conveyed to the Congress herein are among the mightiest in the Constitution; a summary is contained in the Congressional Research Service annotated edition of the Constitution, which notes that under this clause Congress claimed and secured the power to "restrain the circulation of notes not issued under its own authority," to "impose a prohibitive tax upon the circulation of the notes of state banks or of municipal corporations," to "require the surrender of gold coin," to "make Treasury notes legal tender in satisfaction of antecedent debts," and to override "private contracts calling for payment in gold coin, even though such contracts were executed before the legislation was passed."

To provide for the Punishment of counterfeiting the Securities and current Coin[94] of the United States;[95]

94. A coin is current if Congress pegs its value and authorizes it as a valid form of payment. William Blackstone wrote in his *Commentaries on the Laws of England* (1765): "The king may also, by his proclamation, legitimate foreign coin, and make it current here; declaring at what value it shall be taken in payments." It was through the inclusion of the word "current" that Congress received the power to punish counterfeiters of not only American coins but some foreign coins. Chief Justice John Jay wrote to President Washington in 1790: "If the word *current* had been omitted, it might have been doubted whether the Congress could have punished the counterfeiting of foreign coin. Mexican dollars have long been known in our

public acts as *current* coin." In 1857 Congress decided to quit exercising this power, declaring, in its Act Relating to Foreign Coins: "All former acts authorizing the currency of foreign gold and silver coins, and declaring the same a legal tender in payment for debts, are hereby repealed."

95. The plain language of this phrasing would seem to deny Congress the power to punish counterfeiters of noncurrent foreign currencies. But that did not help Ramon Arjona, who, in the 1880s, was charged with counterfeiting the notes of a bank from the Colombian state of Bolivar. The charges were handed up under an 1884 statute that made it a crime to forge any foreign note. Arjona challenged the law as unconstitutional. In *United States v. Arjona*, the Court didn't deign to cite this clause even once, deciding instead that Congress could enact such a law because it was duty bound to prevent violations of the "law of nations" (please see footnote 101), of which counterfeiting foreign notes was one.

In our time, the federal government is using this power to prosecute an activist against the Federal Reserve, Bernard von NotHaus, who mints silver and gold coinage that he calls the Liberty Dollar. The currency contains markings—such as an image of Lady Liberty in profile and the slogan "Trust in God"—that are similar to those on federal coins. Von NotHaus advertises his coins as an inflation-proof alternative to the greenback. Federal agents have seized thousands of the coins and their corresponding bearer certificates in raids in Indiana and Idaho. During the years of soaring precious metals prices, Liberty Dollars far outperformed the dollar issued by the federal government, a fact that, if von NotHaus is prosecuted, could invite this question: Is something counterfeit when it has value that is equal to or greater than the original?

In the 1984 case of *Regan v. Time*, the Supreme Court found in favor of Time, Inc., in its lawsuit against the Treasury secretary after the publisher had been warned by the Secret Service that color reproductions of paper currency in its magazines violated an anti-counterfeiting law. The law said that such reproductions could only be made in black and white and less than three-fourths or greater than one and one-half times the actual size of the bills.

To establish Post Offices and post Roads;[96]

———————

96. A debate waxed during the early decades of the Republic in respect of whether this language granted the federal government the power to make internal improvements. Skeptics, including some justices of the Supreme Court, believed that this clause permitted Congress to designate existing thoroughfares as postal roads, but did not authorize Congress to build new roads. On the subject of post roads, Jefferson wrote to Madison in 1796: "I view it as a source of boundless patronage to the executive, jobbing to members of Congress & their friends, and a bottomless abyss of public money. You will begin by only appropriating the surplus of the post office revenues; but the other revenues will soon be called into their aid, and it will be a scene of eternal scramble among the members, who can get the most money wasted in their State; and they will always get most who are meanest." His sentiment did not seem to survive a decade. In 1806, Jefferson, as president, signed a bill authorizing construction of the Cumberland Road between Maryland and Illinois. In 1817, Madison vetoed the Bonus Bill, which would have funded roads and canals that, Congress insisted, were necessary to promote commerce and the common defense. In his veto message, Madison stated that "it does not appear that the power, proposed to be exercised by the bill, is among the enumerated powers."

Madison worried about Congress's efforts to justify such expenditures by appealing to national security. Said the fourth president: "Such a view of the Constitution would have the effect of giving to Congress a general power of legislation, instead of the defined and limited one hitherto understood to belong to them." Yet Congress would win this battle, and the national defense would eventually come to be seen as acceptable grounds for building a road system. When, in 1956, Congress passed a law for an Interstate Highway System, the president spoke of the "primary importance to the national defense" of what came to be called the Dwight D. Eisenhower National System of Interstate and Defense Highways. In signing the bill, Eisenhower spoke of the Soviets. "In case of an atomic attack on our key cities, the road net must permit quick evacuation of target areas, mobilization of defense forces and maintenance of every essential economic function," Eisenhower said, according to a draft of his speech. "But the present system in critical areas would be the breeder of a deadly congestion within hours of an attack."

The authority to run a postal service is a significant source of federal power in other arenas as well. The government's property interest in the mail was one of the grounds the Supreme Court cited in 1895 for keeping Eugene Debs imprisoned for his role in the Pullman Strike of the preceding year. The strike, among other things, paralyzed mail delivery. The court, also citing the interstate commerce clause, upheld injunctions, requested by the executive branch, that had ordered strike leaders to desist. Debs hadn't obeyed the court order, leading to his imprisonment. The government has at times taken the postal authority to permit it to remove items it deemed treasonous or obscene—as well as contraceptives—from the mail. But mark the First Amendment. Justice Holmes, in a dissenting opinion in 1921 relating to the Espionage Law of 1917, wrote: "The United States may give up the post office when it sees fit, but, while it carries it on, the use of the mails is almost as much a part of free speech as the right to use our tongues, and it would take very strong language to convince me that Congress ever intended to give such a practically despotic power to any one man." The one man to whom Justice Holmes refers is the postmaster general, who had revoked second-class mail privileges of a Milwaukee newspaper, the *Milwaukee Leader*, for its reports during World War I.

To promote the Progress of Science and useful Arts, by securing for limited Times to Authors and Inventors the exclusive Right to their respective Writings and Discoveries;[97]

97. This, one of the most fraught clauses in the Constitution, begins by restricting the motives permitted to Congress in securing the copyrights and patents for authors and inventors. The plain language suggests it may do so only to promote the progress of science and useful arts. It may not do so, the language suggests, to promote progress of nonscientific inquiry or arts that have no use. Nor may it do so for, say, national security reasons. By specifying that Congress may secure the rights for only limited terms, the founders recognized a public interest in the fruits of American creativity. The resulting controversy has escalated for more than two centuries, as authors and the corporations who employ them clamor for greater protections and as the World Wide Web makes creative work accessible to a global audience.

In 1790 Congress granted authors copyrights for fourteen years, renewable at the end of the term for another fourteen years if the author was still living. It extended the length of copyrights in a number of steps over the years and, in 1998, passed the Sonny Bono Copyright Term Extension Act, giving writers a copyright during their lifetime plus seventy years. For company-held copyrights the term would be ninety-five years. An Internet publisher, Eric Eldred, who specializes in issuing books that have gone out of copyright, promptly challenged the Bono Act on the grounds that retroactively extending copyrights for near limitless lengths of time did not comply with the constitutional mandate that the purpose be to promote science and useful arts.

The Supreme Court rejected his claims, but not without a sharp dissent from Justice Breyer: "The economic effect of this 20-year extension—the longest blanket extension since the Nation's founding—is to make the copyright term not limited, but virtually perpetual. Its primary legal effect is to grant the extended term not to authors, but to their heirs, estates, or corporate successors. And most importantly, its practical effect is not to promote, but to inhibit, the progress of 'Science'—by which word the Framers meant learning or knowledge."

Copyrights are not limited to written works. The First Congress passed a copyright act that protected maps and charts in addition to writings. "The only reason why photographs were not included in the extended list in the act of 1802 is probably that they did not exist, as photography, as an art, was then unknown, and the scientific principle on which it rests, and the chemicals and machinery by which it is operated, have all been discovered long since that statute was enacted," the Court wrote in an 1884 case that upheld a congressional act that allowed photographs to be copyrighted. The photograph at the center of the case, *Burrow-Giles Lithographic Company v. Sarony*, was of a seated Oscar Wilde snapped by Napoleon Sarony.

In 1980 the Supreme Court opened the way for patents to be issued in respect of living matter—so long as it didn't occur naturally. The case, *Diamond v. Chakrabarty*, involved a researcher for General Electric, Ananada Chakrabarty, who had genetically altered bacteria to eat oil and help clean up spills. The Supreme Court said this discovery was patentable. Chief Justice Burger wrote: "His claim is not to a hitherto unknown natural phenomenon, but to a nonnaturally occurring manufacture or composition of matter—a product of human ingenuity." The chief justice noted that a 1952 congressional report accompanying a patent act stated that Congress intended for patentable material to "include anything under the sun that is made by man."

A dispute over circus posters designed by one George Bleistein led to a rare moment of humility on the high bench, when, in 1903, Justice Oliver Wendell Holmes, opining for the Court in *Bleistein v. Donaldson Lithographing Co.*, wrote: "It would be a dangerous undertaking for persons trained only to the law to constitute themselves final judges of the worth of pictorial illustrations, outside of the narrowest and most obvious limits. At the one extreme, some works of genius would be sure to miss appreciation. Their very novelty would make them repulsive until the public had learned the new language in which their author spoke. It may be more than doubted, for instance, whether the etchings of Goya or the paintings of Manet would have been sure of protection when seen for the first time. At the other end, copyright would be denied to pictures which appealed to a public less educated than the judge. Yet if they command the interest of any public, they have a commercial value—it would be bold to say that they have not an aesthetic and educational value—and the taste of any public is not to be treated with contempt."

Copyrights and patents are not to be confused with trademarks, which Congress grants under the commerce clause powers. In an 1879 decision, known as the Trademark Cases, the Court held that any attempt "to identify the essential characteristics of a trademark with inventions and discoveries in the arts and sciences, or with the writings of authors, will show that the effort is surrounded with insurmountable difficulties." It noted that "trademark recognized by the common law is generally the growth of a considerable period of use, rather than a sudden invention. It is often the result of accident, rather than design, and when under the act of Congress it is sought to establish it by registration, neither originality, invention, discovery, science, nor art is in any way essential to the right conferred by that act. . . . The trademark may be, and generally is, the adoption of something already in existence as the distinctive symbol of the party using it. At common law, the exclusive right to it grows out of its use, and not its mere adoption."

To constitute Tribunals inferior to the supreme Court;[98]

---

98. All federal courts inferior to the Supreme Court are established under this clause and Article III, Section 1. The thirteen federal circuits and scores of district courts are all created by statutes authorized under this clause. In theory, Congress could, by majority vote, abolish all courts save the Supreme Court and all judgeships

save the chief justice, though were a lawsuit to be brought on the matter it is possible an argument could be adduced that the plain language of the Constitution suggests the founders expected more than one justice to be set up. Anti-Federalists opposed the delegation to the Congress of the power to constitute tribunals inferior to the Supreme Court on the grounds that the creation of a federal court system would displace state courts and dilute local legislative and judicial power. "To have inferior courts appointed under the authority of Congress in the different States," Luther Martin warned in *The Genuine Information*, "would eventually absorb and swallow up the State judiciaries, by drawing all business from them to the courts of the general government, which the extensive and undefined powers, legislative and judicial, of which it possessed, would easily enable it to do."

To define and punish Piracies[99] and Felonies committed on the high Seas,[100] and Offences against the Law of Nations;[101]

99. The first piracy law, passed in 1790, led to a memorable dissent from a Supreme Court justice over the question of a comma. The law and its many clauses and commas left some ambiguity in respect of whether the death sentence was to be imposed on all pirates or only on those pirates who committed sea crimes that would be considered capital had they been committed ashore. Three pirates—John Palmer, Thomas Wilson, and Barney Colloghan—appealed on the question of whether all robberies at sea were to result in the death penalty, or only those robberies that would warrant a death sentence if committed on land. It was in this case, decided in 1818 as *United States v. Palmer*, that the Supreme Court heard the classic formulation: "criminal laws are to be construed liberally as to the offence, and strictly as to the offender." It went on to say that any robbery at sea would result in the death penalty. Justice William Johnson gave as strongly worded a dissent as has ever been penned.

"And singular as it may appear, it really is the fact in this case, that these men's lives may depend upon a comma more or less. . . . Upon such a question I here solemnly declare, that I never will consent to take the life of any man in obedience to any court; and if ever forced to choose between obeying this court, on such a point, or resigning my commission, I would not hesitate adopting the latter alternative."

The justice did not need to resign. While Marshall ruled against the alleged pirates on the point of grammar, he ruled for them on another fine point, that the 1790 act was intended to punish only acts against America—"an act for the punishment of certain crimes against the United States"—and therefore could not be used to prosecute the men for robbing sugar, rum, honey, coffee, silver, and gold from the *Industria Raffaelli*, a ship sailed by Spaniards. This despite the fact that nowhere in the act itself, save for the title, is there any language that would seem to limit violations to pirate attacks in which either the pirates or the victims were American. Congress promptly amended the law to allow for the prosecution of "any person or persons whatsoever" who commit piracy on the high seas.

In 2009 a federal grand jury at New York handed up the first indictment for piracy in more than a century—of one Abdi Wali Muse for allegedly attacking a U.S.-flagged vessel, the *Maersk Alabama*, and kidnapping its captain off the coast of Somalia.

100. Joseph Story, in *Commentaries*, reckons "high seas" embraces

> not only the waters of the ocean, which are out of sight of land, but the waters on the sea coast below the low-water mark, whether within the territorial boundaries of a foreign nation or of a domestic state. Justice Blackstone has remarked that the main sea or high sea begins at the low-water mark. But between the high-water mark and the low-water mark, where the tide ebbs and flows, the common law and the admiralty have divisum imperium, an alternate jurisdiction, one upon the water, when it is full sea; the other upon the land, when it is an ebb. He doubtless here refers to the waters of the ocean on the

seacoast, and not in creeks and inlets. Lord Hale says the sea "is either that, which lies within the body of the county or without. That, which lies without the body of a county, is called the main sea, or ocean. So far, then, as regards the states of the Union, 'high seas' may be taken to mean that part of the ocean, which washes the sea-coast, and is without the body of any county, according to the common law; and, so far as regards foreign nations, any waters on their sea-coast, below low-water mark."

101. Of the law of nations, James Kent, the jurist, in *Commentaries on American Law*, wrote: "By this law we are to understand that code of public instruction which defines the rights and prescribes the duties of nations, in their intercourse with each other." Earlier on the page, Kent wrote: "When the United States ceased to be a part of the British empire, and assumed the character of an independent nation, they became subject to that system of rules which reason, morality, and custom had established among the civilized nations of Europe, as their public law." Of offenses against the law of nations, William Rawle, in *View of the Constitution of the United States*, writes, "the most prominent subjects under this head are those which relate to the per-sons and privileges of ambassadors."

In 1820, Congress broadened the definition of pirates to include those engaged in the slave trade. The law declared that any U.S. citi-zen on a foreign vessel engaged in the slave trade "shall be adjudged a pirate," and, upon conviction, "shall suffer death." The move drew resistance from Chief Justice Marshall.

Marshall, in a decision on a slave ship, *Antelope*, being held at Georgia while both Spain and Portugal pressed for the return of its cargo, wrote in 1825: "However abhorrent this traffic may be to a mind whose original feelings are not blunted by familiarity with the practice, it has been sanctioned in modern times by the laws of all nations who possess distant colonies, each of whom has engaged in it as a common commercial business which no other could rightfully interrupt."

To declare War,[102] grant Letters of Marque and Reprisal,[103] and make Rules concerning Captures on Land and Water;[104]

---

102. Five formal declarations of war were enacted by Congress: against the British Empire on June 18, 1812; against Mexico on May 11, 1846; against Spain on April 24, 1898; against Germany and Austria-Hungary on, respectively, April 6, 1917, and December 7, 1917; and against Japan and Germany on, respectively, December 8, 1941, and December 11, 1941.

It was this power and the Article II powers of the president as commander in chief that the Supreme Court cited when, in *Korematsu v. United States*, it refused to rule unconstitutional President Franklin Delano Roosevelt's internment of Japanese Americans during World War II. Stomach ulcers prevented Fred Korematsu from joining the Navy, and so he contributed to the war effort as a welder in northern California, employment he soon lost due to anti-Japanese sentiment. When his county was declared a military zone, the first step toward internment, Korematsu hoped to mask his ethnicity by undergoing plastic surgery on his eyelids and changing his name. A few months later, after successfully avoiding being shipped to the camps, he was, despite his altered identity, caught on a street corner and arrested. In the opinion, Justice Hugo Black wrote that the Court was "unable to conclude that it was beyond the war power of Congress and the Executive to exclude those of Japanese ancestry from the West Coast war area at the time they did" as the measure had "a definite and close relationship to the prevention of espionage and sabotage." Justice Robert Jackson issued a famous dissenting opinion, one of three, in which he said, "The courts can exercise only the judicial power, can apply only law, and must abide by the Constitution, or they cease to be civil courts and become instruments of military policy."

103. A letter of marque and reprisal authorizes a private citizen to carry out attacks and raids on other nations or their interests. That this authority is given to Congress, and not to the president, has been used to suggest that the founders envisioned Congress as possessing

some oversight of the execution of war. Letters of marque and reprisal have rarely been granted. The Confederacy made use of the instruments during the Civil War. Within a week of the attack on Fort Sumter, Jefferson Davis issued a proclamation inviting those who wanted to help the Rebellion "by service in private armed vessels on the high seas" to make "application for commissions or letters of marque and reprisal to be issued under the seal of these Confederate States." Despite authorization by the Congress, President Lincoln, in the face of dissension within his cabinet, declined to issue letters of marque and reprisal. Secretary of State Seward lobbied Lincoln to grant such letters, while the Navy secretary, Gideon Welles, was opposed. Congress authorized Lincoln to grant such letters in 1863, over opposition from Senator Sumner. A flavor of the debate in Congress is provided by William Salter in his biography of Senator James W. Grimes, who pressed for the grant of letters of marque in, among other places, a speech in which he asked: "What real objection can be urged against the policy of granting letters of marque, that may not be urged against the employment of the militia upon land? I can imagine none. Do not vessels carrying letters of marque have our commission? Do they not sail under our flag? Are they not manned by our countrymen? Are they not responsible to our laws? Must not their captures be condemned under our admiralty laws and in our courts?"

Since September 11, 2001, Representative Ron Paul of Texas has twice proposed legislation that would authorize the president to issue letters of marque and reprisal to "privately armed and equipped persons and entities" to seize the terrorist leader Osama bin Laden or any al Qaeda co-conspirator and take any of their property. The last effort to commission privateers under this Article I power occurred in 1981, when a lawyer in Key West, Florida, petitioned Congress to allow him to plunder drug smugglers, according to a *New York Times* article of December 16, 1981. The petitioner, Randy Ludacer, claimed, according to the *Times* dispatch, to have one hundred volunteers behind him.

In 1998, the *Wall Street Journal* published an op-ed by Seth Gitell pointing out that Congress had created another approach for private citizens to attack the assets of foreign powers responsible for hostile actions against America—tort law. He referred to the Anti-Terrorism and Effective Death Penalty Act of 1996, which authorizes private plaintiffs to sue foreign states that sponsor terrorism. Gitell quoted Stephen Flatow, whose daughter, Alisa, had been killed in a terrorist attack against Israel, as having suggested that "maybe the Anti-Terrorism Act is a letter of marque with a fancy title."

Such suits, sometimes resulting in judgments well in excess of $100 million, have become increasingly common, and have been used against Iran and Cuba, among others. Plaintiffs have, by and large, had difficulty collecting the judgments. The approach arguably raises separation of power questions. Article I delegates authority to Congress to empower private citizens to plunder certain foreign targets. In authorizing plaintiffs to sue foreign states for sponsoring terrorism, Congress arguably is ceding its Article I authority to be the fact finder in questions of foreign policy to Article III judges.

104. This phrase—delegating to Congress the power to make "Rules concerning Captures on Land and Water"—was at the center of the debate between Congress and the administration of President George W. Bush over which would dictate how suspected terrorists are treated. Senator John McCain, in arguing for an amendment that would prohibit detainees from being subjected to "cruel, inhuman, or degrading treatment," said, "I would like to point out the Congress not only has the right but the obligation to act. Article 1, Section 8 of the Constitution of the United States, clause 11: 'To declare War, grant Letters of Marque and Reprisal, and make Rules concerning Captures on Land and Water.'" Executive branch officials argued that Congress could not limit the president's prerogative on how to treat captured terror suspects. The reporter Barton Gellman, in his book on Vice President Cheney, *The Angler*, recounts a conversation at the White House that occurred between Representative Jane Harman, a Democrat of California, and the vice president's attorney, David Addington. Harman, according to Gellman, "wanted to work with the White House on new rules" governing the interrogation of suspected terrorists. Gellman recounts what happened next: "She

came armed with the Constitution. Addington, she figured, would like that. Article 1, Section 8, gave Congress the power to 'make rules concerning captures on land and water.'"

"'That doesn't apply,'" Gellman quotes Addington as replying. "'That's about piracy.'" Addington's response suggested he was familiar with Madison's notes of the debates at the Constitutional Convention, which indicate that piracy was the topic when this clause was hammered out. In the event, Harman understood, the founders chose not to limit Congress's authority on captures to piracy.

To raise and support Armies,[105] but no Appropriation of Money to that Use shall be for a longer Term than two Years;[106]

---

105. These words give Congress the authority to draft citizens into the military. Lincoln, in a legal opinion not made public during the Civil War, called objections to the nation's first conscription law, the Draft Act of 1863, "the first instance, I believe, in which the power of Congress to do a thing has ever been questioned in a case when the power is given by the Constitution in express terms. Whether a power can be implied when it is not expressed has often been the subject of controversy; but this is the first case in which the degree of effrontery has been ventured upon of denying a power which is plainly and distinctly written down in the Constitution." Wrote Lincoln of the power delegated: "It is not a power to raise armies if State authorities consent; nor if the men to compose the armies are entirely willing; but it is a power to raise and support armies given to Congress by the Constitution, without an 'if.'"

The question of the constitutionality of the draft never reached the Supreme Court during the Civil War, but during World War I the Court quickly dismissed any constitutional objections, including one to the draft based on the Thirteenth Amendment's prohibition of slavery. "As the mind cannot conceive an army without the men to compose it, on the face of the Constitution, the objection that it does not give power to provide for such men would seem to be too frivolous for further notice," Chief Justice White wrote in the selective draft law cases of 1918. Noting the dearth of constitutional challenges to the Civil War draft in Union courts, the chief justice actually cited Confederate court decisions.

> And as further evidence that the conclusion we reach is but the inevitable consequence of the provisions of the Constitution as effect follows cause, we briefly recur to events in another environment. The seceding States wrote into the constitution which was adopted to regulate the government which they sought to establish, in identical words, the provisions of the Constitution of the United States which we here have under consideration. And when the right to enforce under that instrument a selective draft law which was enacted, not differing in principle from the one here in question, was challenged, its validity was upheld, evidently after great consideration, by the courts of Virginia, of Georgia, of Texas, of Alabama, of Mississippi, and of North Carolina, the opinions in some of the cases copiously and critically reviewing the whole grounds which we have stated.

106. Of the two-year limit, Akhil Amar, in *America's Constitution: A Biography*, wrote: "America would never be more than two years away from presumptive demilitarization." Yet the Justice Department has not read this to stand in the way of long-term defense contracts that are behind the development of nearly every advanced weapons system. According to the Congressional Research Service annotated edition of the Constitution: "In 1904, the question arose whether this provision would be violated if the Government contracted to pay a royalty for use of a patent in constructing guns and other equipment where the payments are likely to continue for more than two years. Solicitor-General Hoyt ruled that such a contract

would be lawful; that the appropriations limited by the Constitution 'are those only which are to raise and support armies in the strict sense of the word "support," and that the inhibition of that clause does not extend to appropriations for the various means which an army may use in military operations, or which are deemed necessary for the common defense.'" Relying on this earlier opinion, Attorney General Tom Clark ruled in 1948 that there was "no legal objection to a request to the Congress to appropriate funds to the Air Force for the procurement of aircraft and aeronautical equipment to remain available until expended."

To provide and maintain a Navy;[107]

107. Anti-Federalist William Grayson of Virginia thought that building and manning a navy would favor the economies of northern cities. At the Virginia ratifying convention, Grayson said: "All the vessels of the intended fleet would be built and equipped in the Northern States, where they have every necessary material and convenience for the purpose. Will any gentleman say that any ship of war can be raised to the south of Cape Charles? The consequence will be that the Southern States will be in the power of the Northern States." As it turned out, the world's largest naval base, Norfolk, is in Grayson's home state of Virginia. Norfolk traces its roots to the colonial era, and it built two ships for the Continental Navy.

The founders were attracted to a standing navy, although they feared a standing army. Amar points out that the Section 8 prohibition against standing appropriations for longer than two years applies to the army only. And what role did the founders intend for this Navy? Beyond protecting America's merchant fleet, the Navy was to be the new country's picket fence—the protection that America would need to isolate itself from the tumultuous affairs of its neighbors across the Atlantic. Hamilton had high hopes that the Navy would allow America to become involved in hemispheric affairs: the "Arbiter of Europe in America" is how he put it in 11 *Federalist*.

The Air Force took off from a runway other than the Constitution, which provides for two independent branches of the military— not three. Edward Corwin reports that in 1947, shortly after the U.S. Army Air Forces was reorganized into an independent force, there was at least one proposal to amend the Constitution, but it came to naught.

To make Rules for the Government and Regulation of the land and naval Forces;[108]

108. This clause gives Congress wide-ranging authority to govern military personnel in ways that wouldn't be constitutional if applied to the civilian population. This includes exempting women from the draft and setting up a system of military justice. The scope of the authority is laid out in *Parker v. Levy*, brought by an army doctor, Howard Levy, who was sentenced to three years of hard labor for refusing to teach Special Forces medics during the Vietnam War. Quoth the Supreme Court: "For the reasons which differentiate military society from civilian society, we think Congress is permitted to legislate both with greater breadth and with greater flexibility when prescribing the rules by which the former shall be governed than it is when prescribing rules for the latter. . . . While the members of the military are not excluded from the protection granted by the First Amendment, the different character of the military community and of the military mission requires a different application of those protections."

Justice Stevens, in ruling on the appeal filed from Guantanamo by one of Osama bin Laden's chauffeurs, Salim Ahmed Hamdan, quoted a citation of this clause in *Ex Parte Milligan*, a case that curtailed the government's power to use military commissions to try civilians when civilian courts were functioning. "The power to make the necessary laws is in Congress; the power to execute in the President. Both powers imply many subordinate and auxiliary powers. Each includes all authorities essential to its due exercise. But neither can the President, in war more than in peace, intrude upon the proper authority of Congress, nor Congress upon the proper authority of the President. . . . Congress cannot direct the conduct of campaigns, nor can the President, or any commander under him, without the sanction of Congress, institute tribunals for the trial and punishment of offences, either of soldiers or civilians, unless in cases of a controlling necessity, which justifies what it compels, or at least insures acts of indemnity from the justice of the legislature."

To provide for calling forth the Militia to execute the Laws of the Union, suppress Insurrections[109] and repel Invasions;[110]

109. Abolitionists saw in this clause a proslavery bent. A leader in the fight against slavery, Wendell Phillips, wrote that it did "deliberately pledge the whole national force against the unhappy slave if he imitate our fathers and resist oppression—thus making us partners in the guilt of sustaining slavery."

110. Since early in America's history, all three branches of government, as well as the states, had a hand in the execution of this clause. Congress quickly transferred to the president its authority to call the militia, requiring that a federal judge first certify that the laws of the country were being opposed by a force too powerful for the courts or marshals to handle. That requirement was later eliminated. States also have their own concurrent authority to call up their militias.

An early, important test of the militia's power occurred in 1794 during the Whiskey Rebellion. Incensed by a tax on distillers, residents—many of them members of the local militia—attacked collectors and assembled an army in western Pennsylvania. After securing permission from a judge, President Washington responded by summoning nearly 13,000 militiamen from Maryland, New Jersey, Pennsylvania, and Virginia. It was an army larger than any he had led during the Revolution. In a rare case of a sitting president personally leading the troops, Washington marched the army west and dispersed the rebels.

This critical moment in American history demonstrated the federal government's authority in the years following the signing of the Constitution. The president's authority over the militia crystallized following the War of 1812. The war was so unpopular in New England that the state governments of Connecticut, Massachusetts, and Rhode Island refused to summon their militias when it began, despite a call to do so from President Madison. The governors made various legal claims to justify their resistance—for example, that the country first needed to be in imminent danger of invasion and their troops could not serve in the regular army. Historian Donald R. Hickey relates that Governor Strong of Massachusetts and Governor Griswold of Connecticut "argued that, internal disorders aside, the militia could not be called out unless the country were invaded or were in imminent danger of invasion, and that no such contingency existed. Moreover, because the states were constitutionally charged with appointing the militia officers, the Connecticut council and the Massachusetts court held that their troops could not serve under regulars."

It wasn't only governors who protested. A private in a New York militia company, Jacob Mott, challenged the call-up order after he was court-martialed for failing to appear for duty during the war. In the resulting Supreme Court case, *Martin v. Mott*, the Court, in 1827, established that the president gets the benefit of the doubt when he—and he exclusively—decides that the required threat exists: "The power itself is to be exercised upon sudden emergencies, upon great occasions of state, and under circumstances which may be vital to the existence of the Union. A prompt and unhesitating obedience to orders is indispensable to the complete attainment of the object. The service is a military service, and the command of a military nature, and in such cases every delay and every obstacle to an efficient and immediate compliance necessarily tend to jeopard the public interests."

"Besides," the Court added, "in many instances the evidence upon which the President might decide that there is imminent danger of invasion might be of a nature not constituting strict technical proof, or the disclosure of the evidence might reveal important secrets of state which the public interest, and even safety, might imperiously demand to be kept in concealment."

More than a century after *Mott*, the struggle for control of the militia played a critical role in the integration of southern schools. In the wake of *Brown v. Board of Education*, nine black students desegregated Little Rock's Central High School. Governor Orval Faubus responded by summoning the state's National Guard to block the students' entry. He eventually withdrew them, but in doing so left the school in control of the mob. President Eisenhower responded by sending in a thousand Regular Army paratroopers, part of the 101st Airborne Division, to escort the students. He also took command of the state National Guard and sent it in on the side of the United States.

Eisenhower chose to lead with the 101st because it could respond more quickly than the National Guard, and because he wasn't sure he could rely on the Arkansas Guardsmen to follow federal orders.

Five years later, when James Meredith integrated the University of Mississippi at Oxford, the state's National Guard, which President Kennedy had federalized, played a crucial role in rescuing the besieged federal marshals who were being attacked on campus; 28 of them would be shot by the end of the violence. In all, some 30,000 troops, a combination of Guardsmen and active Army troops, would quell the rebellion.

To provide for organizing, arming, and disciplining,[111] the Militia,[112] and for governing such Part of them as may be employed in the Service of the United States,[113]

---

111. In 1916 Enoch Herbert Crowder, judge advocate general, U.S. Army, offered this interpretation of these three gerunds: "'Or-

ganizing' meant proportioning the officers and men; 'arming' meant specifying the kind, size, and caliber of arms; and 'disciplining' meant prescribing a drill book." Crowder, one of the military's most able legal minds and the man who would be tasked with administering the draft in World War I, said the substance of the debate in Philadelphia suggested "that it was prominently writ in the minds of those framers of this particular provision of the Constitution that the militia they were authorizing and regulating was primarily a State force and only contingently and within quite a restricted field could it be a Federal force."

112. "Those of us who are male and able-bodied have almost all been militiamen for most of our lives whether we know it or not, whether we were organized or not, whether our state government supervised our possession and use of arms or not." So wrote Judge Andrew Kleinfeld of the 9th Circuit in 2003, in a dissent in *Silveira v. Lockyer*, a case in which the 9th Circuit held that the Second Amendment does not confer an individual right to keep and bear arms, a holding that was eventually found by the Supreme Court, in *District of Columbia v. Heller*, to be a misreading. Kleinfeld based his definition on the United States Code, Title 10, Section 311, which states: "The militia of the United States consists of all able-bodied males at least 17 years of age and . . . under 45 years of age who are, or who have made a declaration of intention to become, citizens of the United States and of female citizens of the United States who are members of the National Guard."

113. The Constitution contemplates three scenarios in which the militia would be employed in the service of America: to enforce laws, to quell rebellions, and to repel invasions (please see p. 74). Congress has found a way around these limitations. A recent Supreme Court opinion, *Perpich v. DOD*, recounts what happened: "Until 1952, the statutory authority to order National Guard units to active duty was limited to periods of national emergency. In that year, Congress broadly authorized orders to 'active duty or active duty for training' without any emergency requirement, but provided that such orders could not be issued without gubernatorial consent."

reserving to the States respectively, the Appointment of the Officers, and the Authority of training the Militia[114] according to the discipline prescribed by Congress;

---

114. The Constitution is adamant that in peacetime the states retain "Authority of training the Militia." In 1990 the Supreme Court ruled that the federal government could call up National Guard units and send them overseas for training, despite the objections of the governors of states from which those Guard units came. The issue arose in the mid-1980s when Guard units were being dispatched to Honduras to build roads and engage in other infrastructure-building projects that were expected to be of use should America use Honduras as a staging ground for an invasion of neighboring Nicaragua. More generally, the overseas military presence of Guardsmen was a clear warning signal to the neighboring Sandinista government. In 1985 Governor Deukmejian of California refused to "send approximately 450 National Guardsmen to anti-armor training exercises near the Honduras-Nicaragua border," reports a University of Colorado law review article. Governors in more than half a dozen other states either followed Deukmejian's lead or pledged that they would.

Congress's response to these objections was to pass a law that stated: "The consent of a Governor . . . may not be withheld (in whole or in part) with regard to active duty outside the United States, its territories, and its possessions, because of any objection to the location, purpose, type, or schedule of such active duty."

Minnesota's governor, Rudolph Perpich, sued on the grounds that the law unconstitutionally impinged on the authority of states to train the militia, as these overseas assignments were considered training missions. The Supreme Court, in *Perpich v. DOD*, unanimously found that Congress hadn't unconstitutionally removed governors from having a say in where their state's Guard units were sent. The opinion, written by Justice Stevens, turned on the dual nature of the National Guard. Beginning in 1933, when a dual enlistment law was enacted, all soldiers enlisting in a state unit were automatically made part of the Army reserve. Justice Stevens wrote that this "dual enlistment system means that the members of the National Guard of Minnesota who are ordered into federal service with the National Guard of the United States lose their status as members of the State militia during their period of active duty. If that duty is a training mission, the training is performed by the Army in which the trainee is serving, not by the militia from which the member has been temporarily disassociated." Stevens further suggested that Congress had seized from the states so much control over Guard units that they were no longer what the Constitution spoke of when it mentioned the militia. The opinion said states that did not like their units being sent overseas were free to "provide and maintain at its own expense a defense force that is exempt from being drafted into the Armed Forces of the United States." The opinion continued: "As long as that provision remains in effect, there is no basis for an argument that the federal statutory scheme deprives Minnesota of any constitutional entitlement to a separate militia of its own."

To exercise exclusive Legislation[115] in all Cases whatsoever, over such District (not exceeding ten Miles square)[116] as may, by Cession of particular States,[117]

115. In 1973 Congress granted home rule to residents of the District, allowing for a mayor as well as a city council that can pass legislation subject to congressional approval.

116. Not ten square miles. Ten miles square is the equivalent of one hundred square miles. As a surveyor, President Washington proclaimed: "I do hereby declare and make known that the whole of the said territory shall be located and included within the four lines following, that is to say: Beginning at Jones's Point, being the upper cape of Hunting Creek, in Virginia, and at an angle in the outset of 45 degrees west of the north, and running in a direct line 10 miles for the first line."

117. The land for the national city was ceded by Maryland and Virginia in 1788 and 1789, according to Washington's proclamation on the founding of the city. In 1846 Congress ceded the Virginia portion of the land, which included Alexandria, back to that state. The future of slavery in the District was one of the issues affecting the decision. According to the census, the District is now 61.4 square miles, not the original 100. From the creation of the District until Congress would create new laws for the region, the laws of Maryland would remain in effect in the portions of the District ceded by Maryland, and Virginia law would apply in the Virginian portions.

and the Acceptance of Congress, become the Seat of the Government of the United States,[118] and to exercise like Authority over all Places purchased by the Consent of the Legislature of the State in which the Same shall be, for the Erection of Forts, Magazines, Arsenals, dockYards, and other needful Buildings;[119] —And

---

118. The need for a federal city was put into sharp relief by the events of June 20, 1783. On that day, as it is retold by historian Mark Noll, "a mutinous group of soldiers from the Maryland Line, assigned to guard duty in Philadelphia and Lancaster County, surrounded their meeting place, the Pennsylvania State House. This hard-drinking band had heard that Congress planned to discharge them without settling back pay, and so they were taking matters into their own hands. After a standoff lasting three hours, the legislators passed peacefully through the mutineers and then called upon Pennsylvania to disperse the rioters. When nothing happened, Congress resolved to leave Philadelphia."

Of the need for a federal city, Madison wrote in 43 *Federalist*: "Without it, not only the public authority might be insulted and its proceedings be interrupted, with impunity; but a dependence of the members of the general Government, on the State comprehending the seat of the Government for protection in the exercise of their duty, might bring on the national councils an imputation of awe or influence, equally dishonorable to the Government, and dissatisfactory to the other members of the confederacy. This consideration has the more weight as the gradual accumulation of public improvements at the stationary residence of the Government, would be both too great a public pledge to be left in the hands of a single State." According to Elliott's *Debates*, "Mr. Gouverneur Morris did not dislike the idea, but was apprehensive that such a clause might make enemies of Philda. & N. York, which had expectations of becoming the Seat of the Genl. Govt."

"Inside the Beltway," a derisive reference to the capital city, is mild in comparison to the warnings issued at the founding. The Anti-Federalists, who wanted the national government to meet in a place under the jurisdiction of a state, predicted the federal city would become a sort of Gomorrah of politicians and their hangers-on. One, writing in 18 *Federal Farmer*, deemed it "a novel kind of provision in a federal republic" and "repugnant to the spirit of such a government" and reckoned it "must be founded in an apprehension of a hostile disposition between the federal head and the state governments." Thomas Tredwell, at New York's ratifying convention, described the future city as a place "where men are to live, without labor, upon the fruit of the labors of others; this political hive, where all the drones in the society are to be collected to feed on the honey of the land." At the Virginia ratifying convention, George Mason predicted that the federal city would "become the sanctuary of the blackest crimes."

119. In 43 *Federalist*, Madison offers a straightforward explanation for this clause: "The public money expended on such places, and the public property deposited in them, require that they should be exempt from the authority of the particular State. Nor would it be proper for the places on which the security of the entire Union may depend, to be in any degree dependent on a particular member of it.

All objections and scruples are here also obviated by requiring the concurrence of the States concerned, in every such establishment." California cited this clause in defending its effort to tax the sale of alcohol at Yosemite, even though it was national parkland. It suggested that the federal government couldn't exercise jurisdiction over land that it held for purposes other than those enumerated above. Parkland, the state postulated, didn't fit the bill. The Supreme Court, in *Collins v. Yosemite Park & Curry Co.*, said the clause "has not been strictly construed."

Does the founders' use of the word "exclusive" to describe jurisdiction mean that none of the civil rights that state citizens enjoy extend to a so-called federal enclave that might lie within a state? A 1956 report by the Interdepartmental Committee for the Study of Jurisdiction over Federal Areas Within the States noted that in 1841 the Massachusetts Supreme Judicial Court opined that persons living on federal land are, as the Massachusetts court put it, "not entitled to the benefits of the common schools for their children, in the towns in which such lands are situated." When the New Mexico Supreme Court ruled in a pair of decisions that Los Alamos residents weren't state citizens, and therefore could neither vote in state elections nor sue for divorce in state courts, the federal government decided to cede Los Alamos to the state in 1949. In 1936 the federal government began to give states jurisdiction over these so-called federal enclaves in the narrow arena of workmen's compensation laws. The need for that law was illustrated during the construction of the Golden Gate Bridge, the approaches to which stood atop federal land. The 1956 report quoted an earlier investigation by Congress that found private insurance companies were using court precedents that seemed to hold that State Compensation Insurance Acts do not apply, "leaving the workers wholly unprotected" except through common law right to sue.

Is the United Nations headquarters in New York City a "needful building," and who now has "exclusive jurisdiction"? A professor at Columbia Law School, Louis Henkin, in *Foreign Affairs and the United States Constitution*, noted that the New York legislature authorized the governor "to cede to the United States jurisdiction over the territory of the U.N. headquarters, presumably in the expectation that the United States might in turn cede jurisdiction to the United Nations." But he goes on to say: "Neither the governor nor the United States has executed such cession. To the extent that some cession by the United States is implicit in the terms of the U.N. Headquarters Agreement, June 26, 1947, the consent of New York was in effect obtained through the act of its legislature."

To make all Laws which shall be necessary and proper[120] for carrying into Execution the foregoing Powers, and all other Powers vested by this Constitution in the Government of the United States, or in any Department or Officer thereof.

120. From the beginning the Anti-Federalists feared this clause would prove to be a constitutional loophole. "Under such a clause as this can any thing be said to be reserved and kept back from Congress?" wrote An Old Whig. "Can it be said that the Congress have no power but what *is expressed*? 'To make all laws which shall be necessary and proper' is in other words to make all such laws which *the Congress shall think necessary and proper*. . . . What limits are there to their authority?—I fear none at all; for surely it cannot justly be said that they have no power but what is expressly given to them, where by the very terms of their creation they are vested with the powers of making laws in all cases necessary and proper; when from the nature of their power they must necessarily be the judges, what laws are necessary and proper."

During the ratification debates the Virginia Anti-Federalists called this "the sweeping clause," giving rise to Jefferson's famous witticism in a letter, sent in 1800, to Edward Livingston: "Congress are authorized to defend the nation. Ships are necessary for defence; copper is necessary for ships; mines necessary for copper; a company necessary to work mines; and who can doubt this reasoning who has ever played at 'This is the House that Jack built?' Under such a process of filiation of necessities the sweeping clause makes clean work."

In 33 *Federalist*, on the general power of taxation, Hamilton had mounted a defense of the cagey clause. "What is a power, but the ability or faculty of doing a thing? What is the ability to do a thing but the power of employing the *means* necessary to its execution? What is a LEGISLATIVE power but a power of making LAWS? What are the *means* to execute a LEGISLATIVE power but LAWS? What is the power of laying and collecting taxes but a *legislative power*, or a power of *making laws*, to lay and collect taxes? What are the proper means of executing such a power but *necessary* and *proper* laws? . . . Why then was it introduced? The answer is, that it could only have been done for greater caution, and to guard against all cavilling refinements in those who might hereafter feel a disposition to curtail and evade the legitimate authorities of the Union."

It was under this clause that the Supreme Court found, in 1819 in *McCulloch v. Maryland*, that Congress hadn't exceeded its power in creating a national bank. Maryland tried to argue that the purpose of the necessary and proper clause was merely to give Congress the right to legislate. Chief Justice Marshall mocked Maryland: "Could it be necessary to say that a legislature should exercise legislative powers, in the shape of legislation? After allowing each house to prescribe its own course of proceeding, after describing the manner in which a bill should become a law, would it have entered into the mind of a single member of the convention that an express power to make laws was necessary to enable the legislature to make them? That a legislature, endowed with legislative powers, can legislate is a proposition too self-evident to have been questioned."

Concluded Marshall: "The result of the most careful and attentive consideration bestowed upon this clause is that, if it does not enlarge, it cannot be construed to restrain, the powers of Congress, or to impair the right of the legislature to exercise its best judgment in the selection of measures to carry into execution the Constitutional powers of the Government. If no other motive for its insertion can be suggested, a sufficient one is found in the desire to remove all doubts respecting the right to legislate on that vast mass of incidental powers which must be involved in the Constitution if that instrument be not a splendid bauble."

It was also under this clause that the Supreme Court eventually, in a series of cases known as the Legal Tender Cases, validated Congress's power to print the paper money it had started issuing during the Civil War. One of the cases, *Knox v. Lee*, involved payment for 608 sheep that a Mrs. Lee of Pennsylvania had owned and kept in Texas where, during the Civil War, they were taken by the Confederacy and sold to a man named Knox. Years later, when the time came for a jury to be instructed on what to award Mrs. Lee, a lower court issued a cautionary suggestion: "In assessing damages, the jury will recollect that whatever amount they may give by their verdict can be discharged by the payment of such amount in legal tender notes of the United States." It was a not so subtle hint in respect of paper money, originally known as greenbacks, that the Congress first authorized the government to issue during the Civil War. (Please see note 90.)

The jury, apparently discounting for the fact that the payment was going to be made in paper money, gave an award that Knox felt was too high. So he sued and gained a hearing before the Supreme Court on the whole question of paper money. It had been ruled unconstitutional by a 5 to 3 Supreme Court vote in *Hepburn v. Griswold*. Chief Justice Salmon Portland Chase, who had endorsed the greenbacks scheme when he was Treasury secretary, abandoned his support when he mounted the high bench and heard *Hepburn*. But when the Court was expanded to nine members in 1869, the justices heard the case of Mrs. Lee's flock, reversed *Hepburn*, and upheld the greenback.

An associate justice, William Strong, delivered the opinion for the Court, citing the necessary and proper clause as giving Congress the cover it needed. But Chief Justice Chase dissented. He agreed that the question of "whether a law is a necessary and proper means to execution of an express power" is a "judicial question." Congress, he said, "may not adopt any means for the execution of an express power that Congress may see fit to adopt." But "whether the means actually employed in a given case are such or not, the court must decide. The court must judge of the fact, Congress of the degree of necessity."

A hapless farmer, Roscoe Curtiss Filburn of Ohio, seeking shelter under the commerce clause to market his wheat in the face of prohibitions under President Franklin Roosevelt's Agricultural Adjustment Act, went to court against the secretary of agriculture and almost succeeded until he got to the Supreme Court. In an opinion written by Associate Justice Robert Jackson in a case called *Wickard v. Filburn*, the Court accepted the government's argument on the commerce clause, but added, ominously, that even if the act stretched the commerce clause, "it is sustainable as a 'necessary and proper' implementation of the power of Congress over interstate commerce." The "necessary and proper" clause was cited by the Supreme Court against a distinguished physician in New York City, Samuel Lambert, who tried in vain to win the leeway to use his judgment, rather than Congress's, in deciding whether to prescribe modest amounts of liquor for medicinal purposes.

SECTION 9. The Migration or Importation[121] of such Persons as any of the States now existing shall think proper to admit,[122] shall not be prohibited by the Congress prior to the Year one thousand eight hundred and eight,[123] but a Tax or duty may be imposed on such Importation, not exceeding ten dollars[124] for each Person.

---

121. Slaving. Because the Constitution countenanced slavery, some abolitionists believed the union between North and South was beyond redemption. William Lloyd Garrison's abolitionist newspaper, *The Liberator*, carried this message in its columns: "That the compact which exists between the North and the South is 'a covenant with DEATH, and an agreement with HELL'—involving both parties in atrocious criminality—and should be immediately annulled."

122. W.E.B. Du Bois, in his essay on the Federal Convention, wrote that in the debate "the moral arguments were prominent," and he quotes Colonel Mason as denouncing the trade as "infernal" and warning that the crime of slavery might yet bring God's judgment on the nation. South Carolina and Georgia were adamant, however. When General Pinckney first proposed to extend the slave-trading limit to 1808, Du Bois reports, Nathaniel Gorham of Massachusetts seconded the motion. This brought a protest from Madison: "Twenty years will produce all the mischief that can be apprehended from the liberty to import slaves. So long a term will be more dishonorable to the American character than to say nothing about it in the Constitution." Once the Constitution was sent out for ratification, Madison argued in 42 *Federalist*, "It ought to be considered as a great point gained in favor of humanity, that a period of twenty years may terminate for ever within these States, a traffic which has so long and so loudly upbraided the barbarism of modern policy; that within that period it will receive a considerable discouragement from the federal Government, and may be totally abolished by a concurrence of the few States which continue the unnatural traffic, in the prohibitory example which has been given by so great a majority of the Union. Happy would it be for the unfortunate Africans, if an equal prospect lay before them, of being redeemed from the oppressions of their European brethren!" Du Bois concluded that this clause was accepted by the various states "from widely different motives." He quotes James Wilson as saying: "I consider this as laying the foundation for banishing slavery out of this country." It proved to be an overly optimistic view.

123. An act curbing but not prohibiting the slave trade was passed in 1794. It outlawed fitting, equipping, loading, or otherwise preparing vessels used for transporting slaves. A law cited as "An Act to Prohibit the Importation of Slaves into any Port or Place Within the Jurisdiction of the United States, From and After the First Day of January, in the Year of our Lord One Thousand Eight Hundred and Eight" was passed in 1807. The struggle to expunge slavery from American soil would extend through the Civil War.

124. Efforts to pass such a tax on the importation of slaves met with resistance in the First Congress. Even some who opposed slavery argued that to vote for a tax was a form of approval. Roger Sherman of Connecticut stated that although he "approved of the object of the motion . . . he could not reconcile himself to the insertion of human beings as an article of duty, among goods, wares, and merchandise." The measure was argued down by both pro- and antislavery members of Congress, and, according to W.E.B. Du Bois, the first session had been "whirled into a discussion of too delicate and lengthy a nature to allow its further prolongation." The tax proposal was subsequently withdrawn. This clause contains one of but two mentions of dollars in the body of the Constitution. The other is in the Seventh Amendment in conferring the right to a jury trial for all civil disputes exceeding $20. The reference is to the Spanish milled dollar, which was made of silver. A discussion is on page 244.

The Privilege of the Writ of Habeas Corpus[125] shall not be suspended, unless when in Cases of Rebellion or Invasion the public Safety may require it.[126,127]

125. Latin for "you have the body"; the writ is an order for a jailer to produce a prisoner. A judge uses such a writ to inquire into the circumstances of a prisoner's detention with an eye toward freeing him if he is being held illegally.

126. The Constitution does not create the privilege of the writ of habeas corpus, which William Blackstone called "the most celebrated writ in the English law." According to Edward Corwin, the Constitution "simply assumes" that "it will be a part of the law of the land." In addition, the First Congress passed a statute providing for the writ, which has been updated as recently as 2007 and is at Title 28 of the United States Code, Section 2241. This clause of the Constitution prohibits the Congress from suspending the writ absent specified conditions. One of the constitutional questions before the

Supreme Court in recent years is whether the privilege of habeas corpus extends to foreigners being held offshore at the naval base at Guantanamo Bay, Cuba. In June 2008, in *Boumediene v. Bush*, the Supreme Court ruled that, absent formal suspension by Congress, the privilege of the writ of habeas corpus extended even there. That finding undercut the Bush administration's logic for holding terror suspects at the base. Administration lawyers had argued that foreign prisoners, once there, were beyond the review of the federal courts.

Could the Congress, if it desired, suspend habeas corpus in these circumstances? The Supreme Court in *Boumediene* suggested that it was certainly welcome to try. From Justice Kennedy's opinion: "If the privilege of habeas corpus is to be denied to the detainees now before us, Congress must act in accordance with the requirements of the Suspension Clause." Yet Jonathan Adler of Case Western Reserve Law School, one of a number of law professors who comment at a website called the Volokh Conspiracy, is not so sure that, in such circumstances, the Court would consider a suspension of habeas corpus constitutional. He suggests that the Constitution's language seems to impose two separate conditions on the use of the suspension clause: (1) rebellion or invasion and (2) public safety. Even were those requirements "justiciable," he asks, "What showing would the government have to make?" He deems the application to Guantanamo of the constitutional requirements for suspension "problematic at a conceptual level." Justice Scalia, however, characterized the Court's opinion as a "game of bait-and-switch" that "plays upon the Nation's Commander in Chief " and will "make the war harder on us. It will almost certainly cause more Americans to be killed. That consequence would be tolerable if necessary to preserve a time-honored legal principle vital to our constitutional Republic. But it is this Court's blatant *abandonment* of such a principle that produces the decision today."

127. One of the unanswered questions about this clause is who can suspend the writ. In April 1861, Lincoln, fearing that Maryland would secede and leave the District of Columbia surrounded by the rebels, suspended habeas corpus in parts of that state. The military

was then empowered to lock up without interference those who were fomenting a rebellion. Chief Justice Taney, writing as a circuit judge, ordered the release of one of the men held, John Merryman, on the grounds that only Congress—not the president—could suspend habeas. Taney, in his decision, noted that the suspension clause appears in Article I and contains "not the slightest reference to the executive department."

Yet by 1863, Congress agreed with Lincoln and authorized him to suspend habeas anywhere in the country. Congress has formally authorized the suspension of habeas in the states or territories on only three other occasions: in 1871 to assist Reconstruction efforts to suppress the Ku Klux Klan; during the insurrection in the Philippines, which lasted from 1899 to 1902, and in Hawaii following Pearl Harbor.

The most famous American judicial pronouncement in defense of habeas corpus came in 1866, on an appeal by Lambdin Milligan, an antiwar Democrat in Indiana who was sentenced by a military commission to hang for treason. The treason involved a plan to free locally held Confederate prisoners of war and kidnap the governor of Indiana. The Supreme Court released him on the grounds that a military commission did not have the right to try a citizen of Indiana so long as that state was at some semblance of peace and the courthouse was open. "Martial law cannot arise from a *threatened* invasion," Justice Davis wrote.

No Bill of Attainder[128]

---

128. A law that condemns an individual or group to be executed or subjected to lesser punishment. The British Parliament issued bills of attainder as death sentences against political enemies and traitors. The most famous was issued two years after Oliver Cromwell's death, ordering that his body be exhumed and displayed in postmortem punishment. In America during the Revolu-

tionary War, bills of attainder confiscating property were commonplace against British loyalists. Leonard Levy, in *Origins of the Bill of Rights*, numbers the persons against whom New York issued bills of attainder at more than one thousand. Levy reckons that the "most notorious bill of attainder in American history" was the one Jefferson wrote in Virginia condemning a Tory cutthroat, Josiah Philips, to death unless he surrendered within a month. The bill also included this provision: "that from and after the passing of this act it shall be lawful for any person with or without orders, to pursue and slay the said Josiah Philips and any others who have been his associates or confederates." The attainder never went into effect because, within a month of its enactment, Philips was captured and tried in court. He was executed for robbery. In the Virginia ratifying convention, Edmund Randolph, who had been the prosecutor, brought up the Philips bill of attainder. "I cannot contemplate it without horror," Randolph said. He called it "an example so horrid, that, if I conceived my country would passively permit a repetition of it, dear as it is to me, I would seek means of expatriating myself from it."

In 1800 the Supreme Court, in *Cooper v. Telfair*, upheld a bill of attainder that had been passed in 1782, before ratification. In 1965 the Supreme Court, in *U.S. v. Brown*, reversed a conviction under a federal law, the Landrum-Griffin Act, which made it a crime for a member of the Communist Party to serve as an officer of a labor union. Such a law, Chief Justice Warren wrote, violated the prohibition against bills of attainder. The plaintiff, Archie Brown, a Communist who worked as a longshoreman in San Francisco, had been sentenced to six months in prison for serving on the executive board of his local. Wrote Warren: "We do not hold today that Congress cannot weed dangerous persons out of the labor movement. . . . Rather, we make again the point . . . that Congress must accomplish such results by rules of general applicability. It cannot specify the people upon whom the sanction it prescribes is to be levied. Under our Constitution, Congress possesses full legislative authority, but the task of adjudication must be left to other tribunals."

After President Nixon resigned, he invoked the prohibition on bills of attainder to challenge a 1974 law that would have prevented destruction of hundreds of tape recordings made of his conversations while he was in office. Although the law singled out Nixon by name and applied only to his tape recordings, the majority of the Supreme Court was unconvinced that the law qualified as a bill of attainder. Chief Justice Burger wrote in a dissent: "I see no escape, therefore, from the conclusion that, on the basis of more than 180 years' history, the appellant has been deprived of a property right enjoyed by all other Presidents after leaving office, namely, the control of his Presidential papers." Justice Burger wrote at another point in the same opinion: "I need not, and do not, inquire into the motives of Congress in imposing this deprivation on only one named person. Our cases plainly hold that retribution and vindictiveness are not requisite elements of a bill of attainder."

or ex post facto Law[129] shall be passed.

129. A law that retroactively makes a lawful action illegal or one that retroactively increases the penalty for an unlawful act. A number of Supreme Court rulings on ex post facto laws came shortly after the Civil War and concerned newly required loyalty oaths that compelled certain professionals to pledge they had never aided the Confederacy. One case involved a federal law requiring such an oath of lawyers practicing in the federal courts. The oath was challenged by Augustus Hill Garland, who had represented Arkansas in the Confederate Congress, and, though pardoned by President Johnson, could not practice law pursuant to the oath. In *Ex Parte Garland* the high court struck down the law. Garland would go on to be elected to the Senate and eventually serve as attorney general under President Cleveland.

Ex Parte Garland, which was issued in 1876 and found that the law was both ex post facto and an attainder, is brief. A more passionate opinion on the subject was issued in the same year and involved a Catholic priest, John Cummings of Missouri, who'd been born in 1840 and ordained in 1863 and who kept to himself his views on the Civil War. He preached a sermon on Sunday, September 3, 1865, though Missouri had revised its constitution to mandate that an oath be taken by all persons who held public office, managed a private company, taught in school, or preached in church. The oath required that the individual swear that he had never been aligned with the Confederacy or even sympathetic to it. Cummings had never taken the required oath and was sentenced to pay $500. In *Cummings v. Missouri*, the Supreme Court objected to the clauses that, in respect of some acts, "impose additional punishment to that prescribed when the act was committed." As the loyalty oath in the Missouri case was a state enactment—not a federal one—the relevant constitutional prohibition is the Section 10 rule against such state enactments (please see p. 109), not this Section 9 language.

No Capitation,[130] or other direct, Tax[131] shall be laid,

130. A head tax on all inhabitants. "Congress has never enacted a capitation tax," according to scholar Erik Jensen, who has noted that "most people understand the term to refer to a lump-sum charge on each taxed person" and differentiates it from a tax on income. Jensen, *en passant*, notes that slaves were generally included when Congress, in the years leading up to 1861, taxed real estate.

131. "What was the precise meaning of *direct* taxation?" a Massachusetts delegate, Rufus King, asked at the Convention in Philadelphia. His fellow delegates, according to Madison, offered little help. "No one answd," Madison jotted down in his shorthand. There is, as Madison's notes suggest, no generally accepted definition of direct tax. The Supreme Court, in 1796 in *Hylton v. United States*, mulled the question of whether a tax on carriages was a direct tax, and therefore had to be apportioned among the states by population, in accordance

with the second half of this clause. Writing for the Court, Justice Paterson noted: "Whether direct taxes, in the sense of the Constitution, comprehend any other tax than a capitation tax and tax on land is a questionable point." A University of Texas law professor, Calvin Johnson, argues that the "Founders usually used the term 'direct tax' as a synonym for 'internal taxes,' meaning all taxes except taxes on imports or exports."

unless in Proportion to the Census or Enumeration herein before directed to be taken.[132]

132. Were an income tax direct, it would have to be apportioned among the states according to population; such a tax would be impossibly regressive. "Apportioning an income tax among the states on the basis of respective state populations would probably have required different tax rates in different states (or some other rickety structure)," Professor Jensen points out. "Furthermore, to make apportionment come out right, citizens of higher-income states would probably have been subject to tax at *lower* rates than those in lower-income states. Apportionment of that sort could have been handled technically (congressional staffers can do the math to get the numbers right), but such a step would have been almost impossible politically."

The question of whether income taxes had to be apportioned was made moot by the Sixteenth Amendment, which exempted income taxes from apportionment. The amendment responded to the Supreme Court's 1895 decision in the case of *Pollock v. Farmers' Loan & Trust Co.*, which dismantled the federal income tax of 1894 on the grounds that the tax wasn't apportioned among the states. The tax was 2 percent of all corporate and personal income above $4,000. In its decision, the Court suggested that the apportionment requirement was intended to protect wealth by making it more difficult for the have-nots to tax the haves.

In *Hylton*, the riding carriage case, Justice Paterson shed some light on the intent of the founders, of whom he was one: "The provision was made in favor of the southern states. They possessed a large number of slaves; they had extensive tracts of territory, thinly settled and not very productive. A majority of the states had but few slaves, and several of them a limited territory, well settled, and in a high state of cultivation. The southern states, if no provision had been introduced in the Constitution, would have been wholly at the mercy of the other states. Congress in such case might tax slaves at discretion or arbitrarily, and land in every part of the Union after the same rate or measure: so much a head in the first instance, and so much an acre in the second. To guard them against imposition in these particulars was the reason of introducing the clause in the Constitution which directs that representatives and direct taxes shall be apportioned among the states according to their respective numbers."

While there may have been a purpose behind the apportionment clause, modern scholars have been less impressed with the mechanism the founders chose. The apportionment requirement has been called "a glitch, or foul-up, in the core of the Constitution." Professor Johnson illustrates the point by taking the example of the carriage tax. Although the Supreme Court decided not to count it as a direct tax, no less an authority than James Madison declared that he would vote against it on the grounds that it was an unapportioned direct tax. Johnson, to prove the point, assumes a carriage tax is a direct tax.

> To illustrate the absurdity of apportionment, assume that Congress imposes a tax on carriages held for personal use or for hire. . . . Assume that Virginia and New York have equal populations, counted under the apportionment formula, so that they must bear the same amount of direct tax. Carriages are useful in urban centers, but Virginia has few urban centers. Assume, therefore, that there are one thousand carriages in New York and only one hundred carriages in Virginia. To satisfy

the requirement of apportionment by population under these circumstances, Virginia carriages would have to be taxed at a rate ten times higher than the tax rate on New York carriages. The result is necessary and independent of policy. . . . Tax rates must be ten times higher in Virginia solely because Virginia has so few carriages over which to spread its quota. There is no reason to punish Virginia citizens for the state's paucity of carriages. . . . Under apportionment, a state's whole quota might fall on a small group or even just one person. Assume that Vermont has no carriages as of yet. Vermont's entire quota would then float at the state line, waiting to pounce on the first poor soul who crosses over the state border with a carriage.

In respect of the question of how the founders could have failed to see the problem created by apportionment, Jensen has noted that the concept of an income tax "was new in the late eighteenth century," and has suggested "it was probably unknown to most of the founders. (England did not enact an income tax until 1799. Some founders became familiar with Adam Smith's *The Wealth of Nations*, in which Smith discussed income taxes, but it is not clear that Smith was read by many founders before the Constitution was ratified.) The Founders thus had no reason to say anything one way or the other about income taxes at the Constitutional Convention or in the ratification debates."

No Tax or Duty shall be laid on Articles exported from any State.[133]

133. A concession to the South. It made the proposed Constitution more palatable to delegates concerned that agricultural exports such as tobacco, indigo, and rice would be taxed by a Congress controlled by the North. John Langdon of New Hampshire, during de-

bate on this clause, said: "It seems to be feared that the Northern States will oppress the trade of the Southn." For some Southern delegates this was a defining issue. Madison quotes General Pinckney of South Carolina as telling the Federal Convention that absent "security to the Southern States agst. an emancipation of slaves, and taxes on exports, he shd. be bound by duty to his State to vote agst. their Report." The indirectness of the export tax was attractive to some founders who worried that the national government would need money. Gouverneur Morris called them "a necessary source of revenue" and warned that "the people of America will not have money to pay direct taxes" and that to "seize and sell their effects" would "push them into Revolts." His prescience was confirmed in the Whiskey Rebellion of 1794.

In 1998 the Supreme Court ruled that this clause prohibited a so-called harbor maintenance tax, under which importers and exporters were to be charged 0.125 percent of the value of the cargo that goes through the country's ports. The Court ruled that exporters couldn't be charged under this law. Although the government billed it as a "user fee," the Court found that it was really an unconstitutional tax. Justice Ginsburg, writing for the Court in *United States v. United States Shoe Corp.*, said the decision did "not mean that exporters are exempt from any and all user fees designed to defray the cost of harbor development and maintenance. It does mean, however, that such a fee must fairly match the exporters' use of port services and facilities."

No Preference shall be given by any Regulation of Commerce or Revenue to the Ports of one State over those of another; nor shall Vessels bound to, or from, one State, be obliged to enter, clear,[134] or pay Duties in another.

134. "To 'clear' is to obtain from the proper authorities the necessary papers for sailing from the port," Israel Ward Andrews wrote in *Manual of the Constitution of the United States*. The Supreme Court,

in a mid-nineteenth-century case, *Pennsylvania v. Wheeling & Belmont Bridge Company*, wrote: "It is a mistake to assume that Congress is forbidden to give a preference to a port in one state over a port in another. Such preference is given in every instance where it makes a port in one state a port of entry and refuses to make another port in another state a port of entry. No greater preference, in one sense, can be more directly given than in this way, and yet the power of Congress to give such preference has never been questioned. Nor can it be, without asserting that the moment Congress makes a port in one state a port of entry, it is bound at the same time to make all other ports in all other states ports of entry. The truth seems to be that what is forbidden is not discrimination between individual ports within the same or different states, but discrimination between states." In the same opinion, the Court noted that it certainly was within Congress's power to place a lighthouse in one port and not another, even if such an "advantage may incidentally operate to the prejudice of the ports in a neighboring state." This clause ensures that a cabal of congressmen from Boston doesn't pass a law requiring ships bound to Maine from New York to stop in Massachusetts. During the debate in Philadelphia, two delegates from Maryland, Daniel Carroll and Luther Martin, voiced their concerns that absent this protection, Congress could divert traffic from the port of Baltimore to nearby Norfolk.

No Money shall be drawn from the Treasury, but in Consequence of Appropriations made by Law;[135]

---

135. "They in a word hold the purse," wrote Madison in 58 *Federalist*. During the Federal Convention of 1787, George Mason said: "The purse & the sword ought never to get into the same hands whether Legislative or Executive." Hence the leverage of Congress in the field of foreign affairs. Congress's exercise of this authority, via the Boland Amendment, set the stage for the Iran-Contra scandal.

David Abshire and Richard Neustadt wrote in *Saving the Reagan Presidency*: "While the Boland Amendment had some ambiguities, a Reagan authorization of the diversion of funds clearly could have been a heinous offense. That would have constituted 'theft of government property'—stealing and using funds for unauthorized purposes. The U.S. Constitution, Article 1, Section 9, states that 'no money shall be drawn from the treasury, but in consequence of appropriations made by law.' The Anti-Deficiency Act (31 USC 1517, 1519) makes it a felony to spend money without appropriation."

This clause was also tested after the Civil War, when Lincoln and then Andrew Johnson offered pardons and amnesties to former Confederates and sympathizers. Congress pursued a harder line. The question arose as to whether a full pardon meant restoration of property rights. The case came to a head over the finances of Simeon Hart, an El Paso, Texas, man who had sympathized with the Rebellion and helped outfit the Confederate army that invaded New Mexico. He received a pardon in 1865. Hart claimed that he had sold flour, corn, and forage to the United States before the Rebellion and was owed the money. But Congress had passed a resolution in 1867 stating: "Until otherwise ordered, it shall be unlawful for any officer of the United States government to pay any account, claim, or demand against said government, which accrued or existed prior to the thirteenth day of April, ad 1861, in favor of any person who promoted, encouraged, or in any manner sustained, the late rebellion."

So what was the trump card—the president's pardon or a law of the Congress? The court of claims ruled against Hart. The Supreme Court agreed: "No pardon could have had the effect to authorize the payment out of a general appropriation of a debt which a law of Congress had said should not be paid out of it."

and a regular Statement and Account of the Receipts and Expenditures of all public Money shall be published from time to time.[136]

---

136. What about secret intelligence budgets? Louis Fisher, a senior specialist in the Government and Finance Division of the Congressional Research Service, stated in a court affidavit: "In the long period from 1789 to 1935, there were no more than five instances of confidential spending." Fisher drew a distinction between confidential and secret spending. The former refers to money that is publicly appropriated but whose expenditures aren't made public. Secret spending is secretly appropriated. The five instances of early confidential spending that Fisher identified included $40,000 provided to the president in a 1790 statute "for the support of such persons as he shall commission to serve the United States in foreign parts," to be accounted for by the president "as in his judgment may be made public"; $63,000 appropriated in 1899 for diplomatic and consular service emergencies; a "confidential travel fund for the President" created in 1906; "a confidential fund for the Secretary of the Navy" set up in 1916; and funds that were set aside for the FBI in 1935. The first known instance of secret spending, according to Fisher, occurred in 1811, when Congress, "voting in secret session . . . provided President Madison $100,000 to take temporary possession of certain territory south of Georgia." Fisher noted that this expenditure was eventually published in 1818: "World War II marked a sharp decline in budget accountability, most notably in the Manhattan Project. . . . The money was hidden within misleadingly named accounts in appropriation bills." The Fisher affidavit characterizes the text of the 1949 Central Intelligence Act as providing that the CIA can expend money "without regard to the provisions of law and regulations relating to the expenditure of Government funds." His affidavit was given in a lawsuit against the agency by the director of the Project on Government Secrecy at the Federation of American Scientists, Steven Aftergood, who prevailed. In 1974 the Supreme Court considered a suit by a taxpayer who sought to declare uncon-

stitutional the CIA Act of 1949 because of the issue of secret spending. The Supreme Court ruled that the taxpayer lacked standing. The case was *United States v. Richardson.*

No Title of Nobility[137] shall be granted by the United States:

137. The prohibition against titles of nobility, Hamilton wrote in 84 *Federalist,* "may truly be denominated the corner stone of republican government; for so long as they are excluded, there can never be serious danger that the government will be any other than that of the people." Despite the egalitarian bent of this clause, members of the First Congress showed nostalgia for Europe's pomp. In 1789 a Senate committee recommended that the president be addressed "His Highness, the President of the United States of America, and Protector of Their Liberties." The winning formula—"President of the United States"—was the House's idea. Representative James Jackson of Georgia asked: "Would it add to his fame to be called after the petty and insignificant princes of Europe? Would styling him His Serene Highness, His Grace, or Mightiness, add one tittle to the solid properties he possessed?"

During that debate, Representative Thomas Tucker of South Carolina asked: "What, sir, is the intention of this business? Will it not alarm our fellow-citizens? Will it not give them just cause of alarm? Will they not say, that they have been deceived by the convention that framed the constitution? That it has been contrived with a view to lead them on by degrees to that kind of government which they have thrown off with abhorrence? Shall we not justify the fears of those were opposed to the constitution, because they considered it as insidious and hostile to the liberties of the people? . . . Does this look like a democracy, when one of the first acts of the two branches of the Legislature is to confer titles?"

Benjamin Franklin, in a 1784 letter to his daughter, suggested that there was nothing terribly offensive about people "wearing their

Ribband and Badge according to their Fancy," so long as it wasn't passed down to their children. Franklin thought that America ought to look farther east than Europe. "Thus among the Chinese, the most ancient, and from long Experience the wisest of Nations, honour does not *descend*, but *ascends*. If a man from his Learning, his Wisdom, or his Valour, is promoted by the Emperor to the Rank of Mandarin, his Parents are immediately entitled to all the same Ceremonies of Respect from the People. . . . This *ascending* Honour is therefore useful to the State, as it encourages Parents to give their Children a good and virtuous education." In the 1810s the states took the war against titles further, almost passing a constitutional amendment that would have stripped any American of his citizenship if he took a title from a foreign state. The proposed amendment was ratified by twelve states by the end of 1812, short a single state.

And no Person holding any Office of Profit or Trust under them, shall, without the Consent of the Congress, accept of any present,[138] Emolument, Office, or Title, of any kind whatever, from any King, Prince, or foreign State.[139]

---

138. President Washington was a real stickler about this clause. A recent article in *Slate* related: "When an emissary of the French Republic presented its new flag to Washington, he replied, 'The transaction will be announced to Congress, and the colors will be deposited with [the] Archives.'" Currently Congress allows government employees, as well as elected officials, to accept gifts from foreign nations that are worth less than $335. If the gift has a retail value of less than that, it has "minimal value," according to the relevant law, which provides that "Congress consents to . . . the accepting and retaining by an employee of a gift of minimal value tendered and received as a souvenir or mark of courtesy." Congress allows more valuable gifts to be accepted if they are scholarships, medical

treatment, food, lodging, travel arrangements, "or when it appears that to refuse the gift would likely cause offense or embarrassment." In these cases, the gift is accepted on behalf of the United States and the recipient must turn it over to the government. These rules apply to everyone, including the president.

139. Despite the founders' prohibition against accepting, absent the consent of the Congress, a foreign title "of any kind whatever," prominent Americans have received foreign decorations. Such figures as George Marshall, Ronald Reagan, and Norman Schwarzkopf have been knighted by the Queen. Their knighthoods are honorary, and in Reagan's case came at a point when he was no longer holding office. Congress does permit members of the Armed Forces to receive foreign medals and commendations. The relevant law, 5 USC Section 7342, states: "The Congress consents to the accepting, retaining, and wearing by an employee of a decoration tendered in recognition of active field service in time of combat operations or awarded for other outstanding or unusually meritorious performance, subject to the approval agency of such employee. Without this approval, the decoration is deemed to have been accepted on behalf of the United States" and "shall become the property of the United States."

In 1966 a civil court judge of New York, Maurice Wahl, refused to allow an American-born citizen, Robert Paul Jama, age 23, to add "von" to his surname to make it more Germanic. As the decision recounts, Jama "wants a German genealogy and to be accepted as such 'rather than as a person of Slavic genealogy'; further, that all his friends and acquaintances are of Germanic stock, and because the name Jama does not reflect his Germanic origin, so he says, he seeks to Germanize his patronymic." Wahl wrote: "An American should measure himself by the American standard, and paraphrasing the bold Romans of old, proudly proclaim himself Civis Americanus Sum."

SECTION 10. No State shall enter into any Treaty,[140]

---

140. The principle behind this prohibition—that only the federal government has the right to conduct international affairs—was one factor cited by Justice Hugo Black in 1947 in the Court's opinion in *United States v. California*, when he ruled in favor of the federal government over control of "the submerged land off the coast of California between the low water mark and the three-mile limit." At issue was the right to oil reserves within three miles of shore. California maintained a claim to the land. Its own constitution claimed those three miles for the state, and the federal government had made no fuss about it when California was admitted into the Union in 1850. In 1921 California began to grant permits to offshore oil and gas prospectors. Then President Truman issued an executive order proclaiming that the federal government possessed all natural resources lying off the coast of America. Justice Black concluded that the state didn't have the inherent authority to manage a border between the country and the rest of the world. He wrote, "The ocean, even its three-mile belt, is thus of vital consequence to the nation in its desire to engage in commerce and to live in peace with the world; it also becomes of crucial importance should it ever again become impossible to preserve that peace. And as peace and world commerce are the paramount responsibilities of the nation, rather than an individual state, so, if wars come, they must be fought by the nation."

California was also rebuffed in a case in 1999, stemming from the passage in Sacramento of a law known as the Holocaust Victim Insurance Relief Act, which provided for the revocation of a state business license for insurers that failed to provide information about their European business dealings between 1920 and 1945. When one of the insurance companies challenged the state law's constitutionality, Justice Souter, in *American Ins. Assn. v. Garamendi*, wrote: "Resolving Holocaust-era insurance claims that may be held by residents of this country is a matter well within the Executive's responsibility for foreign affairs. . . . The exercise of the federal executive authority means that state law must give way where, as here, there is evidence of clear conflict between the policies adopted by the two."

Alliance,[141]

141. Which is not to say that states or communities have never dabbled in matters beyond the nation's borders. "What is it that prevents the States from making foreign policy decisions, in the Constitution?" Justice Scalia asked in a case about whether states can mandate economic sanctions against nations that abuse human rights. At issue was a 1996 Massachusetts law that forbade state agencies buying anything from companies that do business with the Burmese junta that had ruled since the coup against democratic rule in 1962. Massachusetts law went further than a congressional ban against new American investment in Burma, which had grandfathered preexisting projects. Given that there are "provisions in the Constitution prohibiting the States from entering treaties with foreign countries, from engaging in war, from . . . let's see, entering into any treaty, alliance, or confederation," Justice Scalia suggested that the states had a right to get involved in foreign affairs in any way that didn't violate those express prohibitions: "All of these things would have been unnecessary if there is some overriding, unexpressed principle in the Constitution that the States cannot get involved in foreign affairs." In the end, the Court unanimously struck down the law on the grounds that it was preempted by Congress's Burmese sanctions.

In the 1980s, local communities (mostly cities, not states) established sister-city relationships with Nicaraguan cities in an express show of support for the Sandinistas. The sister-city relationships were intended to oppose President Reagan's Nicaraguan policy. Wisconsin has had a sister-state relationship with Nicaragua dating to 1964 and a sister-state agreement with Hessen (the German state that includes the city of Frankfurt) dating to 1976. Wisconsin is also entangled in a sister-state relationship with a Chinese province

(Heilongjiang). That relationship was formed in 1982. In addition, Wisconsin has sister-state agreements with the Mexican state of Jalisco and a Japanese subdivision (Chiba prefecture). There's also a relationship with Taiwan and with Belgorod, part of the Russian Federation. The state's Commerce Department has opened trade offices in Canada, Germany, Mexico, and South Korea. California, meanwhile, has twenty-five sister-state relationships. The state senate's website says such relationships are "a formal declaration of friendship between two regions, states, or nations. Such an agreement is a symbol of mutual goodwill. In addition, it is an effort to encourage and facilitate mutually beneficial social, economic, educational, and cultural exchange. Sister state agreements are brought to the Senate or Assembly floor by a Member in the form of a resolution and must be passed by a simple majority."

The slave uprising at Saint-Domingue—now Haiti—drew the attention of South Carolina. A colonial agent known as Monsieur Polony arrived in Charleston and presented South Carolina's governor, Charles Pinckney, with a letter from a Saint-Domingue official requesting troops and provisions to protect white people. Amid fear that a slave revolt would spread to America, the appeal was much debated within South Carolina. Pinckney wrote to the Saint-Domingue General Assembly about this clause. "By the Constitution of the United States all foreign affairs were transferred to the General Government who shall have the authority to direct the national force." He continued: "The individual states are expressly constrained from any interference without the consent of Congress." When the South Carolina legislature convened, Pinckney warned that sending the militia to Saint-Domingue would leave South Carolina defenseless should a slave revolt arise at home.

or Confederation;[142] grant Letters of Marque and Reprisal;[143]

142. Bedrock of the Union. Confederating is unconstitutional. In 1862 Senator Sumner offered a series of resolutions in the Senate denouncing states that had attempted to secede. He accused them of having "unconstitutionally and unlawfully confederated together with the declared purpose of putting an end, by force, to the supremacy of the Constitution within their respective limits." The syllabus of the Supreme Court's decision in the 1877 case of *Williams v. Bruffy* opens with this pronouncement: "The Confederate States was an illegal organization, within the provision of the Constitution of the United States prohibiting any treaty, alliance, or confederation of one state with another." The opinion states: "The Constitution of the United States prohibits any treaty, alliance, or confederation by one state with another."

143. "[For states] to grant letters of marque and reprisal, would lead directly to war, the power of declaring which is expressly given to Congress," Chief Justice Marshall wrote in an aside in an 1833 case, *Barron v. Mayor & City Council of Baltimore*, that had nothing to do with letters of marque and reprisal.

coin Money; emit Bills of Credit;[144]

144. "What is a bill of credit?" Chief Justice Marshall inquired in his opinion in the 1830 case involving a farmer, Hiram Craig, who sought protection under this clause against an effort by the state of Missouri to collect on a loan of Missouri paper money that had been advanced to him—and other farmers—by that state. The Supreme Court, in an opinion by Marshall, held for Craig. As a general matter, he found, what Congress intended to forbid states from issuing was not any promises to pay—for a state could surely borrow money—but bills for general circulation. And for good reason. "At a very early

period of our colonial history," Marshall wrote, "the attempt to supply the want of the precious metals by a paper medium was made to a considerable extent, and the bills emitted for this purpose have been frequently denominated bills of credit. During the war of our revolution, we were driven to this expedient, and necessity compelled us to use it to a most fearful extent. The term has acquired an appropriate meaning, and 'bills of credit' signify a paper medium, intended to circulate between individuals, and between government and individuals, for the ordinary purposes of society. Such a medium has been always liable to considerable fluctuation. Its value is continually changing; and these changes, often great and sudden, expose individuals to immense loss, are the sources of ruinous speculations, and destroy all confidence between man and man. To cut up this mischief by the roots, a mischief which was felt through the United States, and which deeply affected the interest and prosperity of all; the people declared in their constitution, that no state should emit bills of credit. If the prohibition means anything, if the words are not empty sounds, it must comprehend the emission of any paper medium, by a state government, for the purpose of common circulation."

This definition of bill of credit, which hinges in part on whether the bills are intended for common circulation, suggests that state bonds (through which states routinely finance their public work projects) are constitutional. In a dissent in the same case, Justice Smith Thompson sought to give the states additional wiggle room in issuing promissory notes. He delivered this important statement about bills of credit: "As used in the Constitution, it certainly cannot be applied to all obligations, or vouchers, given by, or under the authority of a state for the payment of money. The right of a state to borrow money cannot be questioned, and this necessarily implies the right of giving some voucher for the repayment, and it would seem to me difficult to maintain the proposition that such voucher cannot legally and constitutionally assume a negotiable character, and as such to a certain extent pass as or become a substitute for money." David Currie, a University of Chicago law professor, also found Marshall unconvincing: "Surely, as he admitted, the state was not forbidden to issue promissory notes when it borrowed money. The hard problem in the case was to define the difference between such a note and the forbidden bill, and Marshall made no real effort to wrestle with it."

make any Thing but gold and silver Coin a Tender in Payment of Debts;[145] pass any Bill of Attainder, ex post facto Law,[146] or Law impairing the Obligation of Contracts,[147]

145. These clauses prohibit states from issuing their own scrip and seek to force them to accept the monetary policy of Congress. Here is Madison in 44 *Federalist*: "The extension of the prohibition to bills of credit must give pleasure to every citizen in proportion to his love of justice, and his knowledge of the true springs of public prosperity. The loss which America has sustained since the peace, from the pestilent effects of paper money, on the necessary confidence between man and man; on the necessary confidence in the public councils; on the industry and morals of the people, and on the character of Republican Government, constitutes an enormous debt against the States chargeable with this unadvised measure, which must long remain unsatisfied; or rather an accumulation of guilt, which can be expiated no otherwise than by a voluntary sacrifice on the altar of justice, of the power which has been the instrument of it." John K. Porter, one of New York's greatest nineteenth-century attorneys, gave this account of the history of state-issued paper money in the colonies: "South Carolina led the van in 1703. New York and Connecticut followed, and made their notes a legal tender in 1709. Rhode Island fell into their wake in 1720; Pennsylvania in 1722; Maryland in 1733; Delaware in 1739; North Carolina in 1748; Virginia in 1755; Georgia in 1760. In two of the States, tobacco and beaver skins were made a legal tender." The above recitation was made in 1863 during oral arguments before New York's Court of Appeals in the case of *Metropolitan Bank v. Van Dyck*.

Though a state cannot issue paper money, mint gold or silver coins, or require that tobacco or any other commodity be accepted as legal tender, it is permitted under the Constitution to declare that gold and silver coins are legal tender. For a state dissatisfied with the monetary policy of the Federal Reserve, such a move would be one way to attempt to move back to a monetary policy built on gold and silver. A report by the secretary of the U.S. Monetary Commission, organized under an 1876 resolution and published by the Government Printing Office in 1877, argues: "The Constitution, by prohibiting the States from making anything else a legal tender, recognizes the authority of the States to enact and maintain the legal-tender capacity of such coins." Several states are considering bills to enable the use in certain situations of what is called electronic gold currency. One such bill was introduced in January 2009 and was being discussed on the Internet as the Indiana Honest Money Act, though the enthusiasm for such efforts is restricted, at least for the moment, to monetary gadflies.

146. See the note on *Cummings v. Missouri* in Section 9 under the corresponding prohibition on the Congress.

147. Can a state impose a moratorium on mortgage payments during an economic downturn? Luther Martin told Marylanders he'd argued against this clause because he felt the states ought to possess the power to impair contracts in times of "great public calamities and distress" and "of such extreme scarcity of specie" that the government would have a duty to step in. But he thought it a power that "ought only to be exercised on very important and urgent occasions." Fast-forward a century and a half to the Great Depression, when the Supreme Court issued its ruling in a case that resonated in the 2008 crisis in the mortgage industry. At issue was a Minnesota law that authorized courts to put off foreclosure sales to secure additional time for delinquent mortgagers to pay their debts. This was on Minnesota's part an impairment of contracts. Yet the Supreme Court, in a 1934 decision in *Home Building & Loan Association v. Blaisdell*, upheld the law, 5 to 4. Wrote Justice Hughes in a notorious piece of legalese: "The policy of protecting contracts

against impairment presupposes the maintenance of a government by virtue of which contractual relations are worthwhile—a government which retains adequate authority to secure the peace and good order of society. This principle of harmonizing the constitutional prohibition with the necessary residuum of state power has had progressive recognition in the decisions of this Court." Justice Sutherland issued a famous dissent that began: "Few questions of greater moment than that just decided have been submitted for judicial inquiry during this generation. He simply closes his eyes to the necessary implications of the decision who fails to see in it the potentiality of future gradual but ever-advancing encroachments upon the sanctity of private and public contracts."

or grant any Title of Nobility.[148]

148. In *Zobel v. Williams*, the Supreme Court, in 1982, ruled unconstitutional a law of Alaska that doled out oil royalties to Alaskans in accordance with length of residency. The Constitution's antipathy to titles of nobility was cited in a footnote, which observed that the "American aversion to aristocracy developed long before the Fourteenth Amendment" and that the aversion was "reflected" in this clause. The Alaska law paid out dividends from the state's income in mineral royalties. An Alaskan with ten years' residency would receive twice the income as an Alaskan with five years' residency. The law was challenged on equal protection grounds.

No State shall, without the Consent of the Congress, lay any Imposts or Duties on Imports or Exports,[149]

149. This corrected a defect in the Articles of Confederation, which permitted tariffs in trade between the various states, but it

hasn't entirely ended the matter. The clause was tested in the 1860s, when an auctioneer in Alabama refused to pay a tax on auction sales and other property levied by the city of Mobile, Alabama. He argued that because he procured his goods from other states, he was protected from the tax by the import-export clause. The court, in *Woodruff v. Parham*, disagreed. But some modern students of the Constitution, Justice Clarence Thomas among them, maintain that the founders would have understood imports and exports to apply to the trade between the states. Critical of the Supreme Court's commerce clause jurisprudence, Thomas has suggested that the import-export clause, and not the commerce clause, is at times the relevant clause for adjudicating questions involving interstate commerce. He made this point in his dissent to *Camps Newfound/Owatonna, Inc. v. Town of Harrison et al.* It involved a church camp in Maine that applied for a state tax exemption given to nonprofit organizations. Its request was rejected because of a provision in the law that suggested the exemption was for nonprofits that serve Maine residents. The campers were mostly out-of-state residents. The court ruled that the provision in the tax law was unconstitutional because it violated the commerce clause. Thomas argued that the commerce clause had no application. "The tax at issue here is a tax on real estate, the quintessential asset that does not move in interstate commerce," he said. The tax exemption was better tested, he argued, against the import-export clause. He quoted William Crosskey as having "unearthed numerous Founding era examples in which the word 'import' referred to goods produced in other States" and provided a number of examples, including cases involving Virginia's efforts to tax cheese from New England and the efforts of Maryland to tax exports of flour to New England. In the end, Thomas said he would uphold the Maine tax even were the Supreme Court to reinterpret the clause on imports and exports to apply to commerce between states.

except what may be absolutely necessary for executing its inspection Laws:[150]

---

150. In the 1880s, Iowa tried to use this exception to defend a law restricting the transport of alcohol into the state. The Court reckoned the purpose was "protecting its people against the evils of intemperance." The Court rejected that reasoning on the basis that the inspection provision does not allow states to encroach on Congress's power to regulate commerce. In another quirky application of the inspection provision, New York State tried to justify a tax on new immigrants by claiming that it needed the money to fund an immigrant inspection program. Steamship companies would be charged one dollar for every immigrant they brought to the state. That money would be used to identify "criminals, or pauper lunatics, idiots, or imbeciles, or deaf, dumb, blind, infirm, or orphan persons, without means or capacity to support themselves and subject to become public charge." Immigrants falling into these categories would either be turned away or provided for by the state. The Court, in 1883, rejected that reasoning, holding that "imports and exports" refer to property and not to free migrants. It also disputed the idea that a mere inspection would be sufficient to determine the conditions mentioned.

and the net Produce of all Duties and Imposts, laid by any State on Imports or Exports, shall be for the Use of the Treasury of the United States;[151] and all such Laws shall be subject to the Revision and Controul of the Congress.[152]

---

151. To ensure that these duties are used for their proper purpose—to pay for inspectors—and not used to fill a state's coffers. A Pennsylvania lawyer, William Rawle, wrote that "to prevent evasion under colour of only securing the right of inspection, it is

provided that the net produce of all duties and imposts laid by any state on imports or exports, shall be for the use of the treasury of the United States."

152. A Maryland tobacco farmer named Turner tried to get out of an indictment for delivering a hogshead of the divine herb grown on his own farm in the state to a place in Baltimore other than sanctioned by Maryland's inspection laws and then sending it to Bremen, Germany. In *Turner v. Maryland*, handed down in 1883, the Court said Maryland could proceed against the farmer. It marked the point that under this clause Congress could "interpose, if at any time any statute, under the guise of an inspection law, goes beyond the limit prescribed by the Constitution in imposing duties or imposts on imports or exports."

No State shall, without the Consent of Congress, lay any Duty of Tonnage,[153] keep Troops, or Ships of War in time of Peace,[154]

153. "A charge upon a vessel according to its tonnage . . . for entering or leaving a port, or navigating the public waters of the country," the Supreme Court explained in the 1886 case *Huse v. Glover*. Nearly a decade earlier, the Court had held that this prohibition doesn't apply to charges for use of a wharf. In the 1877 case *Packet Company v. Keokuk*, the Court said: "It is a tax or a duty that is prohibited—something imposed by virtue of sovereignty, not claimed in right of proprietorship. Wharfage is of the latter character. . . . When compensation is demanded for the use of the wharf, the demand is an assertion not of sovereignty, but of a right of property. A passing vessel may use the wharf or not, at its election, and thus may incur liability for wharfage or not, at the choice of the master or owner." This prohibition is intended to promote interstate commerce.

154. During negotiations over statehood the Republic of Texas agreed to bow to this clause by ceding the four vessels in its navy—

the *Austin, Wharton, Archer,* and *San Bernard*—to the U.S. Navy. Where did that leave its officers? A former commander in the Texas navy, William Brashear, was rebuffed when he tried to report for duty. So he sued the secretary of the Navy, saying he had been passed into the U.S. Navy along with the four vessels under his command. The court rejected his claim, but eventually Congress gave surviving officers of the Texas navy five years' pay in exchange for their dropping any claims.

enter into any Agreement or Compact with another State,[155]

155. In a constitutional irony, this prohibition, intended to keep the states in check, now looms as an obstacle to a scheme that would curtail drastically the power of states in presidential elections. The context is a movement seeking to have the president elected by popular vote instead of by the Electoral College. The aim is to do this without a constitutional amendment but via an interstate compact in which states would pledge their electors' votes to the presidential candidate who wins the national popular vote. It would end the dominant "winner takes all" approach under which the entirety of a state's electoral votes go to the presidential candidate who wins the majority—or even plurality—of the state's vote. This is vouchsafed by Article II, Section 1 of the Constitution, under which each state apportions its electors as it wishes. The proposed National Popular Vote initiative has taken the form of a compact that goes into effect if enough states to comprise a majority of the Electoral College pass the legislation abandoning the constitutional system. So far four states, accounting for fifty electoral votes, have passed the compact through their state legislatures. The movement is animated by the expectation that an interstate compact would be easier than an amendment to the Constitution requiring approval of three-quarters of the state legislatures. But the compact agreement, absent congressional authorization, would appear on its face to violate this clause of the Constitution.

Not that all issues arising under this clause are so grand. In *Virginia v. Tennessee*, involving a boundary dispute, the Court adopted a flexible reading of this passage: "If Massachusetts, in forwarding its exhibits to the World's Fair at Chicago, should desire to transport them a part of the distance over the Erie Canal, it would hardly be deemed essential for that state to obtain the consent of Congress before it could contract with New York for the transportation of the exhibit through that state in that way. If the bordering line of two states should cross some malarious and disease producing district, there could be no possible reason, on any conceivable public grounds, to obtain the consent of Congress for the bordering states to agree to unite in draining the district, and thus removing the cause of disease. So in case of threatened invasion of cholera, plague, or other causes of sickness and death, it would be the height of absurdity to hold that the threatened states could not unite in providing means to prevent and repel the invasion of the pestilence without obtaining the consent of Congress, which might not be at the time in session." In the 1943 case *Ham v. Maine-New Hampshire Interstate Bridge Authority*, the Court ruled that the creation of a bridge authority did not require congressional consent. On September 20, 2001, the Northeast Dairy Compact, which had set milk prices in New England, went out of business after Congress decided to withhold its consent.

or with a foreign Power,[156] or engage in War,[157] unless actually invaded, or in such imminent Danger as will not admit of delay.

156. An accused murderer, George Holmes, had to drag the governor of Vermont, Silas H. Jennison, all the way to the Supreme Court in 1840 to prevent the governor from extraditing him to Canada in violation of this clause. The chief justice, Roger Taney, issued a decision memorable for its fastidiousness about language: "In expounding the Constitution of the United States, every word

must have its due force and appropriate meaning, for it is evident from the whole instrument that no word was unnecessarily used or needlessly added . . . and this principle of construction applies with peculiar force to the two clauses of the tenth section of the first article, of which we are now speaking, because the whole of this short section is directed to the same subject—that is to say it is employed altogether in enumerating the rights surrendered by the states; and this is done with so much clearness and brevity that we cannot for a moment believe that a single superfluous word was used, or words which meant merely the same thing. When, therefore, the second clause declares that no state shall enter into 'any agreement or compact' with a foreign power without the assent of Congress, the words 'agreement' and 'compact' cannot be construed as synonymous with one another; and still less can either of them be held to mean the same thing with the word 'treaty' in the preceding clause, into which the states are positively and unconditionally forbidden to enter, and which even the consent of Congress could not authorize." In other words, even a minor agreement such as an extradition is, in respect of a foreign power, forbidden to the states.

157. The Articles of Confederation permitted a state to wage war not only if it were invaded but if it "shall have received certain advice of a resolution being formed by some nation of Indians to invade such State, and the danger is so imminent as not to admit of a delay till the United States in Congress assembled can be consulted." Skirmishes between Georgia and various Indian tribes were an issue in the first decades of the Republic. Henry Cabot Lodge, in his book on his grandfather, George Cabot, recounts: "In 1812, Georgia was dissatisfied with the President's decision against the seizure of East Florida. Despite express orders from Washington, Governor Mitchell not only refused to withdraw the State troops from Florida, but sent another expedition. The Georgia Legislature soon after resolved that, whether Congress authorized it or not, the possession of Florida was essential to their safety, and they passed an act to raise a State army, which thereupon invaded the peninsula. The Constitution says that no State shall 'engage in war, unless actually invaded;'

and yet Georgia carried on a war of conquest, in the teeth of a direct prohibition from the general government."

In 1899 Texas ran an embargo against New Orleans. In the ensuing case, *Louisiana v. Texas,* the justices let it pass, though Justice Brown wondered whether Texas was not, in fact, approaching a state of war with New Orleans. He wrote, "An embargo, though not an act of war, is frequently resorted to as preliminary to a declaration of war, and may be treated under certain circumstances as a sufficient *casus belli.* The case made by the bill is the extreme one of a total stoppage of all commerce between the most important city in Louisiana and the entire State of Texas, and while I fully agree that resort cannot be had to this Court to vindicate the rights of individual citizens, or any particular number of individuals, where a state has assumed to prohibit all kinds of commerce with the chief city of another state, I think her motive for doing so is the proper subject of judicial inquiry."

ARTICLE II.

SECTION 1. The executive Power shall be vested in a President of the United States of America.[158]

---

158. "A considerable pause" greeted James Wilson's proposal that the executive branch be vested in a single person, according to Madison's notes of the Federal Convention. Faced with their silence, the chairman prepared to move ahead and put the proposal to a vote. It was delayed on the intervention of Benjamin Franklin, who, according to Madison's notes, "observed that it was a point of great importance and wished that the gentlemen would deliver their sentiments on it before the question was put."

Those in favor of a plural executive, meaning a council of executive officers, argued that a single president smacked of English kingship. Edmund Randolph regarded a unitary executive as "the foetus of monarchy." Franklin also wanted several to share executive power, believing that "government policy would thereby be less changeable and more predictable, something that was particularly important in foreign policy," as it is characterized by Richard Ellis in *Founding the American Presidency*. He reports that Franklin also maintained that a plural executive "obviated the problems of succession, illness, or death that inescapably marred a single elected executive." Those who argued for a single president claimed it would result in a swifter and more energetic executive. They also said the president would feel a greater responsibility toward the people if he alone were held accountable.

As for the particular pause Madison describes, Richard Brookhiser suggests it was because George Washington was in the hall. "If there was going to be a national executive, and if it was going to be one man, he was the man. A 'considerable pause' ensued because, for all the boldness of the delegates, not one of them seems to have been bold enough to begin the work of cutting and trimming Washington's next job in his presence. It is significant that the man to break the logjam was Franklin, the only other delegate with anything like Washington's prestige."

This clause has been used to justify expansive presidential power. Article I begins, "All legislative Powers herein granted shall be vested in a Congress of the United States." Article II reads simply, "The executive Power shall be vested in a President of the United States of America." Legislative power is limited to the powers "herein granted," namely, powers specifically enumerated in the Constitution. The president is given a more general executive power, above and beyond the authority outlined in the subsequent clauses of Article II. Only "executive" powers specifically given to other branches, or specifically denied to the president in the Constitution, are off-limits.

Alexander Hamilton noted this in defending President Washington's Neutrality Proclamation during the war between Britain and France. He wrote that "the difficulty of a complete and perfect specification of all the cases of Executive authority would naturally dictate the use of general terms—and would render it improbable that a specification of certain particulars was design[e]d as a substitute for those terms," and added: "The different mode of expression employed in the constitution in regard to the two powers the Legislative and the Executive serves to confirm this inference." And he warned in respect of the Congress that "the enumeration ought rather therefore to be considered as intended by way of greater caution," while presidential authority would "flow from the general grant of that power, interpreted in conformity to other parts of the constitution and to the principles of free government."

The Supreme Court alluded to Hamilton's distinction when it ruled in *Myers v. United States* that the president has the power to remove officials in the executive branch who had been confirmed by the Senate (please see p. 151). But executive power does have limits, a fact underlined by the Court after President Truman seized the steel industry to end a strike during the Korean War. The court found against the president in *Youngstown Sheet & Tube Co. v. Sawyer*. Justice Robert Jackson wrote a concurring opinion but included a memorable warning: "I have no illusion that any decision by this Court can keep power in the hands of Congress if it is not wise and timely in meeting its problems. A crisis that challenges the President equally, or perhaps primarily, challenges Congress. If not good law, there was worldly wisdom in the maxim attributed to Napoleon that 'The tools belong to the man who can use them.' We may say that power to legislate for emergencies belongs in the hands of Congress, but only Congress itself can prevent power from slipping through its fingers."

He shall hold his Office during the Term of four Years,[159] and, together with the Vice President, chosen for the same Term, be elected, as follows:

---

159. Disagreements emerged among the founders over how long and for how many terms a president should serve—and over who decides if he is qualified to remain in office. They decided to strike out

a prohibition of a second term. To Gouverneur Morris, such a prohibition "tended to destroy the great motive to good behavior, the hope of being rewarded by a re-appointment. It was saying to him, make hay while the sun shines."

The founders also wrestled with whether to vest reappointment in the legislature. This was rejected in favor of the separation of powers. As James Madison put it: "If it be essential to the preservation of liberty that the Legisl: Execut: & Judiciary powers be separate, it is essential to a maintenance of the separation, that they should be independent of each other. The Executive could not be independent of the Legislure, if dependent on the pleasure of that branch for a reappointment. Why was it determined that the Judges should not hold their places by such a tenure? Because they might be tempted to cultivate the Legislature, by an undue complaisance, and thus render the Legislature the virtual expositor, as well the maker of the laws. In like manner a dependence of the Executive on the Legislature, would render it the Executor as well as the maker of laws; & then according to the observation of Montesquieu, tyrannical laws may be made that they may be executed in a tyrannical manner."

As for the length of the term itself, suggestions ranged from three years to twenty years to "a term for good behavior" that would be judged by the legislature. Good behavior was rejected as allowing too much potential for abuse. George Mason "considered an Executive during good behavior as a softer name only for an Executive for life. And that the next would be an easy step to hereditary Monarchy. If the motion should finally succeed, he might himself live to see such a Revolution." The four-year term that was ultimately chosen was the midpoint between the two-year term in the House and the six-year term in the Senate, meaning that most of Congress will have been reevaluated by voters by the time the president is up for reelection.

Each State[160] shall appoint, in such Manner as the Legislature thereof may direct, a Number of Electors, equal to the whole Number of Senators and Representatives to which the State may be entitled in the Congress: but no Senator or Representative, or Person holding an Office of Trust or Profit under the United States, shall be appointed an Elector.

---

160. The word "state" appears ten times in this and the following paragraph describing the procedure for choosing the president; the word "people" does not appear at all.

The Electors shall meet in their respective States, and vote by Ballot for two Persons,[161] of whom one at least shall not be an Inhabitant of the same State with themselves.

---

161. This clause provides that electors cast their votes for president only, with the vice presidency going to the candidate who came in second place. The procedure was changed in the Twelfth Amendment, ratified in 1804, which provided that electors specify their votes for president and vice president. The change came about after the election of 1800. President Jefferson and his running mate, Aaron Burr, defeated President Adams. But Jefferson's electors neglected to make sure that at least one of them cast two ballots for Jefferson rather than casting one each for Jefferson and Burr. As a result, Jefferson and Burr tied at seventy-three votes. The decision was then put before the House, which was controlled by lame-duck Federalists and had to vote thirty-six times before Jefferson finally achieved a majority and the Republic was spared a collapse.

And they shall make a List of all the Persons voted for, and of the Number of Votes for each; which List they shall sign and certify, and transmit sealed to the Seat of the Government of the United States, directed to the President of the Senate.[162]

---

162. The founders expected that electors would bow to neither political party nor popular vote, but would exercise their own judgment. That expectation was betrayed as early as 1792, when the Jefferson-led Democratic-Republicans and the Federalists battled over the vice presidency. In 1952 the Supreme Court, in *Ray v. Blair*, ruled that the Alabama Democratic Party could withhold certification of elector Edmund Blair, who had refused to pledge to support the presidential and vice presidential nominees of the national party convention. Justice Jackson dissented with this flourish: "No one faithful to our history can deny that the plan originally contemplated what is implicit in its text—that electors would be free agents, to exercise an independent and nonpartisan judgment as to the men best qualified for the Nation's highest offices. Certainly, under that plan, no state law could control the elector in performance of his federal duty, any more than it could a United States Senator who also is chosen by, and represents, the State." He went on: "This arrangement miscarried. Electors, although often personally eminent, independent, and respectable, officially became voluntary party lackeys and intellectual nonentities to whose memory we might justly paraphrase a tuneful satire: They always voted at their Party's call / And never thought of thinking for themselves at all. As an institution, the Electoral College suffered atrophy almost indistinguishable from rigor mortis."

The President of the Senate shall, in the Presence of the Senate and House of Representatives, open all the Certificates, and the Votes shall then be counted. The Person having the greatest Number of Votes shall be the President, if such Number be a Majority of the whole Number of Electors appointed; and if there be more than one who have such Majority, and have an equal Number of Votes, then the House of Representatives shall immediately chuse by Ballot one of them for President; and if no Person have a Majority, then from the five highest on the List the said House shall in like Manner chuse the President. But in chusing the President, the Votes shall be taken by States, the Representation from each State having one Vote; A quorum for this Purpose shall consist of a Member or Members from two thirds of the States, and a Majority of all the States shall be necessary to a Choice. In every Case, after the Choice of the President, the Person having the greatest Number of Votes of the Electors shall be the Vice President.[163] But if there should remain two or more who have equal Votes, the Senate shall chuse from them by Ballot the Vice President.[164]

163. Save for the Twelfth Amendment, Albert Gore would have been President George W. Bush's vice president and John McCain President Barack Obama's. The thirty-second president of the United States would have been Thomas Dewey.

164. This has all been superseded by the Twelfth Amendment.

The Congress may determine the Time of chusing the Electors, and the Day on which they shall give their Votes; which Day shall be the same throughout the United States.[165]

165. From this clause—and a clause in Article I, Section 4, footnoted on page 21—emerged our modern Election Day. In 1792 Congress legislated that elections for electors could be held any time

during a thirty-four-day period before the first Wednesday of December. The arrangement led to a corruption of the election process, as states that voted later could, as it was put by William C. Kimberling, "swell, diminish, or be influenced by a candidate's victories in the States which voted earlier." Criticism of the thirty-four-day range mirrored later criticism of the modern primary schedule, in which states voting earlier wield outsize influence. The multiday range was also problematic because it facilitated frauds such as voting in more than one state. Congress sought to do away with the problem in 1845, when it established a uniform national Election Day, the first Tuesday after the first Monday in November. Early November was chosen because it came after the fall harvest but before the weather got bad enough in much of the country to restrict travel. Tuesday was chosen because holding elections on Monday would have required many voters to begin traveling on the Christian Sabbath. According to an account of the congressional debate, another reason was apparently a technicality—"to avoid the necessity of changing the laws in relation to the day on which the electoral colleges now meet; for the first Tuesday of November might, in some cases, be more than thirty days from the first Wednesday in December."

The founders did not envision political parties being a part of the electoral system, but a system evolved under which electors were nominated at state party conventions or by a vote of the central committee of the state party. On Election Day, states cast popular votes not for candidates directly but rather for electors who have pledged to represent the candidates' parties in the Electoral College. The electors' actual names may or may not appear on the ballot along with the name of the presidential candidate of the party to which they're pledged. The Supreme Court, in *Ray v. Blair*, condones the practice: "History teaches that the electors were expected to support the party nominees. Experts in the history of government recognize the long-standing practice. Indeed, more than twenty states do not print the names of the candidates for electors on the general election ballot. Instead, in one form or another, they allow a vote for the presidential candidate of the national conventions to be counted as a vote for his party's nominees for the electoral college. This long continued practical interpretation of the constitutional propriety of an implied or oral pledge of his ballot by a candidate for elector as to his vote in the electoral college weights heavily in considering the constitutionality of a pledge, such as the one here required, in the primary." There is no federal law requiring electors to respect the state's popular vote for president once they are elected, but in *Ray v. Blair* the Supreme Court established that political parties may demand pledges from the electors, because the Constitution does not require that the electors vote completely according to their own free will. Some states have laws punishing faithless electors with fines or disqualification.

No Person except a natural born[166] Citizen,[167]

---

166. It's unclear whether "natural born" covers citizens born to American parents outside the United States. On the one hand, if all citizens are either "born or naturalized in the United States," one who was not physically born in America must have been "naturalized," a term that would appear to preclude being natural born. On the other hand, the Naturalization Act of 1790, which was passed by a Congress that included some of the framers, stated, "the children of citizens of the United States, that may be born beyond sea, or out of the limits of the United States, shall be considered as natural born citizens." The "natural born" language was struck in later legislation.

The debate over "natural born" erupted in the 2008 presidential election, when some argued that Senator John McCain might not meet this requirement. McCain was born in 1936 at the Panama Canal Zone, where his father was serving as a Navy officer. Much of the discussion about his eligibility centered on the meaning of "natural born" citizen, as well as the principle that children of military families should not be punished because their parents served abroad.

Some scholars argued that McCain counts as a natural born citizen via his parentage, his birth at an American military installation, and that America held sovereignty over the Canal Zone.

An argument against McCain's eligibility was made by a law professor of the University of Arizona, Gabriel J. Chin, who pointed out that the future senator was not actually a citizen at birth. When he was born, the law granted citizenship to children of an American parent born "out of the limits and jurisdiction of the United States." As the Canal Zone was outside of U.S. borders but not outside its jurisdiction, Chin argued, the citizenship requirement technically did not apply to McCain. Congress fixed this loophole in 1937, conferring citizenship to persons born in the Canal Zone but leaving a short period in which McCain was not a U.S. citizen. "It's preposterous that a technicality like this can make a difference in an advanced democracy," Chin told the *New York Times.* "But this is the constitutional text that we have." The Senate weighed in on this issue in April 2008, unanimously passing a nonbinding resolution that declared McCain a natural born citizen. In September 2008, a federal judge threw out a lawsuit seeking to strike McCain from the California ballot, ruling that he is considered a natural born citizen via the 1937 law, even if he was not one already.

Other presidential candidates have also been dogged by the natural born citizen issue. Barry Goldwater, who was born in Arizona before it became a state, ran for president in 1964. George Romney, who was born in Mexico, ran in 1968. Neither won, so their eligibility wasn't truly tested. McCain's supporters have also pointed to Vice President Curtis, who served under President Hoover and was born in Kansas a year before it gained statehood. President Chester A. Arthur's presidency was challenged based on rumors that he was born in Canada rather than Vermont.

167. Joseph Story wrote: "It cuts off all chances for ambitious foreigners, who might otherwise be intriguing for the office; and interposes a barrier against those corrupt interferences of foreign governments in executive elections, which have inflicted the most serious evils upon the elective monarchies of Europe. Germany,

Poland, and even the pontificate of Rome, are sad, but instructive examples of the enduring mischiefs arising from this source." It also precluded the possibility of a presidential run by Governor Arnold Schwarzenegger of California.

or a Citizen of the United States, at the time of the Adoption of this Constitution,[168] shall be eligible to the Office of President; neither shall any Person be eligible to that Office who shall not have attained to the Age of thirty five Years,[169] and been fourteen Years a Resident within the United States.

168. The phrase "at the time of the Adoption of this Constitution" was added to protect the rights of would-be presidents who had proven their loyalty during the Revolution. Of the thirty-nine signers of the Constitution, seven were born in foreign lands, including Alexander Hamilton (the West Indies), Robert Morris (England), James Wilson (Scotland), and Pierce Butler, Thomas Fitzsimmons, William Paterson, and James McHenry (all Ireland). Edward Corwin has observed that Wilson, who served on the Committee of Detail, "seems to have felt the need of such a clause in his own behalf especially keenly."

169. Nearly a quarter of the signers of the Constitution, including Hamilton, hadn't yet reached the age of thirty-five. This age requirement, Yale's Akhil Amar has suggested, was intended to prevent the presidency from becoming a hereditary position. A relatively high age minimum would diminish the likelihood that a sitting or ex-president would possess an eligible heir to run for the office. A nineteen-year-old favorite son might die before he could seek election at the age of thirty-five. "In the course of nature very few fathers leave a son who has arrived to that age," is what A Native of Virginia had to say in the "Observations Upon the Proposed Plan of Federal Government" of 1788.

The first son of a president to be elected president was John Quincy Adams, who was in his fifties. It is difficult to overstate how concerned some of the founders were that the executive branch would come under the control of a single family, and that the Republican experiment would devolve into a monarchy. In a part of the draft of his First Inaugural Address that wasn't included in the final speech, Washington dwelled on the fact that he was childless: "I have no child for whom I could wish to make a provision—no family to build in greatness upon my Country's ruins." In one passage in 14 *Federal Farmer*, arguing against permitting a presidency of more than a single term, the anonymous anti-Federalist underscores these concerns: "When a man shall get the chair, who may be re-elected, from time to time, for life, his greatest object will be to keep it; to gain friends and votes, at any rate; to associate some favourite son with himself, to take the office after him: whenever he shall have any prospect of continuing the office in himself and family, he will spare no artifice, no address, and no exertions, to increase the powers and importance of it." The Federalist Farmer argued that a man should not be "eligible till he arrive to the age of forty or forty-five years."

In Case of the Removal of the President from Office, or of his Death, Resignation, or Inability to discharge the Powers and Duties of the said Office, the Same shall devolve on the Vice President, and the Congress may by Law provide for the Case of Removal, Death, Resignation or Inability, both of the President and Vice President, declaring what Officer shall then act as President, and such Officer shall act accordingly, until the Disability be removed, or a President shall be elected.[170]

170. The ambiguities in this clause—such as what constitutes an "inability to discharge the powers" and who decides when it has occurred—led to a reworking of the succession procedure in the

Twentieth and Twenty-fifth Amendments in 1933 and 1967, respectively. Until then, the executive branch was forced to rely on its own interpretations. One of the most notable questions was whether the vice president inherits the presidency itself or merely the "powers and duties of the office." In the former instance, he becomes the country's true president; in the latter, he is acting as a steward only until a new president is elected. Vice President John Tyler, when he succeeded President William Henry Harrison in 1841, asserted the complete power of the presidency, earning the nickname "His Accidency." His precedent was followed by subsequently elevated vice presidents until it was formalized in the Twenty-fifth Amendment.

Tyler's decision led to a second problem: If the vice president indeed becomes the country's president, it's not clear from the succession clause that he can give the presidency back, even if the original president is only temporarily disabled. In addition, because the Constitution did not specify who gets to decide when the president is unable to discharge his powers, a vice president who, in such circumstances, asserted the office might be seen as a usurper. As a result, vice presidents have hesitated to step up when presidents were injured. Such was the case in the eighty-day period between the shooting of President Garfield and his death, as well as in the periods following President Wilson's stroke and President Eisenhower's heart attack.

The President shall, at stated Times, receive for his Services, a Compensation, which shall neither be increased nor diminished during the Period for which he shall have been elected,[171] and he shall not receive within that Period any other Emolument[172] from the United States, or any of them.[173]

171. Taft was the highest-paid president and Clinton the lowest, according to a chart of inflation-adjusted presidential salaries pub-

lished in 2005 by Robert C. Sahr of Oregon State University. Washington made about $600,000. The current presidential salary is $400,000. This clause furthers the separation of powers by protecting the president from the threat of salary cuts by Congress. At the same time, it insulates him from being bribed by Congress, or, via the emoluments prohibition, the states individually. The point about separated powers and the president's pay was marked by Hamilton in 73 *Federalist.* "It is evident," he wrote, "that without proper attention to this article, the separation of the executive from the legislative department would be merely nominal and nugatory." He underlined the point by saying that a legislature that had "a discretionary power over the salary and emoluments of the Chief Magistrate" could "render him as obsequious to their will, as they might think proper to make him" and could "either reduce him by famine, or tempt him by largesses, to surrender at discretion his judgment to their inclinations." He noted that there were "men who could neither be distressed nor won into a sacrifice of their duty," but famously noted that "this stern virtue is the growth of few soils."

The historical question of whether a president can be taxed is more complicated. In 1869 Attorney General Ebenezer Hoar offered a written opinion that "a specific tax by the United States upon the salary of an officer" would be "a diminution of the compensation to be paid to him, which, in the case of the President and the judges, would be prohibited by the Constitution of the United States, if the Act of Congress levying the tax were passed during the official term of the President or of the judges respectively concerning whom the question should arise."

172. And the White House? The Supreme Court of South Dakota, in a 1915 decision about whether the justices would receive a cost of living adjustment, noted that Congress "had enacted legislation under which the President . . . had been furnished a home, horses, carriages, servants, household equipment, and many other things incidental to and appropriate to his high office. . . . such federal legislation had never been questioned either as regards its propriety or its constitutionality." A law professor who looked into the matter, David Currie,

found that the First Congress did debate the constitutionality of furnishing President Washington with an allowance for a home and staff. "The House committee had proposed that in addition to his salary the President be given a separate allowance to pay for a house, furniture, secretaries, clerks, carriages and horses, and Representative [John] Laurance [of New York] objected that this provision conferred an 'emolument beyond the compensation contemplated in the constitution,'" Currie wrote, adding: "Congress chose to avoid the hornet's nest by dropping all references to expenses and voting a salary intended to be high enough to cover them."

173. "The Gipper is a dipper." So claimed a watchdog group, the National Taxpayers Union, in response to the fact that President Reagan was collecting a pension of $29,188 a year from the state of California, which he'd served as governor. The taxpayers group asserted that the pension violated the ban against presidents receiving emoluments from a state. The Justice Department's Office of Legal Counsel, however, had concluded that a pension wasn't banned by this language. Professor Robert Delahunty, a veteran of the OLC office, summarized the office's reasoning this way: "Given that President Reagan's retirement benefits were a vested right under California law rather than a gratuity that the state could withhold, the purpose of the clause would not be furthered by preventing him from receiving them."

Before he enter on the Execution of his Office, he shall take the following Oath or Affirmation:—"I do solemnly swear (or affirm) that I will faithfully execute the Office of President of the United States, and will to the best of my Ability, preserve, protect and defend the Constitution of the United States."[174]

174. After Chief Justice Roberts misspoke the oath he was administering during President Obama's inaugural, the new president was sufficiently worried that he had failed to fulfill this constitutional

requirement that he retook the oath the following day. In the initial exchange, the chief justice haltingly instructed Obama to swear that he would "execute the office of president to the United States faithfully," rather than "faithfully execute the office of president of the United States." A professor at Harvard, Steven Pinker, attributed Roberts's misquote to an aversion to split verbs. He wrote in a January 21, 2009, *New York Times* op-ed: "On Tuesday his inner copy editor overrode any instincts toward strict constructionism and unilaterally amended the Constitution by moving the adverb 'faithfully' away from the verb." According to a statement released by the White House counsel, the decision to retake the oath was made "out of an abundance of caution," though one can speculate that in the legal sense the caution might have been in overabundance.

Not that he was the only one. Two other presidents have retaken the oath when questions arose as to the validity of the first try. President Coolidge did so two weeks after his father, a notary public, originally swore him in at the downstairs parlor of the father's Vermont home at 2:47 AM after learning of President Harding's death. Coolidge retook the oath in Washington to settle doubts about whether it was proper for a state official, his father, to swear in the president. President Arthur also took the oath a second time, in Washington, after an initial swearing in by a New York State judge.

For a discussion about the moment the president's term begins, see page 277.

For a discussion about the moment the president's term begins, see page 277.

SECTION 2. **The President shall be Commander in Chief of the Army and Navy of the United States,[175] and of the Militia of the several States, when called into the actual Service of the United States; he may require the Opinion, in writing,[176] of the principal Officer in each of the executive Departments,[177]**

---

175. It was this authority—and no other—that Lincoln cited when he issued the Emancipation Proclamation freeing the slaves in

regions of the rebellious South that had not yet been returned to Union control—and not in other areas, such as border states whose populations had been riven by the war. The proclamation declared emancipation to be "a fit and necessary war measure for suppressing" the Rebellion. Lincoln described it at another point as "an act of justice, warranted by the Constitution, upon military necessity." In a letter to his friend James Conkling in August 1863, Lincoln expounded on what he saw as the constitutional basis for emancipation. The letter was intended by Lincoln to be read aloud at a rally in Springfield, Illinois, and it was: "You dislike the emancipation proclamation; and, perhaps would have it retracted—You say it is unconstitutional—I think differently. I think the constitution invests its commander-in-chief, with the law of war in time of war—The most that can be said, if so much, is that slaves are property. Is there—has there ever been—any question that by the law of war, property, both of enemies and friends, may be taken when needed? And is it not needed whenever taking it, helps us, or hurts the enemy? Armies, the world over, destroy enemie's property when they can not use it."

The president's status as commander in chief, in conjunction with the oath that he will to the best of his ability "preserve, protect and defend the Constitution of the United States," forms the basis for the executive war powers that presidents have asserted at the expense of, from time to time, Congress's power to declare war. In the Prize Cases Lincoln ordered a blockade of southern ports. Owners of the seized ships, claimed by their captors as prizes, objected that the president lacked authority to seize them because Congress had not expressly declared war. Lincoln had feared that declaring war on the Confederacy might legitimate the insurrection. The Supreme Court ruled that the president's status as commander in chief gave him constitutional authority to order the blockade:

> Whether the President, in fulfilling his duties as Commander-in-chief in suppressing an insurrection, has met with such armed hostile resistance and a civil war of

such alarming proportions as will compel him to accord to them the character of belligerents is a question to be decided by him, and this Court must be governed by the decisions and acts of the political department of the Government to which this power was entrusted. "He must determine what degree of force the crisis demands." The proclamation of blockade is itself official and conclusive evidence to the Court that a state of war existed which demanded and authorized a recourse to such a measure under the circumstances peculiar to the case.

Although the United States has used force abroad more than three hundred times in its history, Congress has declared war only five times. After the Vietnam conflict, Congress moved against the presidency with the War Powers Act, which starts a sixty-day clock whenever presidents send the Armed Forces into hostilities. If Congress doesn't approve his action within that time, the law would require a retreat. The act is based on a narrow reading of the commander in chief clause: "The constitutional powers of the President as Commander-in-Chief to introduce United States Armed Forces into hostilities, or into situations where imminent involvement in hostilities is clearly indicated by the circumstances, are exercised only pursuant to (1) a declaration of war, (2) specific statutory authorization, or (3) a national emergency created by attack upon the United States, its territories or possessions, or its armed forces."

President-elect Obama, according to the *New York Times,* met with leaders of a commission assembled by the University of Virginia that proposed a "War Powers Consultation Act" that would require Congress to vote "one way or the other within 30 days of the commencement of military action." It would also create "a Joint Congressional Consultation Committee, composed of the majority and minority leaders of both the Senate and House, as well as the chairmen and ranking members of key committees. This panel would be provided the same intelligence shown the president and have a standing bipartisan staff."

176. James Iredell, who would go on to become one of the six original justices of the Supreme Court, said at the North Carolina ratifying convention: "Their opinion is to be given him in writing. By this means he will be aided by their intelligence; and the necessity of their opinions being in writing, will render them more cautious in giving them, and make them responsible should they give advice manifestly improper. This does not diminish the responsibility of the President himself. They might otherwise have colluded, and opinions have been given too much under his influence." While Iredell supported the Constitution, the state failed to ratify it at this juncture, ultimately becoming one of only two states outside of the Union at Washington's inauguration.

177. After President Washington declared U.S. neutrality in 1793, Secretary of State Jefferson wrote the Supreme Court on the president's behalf seeking advice on the legal implications of neutrality. Chief Justice John Jay and the associate justices rebuffed the president's invitation to serve as his legal advisers. Noting that the Constitution gives the president the power to call on the heads of his departments for opinions, the Supreme Court wrote back to Washington that the principles of separated powers and the justices' role as "a court in the last resort" weighed against "the propriety of our extrajudicially deciding the questions alluded to."

upon any Subject relating to the Duties of their respective Offices, and he shall have Power to grant Reprieves and Pardons[178] **for Offences against the United States,**[179] **except in Cases of Impeachment.**

178. One of the least fettered of the presidential powers. A president is not required to wait for charges to be handed up, a verdict to be brought in, or a sentence to be handed down, nor must he seek the advice and consent of the Senate or, for that matter, the Justice Department. He may pardon fugitives from justice, as did, to cite but one example, President Jimmy Carter when he pardoned

Vietnam-era draft evaders. But must a pardon be delivered to and accepted by the recipient to go into effect?

Chief Justice Marshall, in *U.S. v. Wilson*, ruled that it did, permitting one George Wilson—who had been sentenced to die for robbing a mail train—to refuse a pardon from President Jackson. "A pardon is a deed to the validity of which delivery is essential, and delivery is not complete without acceptance. It may then be rejected by the person to whom it is tendered, and if it be rejected, we have discovered no power in a court to force it on him." Another explanation as to why a pardon can't take effect if the intended recipient refuses to accept it was made by the Supreme Court in the case of the *Tribune* and the tiara, in which a former city editor of the *New York Tribune*, George Burdick, and one of its reporters were held in contempt for refusing to disclose their sources of news on the pending indictment of an ex-congressman who, on entering America after a foreign trip, had been arrested for failing to declare a diamond and pearl tiara.

President Wilson, in an effort to entice them to testify, pardoned the editor and reporter. Neither would talk, choosing instead to leave the pardons on a table in the courthouse. The Supreme Court released Burdick from custody but allowed him to refuse the pardon, noting that "the grace of a pardon, though good its intention," could involve "consequences of even greater disgrace than those from which it purports to relieve." It said: "Circumstances may be made to bring innocence under the penalties of the law. If so brought, escape by confession of guilt implied in the acceptance of a pardon may be rejected, preferring to be the victim of the law rather than its acknowledged transgressor, preferring death even to such certain infamy."

The delivery and acceptance standard doesn't seem to have been consistently applied—at least not in the case of the general pardons and amnesties issued by Lincoln and Johnson during and after the Civil War or extended by Carter to those who dodged the draft during the Vietnam conflict. "Delivery and acceptance" would also be an illogical requirement in the case of posthumous pardons. President George W. Bush tried to revoke the pardon granted to real estate developer Isaac Toussie. The Justice Department argued it could be revoked because it hadn't been delivered. But one law professor, Brian C. Kalt, wrote in the *Washington Post* that while pardons were once viewed as what Chief Justice Marshall called "acts of grace," they are now viewed as what Kalt called "unilateral policy decisions made by politically accountable executives." As such, the old delivery requirement doesn't apply anymore. Kalt argued that even were delivery and acceptance essential, Toussie was informed of his pardon over the phone and accepted it.

179. This limits the pardon power to federal crimes. In *Ex Parte Grossman*, the Supreme Court stated the limitation explicitly, citing the founders' records. Wrote Chief Justice Taft: "The words 'for offenses against the United States' were inserted by a Committee on Style, presumably to make clear that the pardon of the President was to operate upon offenses against the United States as distinguished from offenses against the states." Taft noted this almost as an aside; the actual case concerned whether the president can pardon contempt of court. The court said yes.

He shall have Power, by and with the Advice and Consent of the Senate,[180] to make Treaties, provided two thirds of the Senators present concur;[181]

180. In 2005 the Senate leadership turned to Alexander Hamilton to defuse a partisan crisis that threatened to shut down the Senate over the issue of appointing judges. Democrats had blocked a confirmation vote on ten of President Bush's appellate nominees. Senate Republicans became so frustrated that they threatened what came to be known as the "nuclear option"—ending the filibuster through a majority vote. Democrats countered that they would retaliate by bringing Senate business generally to a halt. That collapse was averted when a handful of Democratic and Republican senators,

known as the Gang of Fourteen, sat down together to reread the Constitution. The *New York Times* reported that Senator Byrd and Senator Warner parsed Hamilton's refutation in 66 *Federalist* of the notion that the Senate might be reluctant to impeach officers whom the members themselves confirmed under the appointments clause. This is because, Hamilton argued, the Senate is not meant to use its power to "choose" government officers.

> It will be the office of the President to nominate, and, with the advice and consent of the Senate, to appoint. There will, of course, be no exertion of choice on the part of the Senate. They may defeat one choice of the Executive, and oblige him to make another; but they cannot themselves choose—they can only ratify or reject the choice of the President. They might even entertain a preference to some other person, at the very moment they were assenting to the one proposed, because there might be no positive ground of opposition to him; and they could not be sure, if they withheld their assent, that the subsequent nomination would fall upon their own favorite, or upon any other person in their estimation more meritorious than the one rejected. Thus it could hardly happen, that the majority of the Senate would feel any other complacency towards the object of an appointment than such as the appearances of merit might inspire, and the proofs of the want of it destroy.

181. President Washington took this literally at first, approaching the Senate to discuss a treaty he was planning to craft with the Creek Indians. But he found the discussions infuriating and changed his approach. John Quincy Adams later recounted a description he had heard of Washington's visit: "They debated it and proposed alterations, so that when Washington left the Senate-chamber he said he would be damned if he ever went there again."

Washington later negotiated the Jay Treaty with Britain without the participation of the full Senate and set the precedent that treaty negotiations are carried out by the chief executive alone. The Senate's history relates that Washington "sent Jay to London at the urging of five Federalist party senators but failed to consult the full Senate in 1795 before requesting their advice and consent to the completed treaty." Instead of actually supervising the negotiations, the Senate can exercise its advice and consent power by rejecting a treaty or adding conditions to it, such as amending it, once the president submits it for approval.

If the president needs a Senate vote to approve a treaty, does he also need a Senate vote to rescind one? The courts explored this after President Carter abandoned the free Chinese government, the Republic of China, in pursuit of normalized relations with the Communist regime, the People's Republic of China. Senator Goldwater filed suit, claiming that the president lacked the constitutional authority to do so. The case, *Goldwater v. Carter*, was dismissed by the Supreme Court. So while the Court failed to answer the constitutional question, it was effectively a defeat for Congress. "The Supreme Court's dismissal of the case indicates that any presidential termination of a treaty would be unreviewable in the courts. This has the practical result of leaving any unilateral presidential decision to terminate undisturbed," wrote a professor of law at University of California's Berkeley Law School, John Yoo, in *The Powers of War and Peace*. Yoo is a former deputy assistant attorney general in the Office of Legal Counsel of the Justice Department.

A dispute over the power to terminate treaties arose in 2001, when President Bush withdrew from the Anti-Ballistic Missile Treaty to pursue a missile defense system. He prevailed over the objections of many scholars, including Yale Professor Bruce Ackerman, who called for Congress to make a stand: "If President Bush is allowed to terminate the ABM treaty, what is to stop future presidents from unilaterally taking America out of NATO or the United Nations? The question is not whether such steps are wise, but how democratically they should be taken. America does not enter into treaties lightly. They are solemn commitments made after wide-ranging democratic debate. Unilateral action by the president does not measure up to this standard," Ackerman wrote in the *New York Times.* Congress, however, declined to act.

and he shall nominate, and by and with the Advice and Consent of the Senate, shall appoint Ambassadors, other public Ministers and Consuls,[182]

182. The president's power to nominate diplomatic representatives supports his primacy in foreign affairs. While their choices are checked by the Senate, presidents have been able to circumvent this by appointing special or secret diplomatic agents who arguably could not be characterized as holding offices. President Cleveland used this tactic in 1893, when he sent James H. Blount to Hawaii to report on a revolution that replaced Queen Liliuokalani with a government backed by American landowners. The new government requested annexation by the United States, but Cleveland had his doubts. When Blount reported that the natives did not support annexation and that the U.S. military had participated in deposing the queen, Cleveland halted the annexation negotiations.

Although Blount's appointment was not submitted for confirmation by the Senate, Cleveland vested him with extraordinary authority. According to instructions given to Blount by the State Department, "Your authority in all matters touching the relations of this government of the Islands, and the protection of our citizens therein, is paramount, and in you alone, acting in co-operation with the commander of the naval forces, is vested full discretion and power to determine when such forces should be landed or withdrawn." Blount used that authority to withdraw a contingent of Marines and restore the Hawaiian flag, which had been replaced with the American flag. The Blount report has been cited as an example of how "executive agents are also useful to the president when a disagreement with Congress precludes a request for advance approval."

Judges of the supreme Court,[183]

183. It was in the confirmation battles over nominations to the Supreme Court that the verb "to bork" entered the language. It emerged with the defeat, through an organized campaign of vilification, of President Reagan's nomination of a former judge of the Court of Appeals for the District of Columbia Circuit, Robert Bork. President George H. W. Bush nominated to the high bench another judge from the District of Columbia Circuit, Clarence Thomas, who had come to oppose affirmative action and was suspected of opposing abortion. One activist, appearing at a convention of the National Organization of Women, vowed: "We're going to bork him. We're going to kill him politically."

The nomination hearings for Thomas became the bitterest in American history. The Judiciary Committee referred Thomas to a full Senate vote without a recommendation that he be confirmed. Three days before the vote was to take place, Thomas was accused of sexual harassment by a law professor, Anita Hill, who had worked with him at the Equal Employment Opportunity Commission and at the Education Department. The charges spurred three days of highly publicized hearings. In the end, he was confirmed by a vote of 52 to 48, the narrowest margin for a Supreme Court nominee in more than one hundred years.

The recent era of high tension confirmation hearings for justices of the Supreme Court began under President Nixon with the nominations of, in 1969, Clement Haynsworth Jr., and, in 1970, G. Harrold Carswell, both of whom failed in the Senate. Some have suggested that the nature of the confirmation hearings reflects neither on the nominees nor the presidents who appointed them, or even on the Senate, so much as on the preparedness of the Supreme Court to decide highly fraught issues—such as school prayer, abortion, and laws in respect of sexual relations—that had previously been left to the legislatures at the state and national levels. But the modern era is not the only one that saw bitter confirmation fights. Between 1789 and our time, some 30 of 145 nominations have failed to win confirmation.

and all other Officers of the United States, whose Appointments are not herein otherwise provided for, and which shall be established by Law:[184] but the Congress may by Law vest the Appointment of such inferior Officers, as they think proper, in the President alone, in the Courts of Law, or in the Heads of Departments.[185]

184. The founders feared congressional despotism. Wrote Justice Scalia in 1991 in *Freytag v. Commissioner*, "The foremost danger was that legislators would create offices with the expectancy of occupying them themselves." By providing that the president, or his appointees (see the next footnote), were responsible for filling whatever offices the Congress might gin up, the founders built a bulwark against legislative self-dealing.

Scalia identifies accountability as a second principle at work here. The people have a right to know at whom they should wag their fingers whenever cronyism or incompetence emerge in the executive branch. James Wilson, in his famous *Lectures on Law*, put it this way: "The person who nominates or makes appointments to offices, should be known. His own office, his own character, his own fortune should be responsible. He should be alike unfettered and unsheltered by counsellors. No constitutional stalking horse should be provided for him to conceal his turnings and windings, when they are too dark and too crooked to be exposed to publick view."

When the appointing power isn't installed in a single office, as it is in the president, then there is no "practicability of tracing the poison to its source." Wilson continues: "Ignorant, vicious, and prostituted characters are introduced into office; and some of those, who voted, and procured others to vote for them, are the first and loudest in expressing their astonishment that the door of admission was ever opened to men of their infamous description. The suffering people are thus wounded and buffeted, like Homer's Ajax, in the dark; and have not even the melancholy satisfaction of knowing by whom the blows are given."

Congress has from time to time placed limits on appointments; in respect of the Federal Election Commission, for example, the law prevents the president from appointing more than three Democrats or three Republicans to the six-person commission.

185. A company that developed circuit technology is invoking the appointments clause to argue that all patent appeals judges seated since 2000 were appointed by someone other than the head of the department and are therefore wielding power unconstitutionally. The alleged flaw was discovered by John Duffy of George Washington University Law School. He argues that a 1999 law governing the appointment of patent judges violates this clause because it provides that they be appointed by the director of the Patent and Trademark Office rather than the head of the department, who is the secretary of commerce, and who previously wielded that power. The case, according to Adam Liptak of the *New York Times,* appears "poised to undo thousands of patent decisions concerning claims worth billions of dollars."

The President shall have Power to fill up all Vacancies that may happen during the Recess of the Senate, by granting Commissions which shall expire at the End of their next Session.[186]

———————

186. President Theodore Roosevelt used this clause to maneuver around racism in the case of William Crum, an African American physician he had named customs collector for Charleston, South

Carolina. The appointment was met with a public outcry in the South and delaying tactics in the Senate. Roosevelt repeatedly reinstalled Crum in office via recess appointments, and eventually Crum was confirmed. Louis Harlan, a scholar on Booker T. Washington, describes the toll the fight took on Crum, who "felt like a hollow man when he entered office in March 1903" and who "would receive no pay until confirmed, so he had to continue his medical practice in his off hours."

President Eisenhower was a champion recess appointer. He appointed three Supreme Court justices—Brennan, Warren, and Stewart—during recess. The Senate eventually confirmed each, but it became fed up with the tactic and in 1960 issued a resolution stating that making such appointments "is not wholly consistent with the best interests of the Supreme Court, the nominee who may be involved, the litigants before the Court, nor indeed the people of the United States" and should only be used "under unusual circumstances and for the purpose of preventing or ending a demonstrable breakdown in the administration of the Court's business."

In 1999 President Clinton moved during recess to appoint James C. Hormel as ambassador to Luxembourg after Republican leaders declined to permit a vote on his nomination. When Senator James Inhofe threatened to block all of Clinton's nominees, the president said he would refrain from recess appointments unless he notified Senate leaders of his intentions before the recess began. President George W. Bush exercised his recess appointment power to install an outspoken critic of the United Nations, John Bolton, as the U.S. permanent representative at the world body. When the Senate broke for Thanksgiving in 2007, the majority leader, Harry Reid, scheduled a series of thirty-second meetings so that the body would technically remain in session.

SECTION 3. He shall from time to time give to the Congress Information of the State of the Union, and recommend to their Consideration such Measures as he shall judge necessary and expedient;[187] he may, on extraordinary Occasions, convene both Houses, or either of them,[188] and in Case of Disagreement between them, with Respect to the Time of Adjournment, he may adjourn them to such Time as he shall think proper;[189]

---

187. Washington gave annual State of the Union addresses to Congress, as did Adams. Jefferson demurred, which writers for the American Presidency Project of the University of California at Santa Barbara summarize this way: "Jefferson was concerned that the practice of appearing before the representatives of the people was too similar to the British monarch's ritual of addressing the opening of each new Parliament with a list of policy mandates, rather than 'recommendations.'" It wasn't until 1913 that a regular speech to Congress was resumed by President Wilson, although health reasons prevented him from addressing the Congress in 1919 and 1920. Both messages, in 1921 and 1922, were oral, as was Coolidge's, in 1923, though Silent Cal's remaining State of the Union messages and all of Hoover's were written. "Franklin D. Roosevelt established the modern tradition of delivering an oral State of the Union beginning with his first in 1934," project writers note. The exceptions they cite are Truman's first in 1946 and last in 1953, Eisenhower's last in 1961, Carter's last in 1981, and Nixon's fourth in 1973. Roosevelt's last message, in 1945, and Eisenhower's fourth, in 1956, were "technically written messages although they addressed the American people via radio summarizing their reports."

188. Presidents have convened Congress twenty-seven times, starting with President Adams's decision to call a special session in 1797 to prepare for war with France. The French had broken off diplomatic relations and seized American ships following the passage of the Jay Treaty. At the session, "A bill was passed to complete

and man three new frigates, provision was made for coast defense, and it was enacted that 80,000 militia should be ready to march at a moment's warning."

The last president to convene Congress was Harry Truman, who announced the decision during his Democratic presidential nomination acceptance speech in 1948. He was far behind in the race against Governor Dewey of New York, and in a ploy to regain momentum, he challenged the Republican-controlled Congress by calling it into session: "In accepting the Democratic presidential nomination at 1:45 AM in a stifling Philadelphia convention hall," one columnist recalled, "Truman stunned delegates by calling on the Republican majority to live up to its party platform by passing laws that bolstered civil rights, extended Social Security and created a national health care program. 'They can do this job in 15 days if they want to do it,' he said." The Republicans balked, and Senator Robert Taft blocked all voting during the session, alleging that Truman had abused his power. But Taft's move backfired when he handed Truman a campaign slogan, "Do-Nothing Eightieth Congress," that helped him win the presidential election. Nowadays Congress's session schedule affords the president little occasion to exercise his convening power.

189. No president has exercised the adjournment power, which is reserved for when the two houses of Congress can't agree on an adjournment time.

he shall receive Ambassadors and other public Ministers;[190]

190. The authority to receive foreign officers has been used by presidents to assert the authority to recognize or not recognize foreign governments. Washington established that authority when he recognized the Republic of France following the revolution there. At the same time, he pledged that the United States would not become

involved in the war between Britain and France, despite a previous alliance with the French. The Neutrality Proclamation set off a rousing public debate about whether Congress or the president was better suited to steer America's foreign policy. Hamilton, who backed Washington's assertion of authority, was pitted against Madison, who backed a stronger legislative role in foreign affairs. Hamilton, using the pseudonym "Pacificus," wrote a series of newspaper essays to build support for the proclamation among the public. The first explained why the president was allowed to determine that a neutrality proclamation did not violate America's prior agreements with France. In the process, Hamilton laid out the case for executive recognition of foreign governments.

"The right of the Executive to receive ambassadors and other public Ministers," Hamilton wrote,

> may serve to illustrate the relative duties of the Executive and Legislative Departments. This right includes that of judging, in the case of a Revolution of Government in a foreign Country, whether the new rulers are competent organs of the National Will and ought to be recognised or not: And where a treaty antecedently exists between the UStates and such nation that right involves the power of giving operation or not to such treaty. For until the new Government is acknowleged, the treaties between the nations, as far at least as regards public rights, are of course suspended.
>
> This power of determining virtually in the case supposed upon the operation of national Treaties as a consequence, of the power to receive ambassadors and other public Ministers, is an important instance of the right of the Executive to decide the obligations of the Nation with regard to foreign Nations.

Jefferson, who was serving as Washington's state secretary, prevailed on Madison to respond to Hamilton's argument: "The presi-

dent's proclamation, and especially Hamilton's interpretation of it,"
wrote one historian, James Roger Sharp, "were seen not only as an
apology for the aggrandizement of executive power but also as a
threat to peace in the United States. 'For god's sake, my dear Sir,'
Jefferson exhorted Madison about Hamilton, 'take up your pen, select the most striking heresies and cut him to pieces in the face of the
public.'" Madison responded, under the pen name "Helvidius," that
the "receive ambassadors" clause was being blown out of proportion:
"It is evident, therefore, that if the executive has a right to reject a
public minister, it must be founded on some other consideration
than a change in the government, or the newness of the government;
and consequently a right to refuse to acknowledge a new government
cannot be implied by the right to refuse a public minister."

**he shall take Care that the Laws be faithfully executed,[191] and shall
Commission all the Officers of the United States.**

191. Here is one of the most powerful weapons in the president's
arsenal. It establishes him as guardian not only of congressional
statutes but of the Constitution itself. One test of the president's
powers came in 1888, over whether the president could appoint a
bodyguard for a judge. The Supreme Court, in *In re Neagle*, wrote:

> The Constitution, section 3, Article 2, declares that the
> President "shall take care that the laws be faithfully exe-
> cuted," and he is provided with the means of fulfilling
> this obligation by his authority to commission all the
> officers of the United States, and, by and with the advice
> and consent of the Senate, to appoint the most important
> of them and to fill vacancies. He is declared to be
> commander-in-chief of the army and navy of the United
> States. The duties which are thus imposed upon him he is
> further enabled to perform by the recognition in the

Constitution, and the creation by acts of Congress, of executive departments, which have varied in number from four or five to seven or eight, the heads of which are familiarly called cabinet ministers. These aid him in the performance of the great duties of his office, and represent him in a thousand acts to which it can hardly be supposed his personal attention is called, and thus he is enabled to fulfill the duty of his great department, expressed in the phrase that "he shall take care that the laws be faithfully executed."

Is this duty limited to the enforcement of acts of Congress or of treaties of the United States according to their express terms, or does it include the rights, duties and obligations growing out of the Constitution itself, our international relations, and all the protection implied by the nature of the government under the Constitution?

The president's authority to use the Armed Forces in law enforcement was limited by the Posse Comitatus Act of 1878, passed with the end of Reconstruction. In the lead-up to the Civil War, Attorney General Caleb Cushing issued an opinion asserting that U.S. marshals could invoke posses comitatus to enforce fugitive slave laws—marshals could summon the military to capture fugitive slaves and stand guard between them and abolitionists who might try to free them. The authority read: "A marshal of the United States, when opposed in the execution of his duty by unlawful combinations, has authority to summon the entire able-bodied force of his precinct as a *posse comitatus*. This authority comprehends not only bystanders and other citizens generally but any and all organized armed force, whether militia of the State, or officers, soldiers, sailors, and marines of the United States."

The shoe was on the other foot when, after the Civil War, the Army was used to support Reconstruction governments in the southern states and protect African American participation in elections. Infuriated by this use of executive power, the Democratic

Party passed the Posse Comitatus Act of 1878, which provided that: "Whoever, except in cases and under circumstances expressly authorized by the Constitution or Act of Congress, willfully uses any part of the Army or the Air Force as a posse comitatus or otherwise to execute the laws shall be fined under this title or imprisoned not more than two years, or both." The law does not prevent the president from acting to quell insurrection.

In the wake of the terrorist attacks of September 11, 2001, and Hurricane Katrina in 2005, efforts have been made to relax the Posse Comitatus Act or to provide for the use of the Armed Forces in certain domestic situations, though these efforts have met with criticism.

SECTION 4. The President, Vice President and all civil Officers of the United States, shall be removed from Office on Impeachment for, and Conviction of,[192] Treason, Bribery, or other high Crimes and Misdemeanors.[193]

192. The question of whether a president can elect to remove a cabinet member led to the impeachment of President Johnson. In 1867 Congress passed the Tenure of Office Act to prevent Johnson from replacing members of Lincoln's cabinet. The law required the president to obtain the consent of the Senate before dismissing any official whose appointment had required Senate confirmation. The context was Johnson's temporizing during Reconstruction. Johnson ignored the act and dismissed Secretary of War Stanton. In 1868 the House impeached Johnson for violating the Tenure of Office Act, but the Senate acquitted him by a single vote. The act he had been accused of violating was shown to be unconstitutional in 1926, when the Supreme Court decided *Myers v. U.S.* and issued an opinion written by the only chief justice who had previously been president, William Howard Taft. The case involved a postmaster of Portland, Oregon, Frank S. Myers, who in 1920 had been fired by the postmaster general on authority of the president. Taft went back

to *The Records of the Federal Convention* to craft a ruling that left the power to fire with the president.

193. "What, then, is an impeachable offense?" So asked Representative Gerald Ford in 1970 when he was seeking the impeachment of Justice William O. Douglas. Ford famously answered his own question: "The only honest answer is that an impeachable offense is whatever a majority of the House of Representatives considers it to be at a given moment in history."

ARTICLE III.

SECTION 1. The judicial Power of the United States,[194]

194. The Supreme Court defined this phrase in *Muskrat v. United States*, a 1911 case involving Indian lands. The Court dismissed the litigation on the grounds that it was little more than an attempt by the Congress to obtain an advisory opinion. The judicial power, Justice William Day wrote, "is the right to determine actual controversies arising between adverse litigants, duly instituted in courts of proper jurisdiction. The right to declare a law unconstitutional arises because an act of Congress relied upon by one or the other of such parties in determining their rights is in conflict with the fundamental law. The exercise of this, the most important and delicate duty of this Court, is not given to it as a body with revisory power over the action of Congress, but because the rights of the litigants in justiciable controversies require the court to choose between the fundamental law and a law purporting to be enacted within constitutional authority, but in fact beyond the power delegated to the legislative branch of the government."

In 78 *Federalist* Hamilton sought to allay concerns of New Yorkers considering ratification: "Whoever attentively considers the different departments of power must perceive, that in a government in which they are separated from each other, the judiciary, from the nature of its functions, will always be the least dangerous to the political rights of the constitution; because it will be least in a capacity to annoy or injure them. The executive not only dispenses the honors, but holds the sword of the community. The legislature not only commands the purse, but prescribes the rules by which the duties and rights of every citizen are to be regulated. The judiciary, on the contrary, has no influence over either the sword or the purse, no direction either of the strength or of the wealth of the society, and can take no active resolution whatever. It may truly be said to have neither Force nor Will, but merely judgment; and must ultimately depend upon the aid of the executive arm even for the efficacy of its judgments."

shall be vested in one supreme Court,[195]

195. The Constitution is silent on the composition of the Court or the federal judiciary in general, save for a reference in Article I to a chief justice who presides over impeachment proceedings against the president. The court system was established by the Judiciary Act of 1789. The first Supreme Court consisted of a chief justice of the United States and five associate justices.

and in such inferior Courts as the Congress may from time to time ordain and establish.[196]

196. Today there are more than 850 Article III judgeships. The question of whether there should even be *any* federal courts beneath the Supreme Court was debated hotly at Philadelphia. Some founders opposed the idea of an expansive federal judiciary with judges across the country. They preferred that state courts handle questions relating to the U.S. Constitution, with a federal Supreme Court reviewing their decisions.

This point was made by John Rutledge of South Carolina, who argued, as Madison noted, "that the State Tribunals might and ought to be left in all cases to decide in the first instance the right of appeal to the supreme national tribunal being sufficient to secure the national rights & uniformity of Judgmts: that it was making an unnecessary encroachment on the jurisdiction of the States, and creating unnecessary obstacles to their adoption of the new system." Madison noted that the motion was seconded by Roger Sherman of Connecticut, who, Madison said, "dwelt chiefly on the supposed expensiveness of having a new set of Courts, when the existing State Courts would answer the same purpose." But John Dickinson of Delaware "contended strongly that if there was to be a National Legislature, there ought to be a national Judiciary, and that the former ought to have authority to institute the latter."

In 1 *Brutus* a leading Anti-Federalist warned that the power of the federal courts was "very extensive; their jurisdiction comprehends all civil causes, except such as arise between citizens of the same state; and it extends to all cases in law and equity arising under the constitution. One inferior court must be established, I presume, in each state, at least, with the necessary executive officers appendant thereto. It is easy to see, that in the common course of things, these courts will eclipse the dignity, and take away from the respectability, of the state courts. These courts will be, in themselves, totally independent of the states, deriving their authority from the United States, and receiving from them fixed salaries; and in the course of human events it is to be expected, that they will swallow up all the powers of the courts in the respective states."

The Judges,[197] both of the supreme and inferior Courts, shall hold their Offices during good Behaviour,[198]

---

197. The titles chief justice and associate justice for members of the Supreme Court are established in Section 1 of the Judiciary Act

of 1789. Chief Justice Rehnquist was a stickler for the usage of the legislated titles. One lawyer, appearing before the high bench for the first time, began her response to a question from Justice Kennedy by saying, "Well, Judge—"

"That's Justice Kennedy," Chief Justice Rehnquist snapped, according to an account in the *New York Times* by Stanford law professor Jeffrey L. Fisher, a former clerk to Justice John Paul Stevens.

The lawyer, though shaken, plunged on, only to respond, a few minutes later to a question from Associate Justice Souter by saying, "Yes, Judge."

Again the chief justice corrected her, saying: "That's Justice Souter."

Then, a couple of minutes later, our hapless heroine called Chief Justice Rehnquist himself a judge. The chief justice, according to Fisher's account in the *Times*, "leaned forward, his deep voice now at its sternest, to say, 'Counsel is admonished that this court is composed of justices, not judges.'"

But, according to the account in the *Times,* before the lawyer could say anything, Justice Stevens interjected: "It's O.K., Counsel. The Constitution makes the same mistake."

198. Meaning life tenure. The prospect of a bench filled with elderly judges who occasionally nodded off during cases or forgot basic facts didn't seem to worry Hamilton in 79 *Federalist*:

> The constitution of New-York, to avoid investigations that must forever be vague and dangerous, has taken a particular age as the criterion of inability. No man can be a judge beyond sixty. I believe there are few at present, who do not disapprove of this provision. There is no station in relation to which it is less proper than to that of a judge. The deliberating and comparing faculties generally preserve their strength much beyond that period, in men who survive it; and when in addition to this circumstance, we consider how few there are who outlive the season of intellectual vigor, and how improbable it is that any considerable

portion of the bench, whether more or less numerous, should be in such a situation at the same time, we shall be ready to conclude that limitations of this sort have little to recommend them. In a republic, where fortunes are not affluent, and pensions not expedient, the dismission of men from stations in which they have served their country long and usefully, on which they depend for subsistence, and from which it will be too late to resort to any other occupation for a livelihood, ought to have some better apology to humanity, than is to be found in the imaginary danger of a superannuated bench.

More than two hundred years later, a debate is growing over the wisdom of life tenure. Writing in the *Wall Street Journal*, two law professors, Steven G. Calabresi and James Lindgren, called the Supreme Court "a gerontocracy—like the leadership cadre of the Chinese Communist Party." Between 1789 and 1970, they reported, "justices served an average of 14.9 years. Those who have stepped down since 1970, however, have served an average of 25.6 years." They said that the "typical one-term president now gets to appoint only one instead of two justices, and with the recent 11-year drought of vacancies a two-term presidency could in theory go by without being able to make even a single Supreme Court appointment." They called such a situation "unacceptable," arguing: "No powerful government institution in a modern democracy should go for 11 years without any democratic check on its membership. Nor should powerful officials hold office for an average of 25.6 years with some of them serving for 35 years or more." They called the tenure rule "a relic of the 18th century and of pre-democratic times."

Akhil Amar notes in *America's Constitution: A Biography*: "Neither of America's first two chief justices served for life or anything close to it. Instead, John Jay left the bench after six years to become governor of New York, and Oliver Ellsworth quit after four and a half years . . . together these two chiefs spent only ten years on the Court and lived for some forty years thereafter."

and shall, at stated Times, receive for their Services, a Compensation, which shall not be diminished during their Continuance in
Office.[199]

---

199. Judges' pay was a sore point with the revolutionaries who declared American independence. The Declaration itself lists as one of
the complaints against George III: "He has made Judges dependent
on his Will alone for the tenure of their offices, and the amount and
payment of their salaries." The founders saw a steady income, which
wouldn't fluctuate according to congressional displeasure with the
courts, as the backbone of an independent judiciary. A number of
judges have claimed that this language exempts them from paying
income tax, as any income tax would reduce the amount that Congress had set for them to receive. In 1862 the federal government, to
help with the war effort, enacted a 3 percent income tax for all federal employees. The next year Chief Justice Taney wrote to the
Treasury secretary, Salmon Chase: "I regard an act of Congress retaining in the Treasury a portion of the compensation of the judges
as unconstitutional, and void."

This letter is cited in the 1920 Supreme Court case *Evans v. Gore*,
in which the high court sided with a district court judge of Kentucky, Walter Evans, a former commissioner of internal revenue under President Arthur. Evans had objected to a provision in the 1919
tax law that, in a departure from earlier revenue acts, included the
judges' salaries as taxable income. The Court wrote: "Here, the
plaintiff was paid the full compensation, but was subjected to an involuntary obligation to pay back a part, and the obligation was
promptly enforced. Of what avail to him was the part which was
paid with one hand, and then taken back with the other? Was he not
placed in practically the same situation as if it had been withheld in
the first instance? Only by subordinating substance to mere form
could it be held that his compensation was not diminished."

The ruling was reversed in 1939, when the Supreme Court decided *O'Malley v. Woodrough*: "To suggest that it makes inroads upon

the independence of judges who took office after Congress had thus charged them with the common duties of citizenship, by making them bear their aliquot share of the cost of maintaining the Government, is to trivialize the great historic experience on which the framers based the safeguards of Article III, § 1. To subject them to a general tax is merely to recognize that judges are also citizens, and that their particular function in government does not generate an immunity from sharing with their fellow citizens the material burden of the government whose Constitution and laws they are charged with administering." The plaintiff, Joseph W. Woodrough, became the longest-serving federal judge in American history—his term ran sixty-one years—and the oldest federal judge; he was still on the bench when he died in 1977 at the age of 104.

Justice William O. Douglas, then in his first term, voted with the majority. "As I entered my vote in the docket book," Douglas wrote, "I decided that I had just voted myself first-class citizenship. The tradition had been that Justices never even voted in public elections . . . I took a different course. Since I would be paying as heavy an income tax as my neighbor, I decided to participate in local, state, and national affairs. . . . That meant I would register and vote . . . I would travel and speak out on foreign affairs."

Before the 2008 recession, the question of judicial pay had popped back into prominence, as some judges, state as well as federal, grew resentful of the soaring salaries their former clerks were making at law firms. In Manhattan, a first-year associate might make upward of $30,000 more than the district judge she had clerked for the year before. Chief Justice Roberts, who currently makes a salary of $217,400, devoted his annual report on the judiciary in 2006 to the pay issue. He said judicial salaries had "now reached the level of constitutional crisis that threatens to undermine the strength and independence of the federal judiciary."

The issue erupted in headlines in New York in 2008, when the chief judge of the Empire State's highest court, Judith Kaye of the Court of Appeals, sued in a court inferior to her own for a pay raise for the entire state judiciary. The lawsuit was brought under New York State's constitution, which also contains a prohibition against lowering the salary of a sitting judge. One of the arguments in the case is that by neglecting to give judges cost of living adjustments, the state has effectively undercut judicial pay. The New York lawsuit echoed a federal lawsuit filed in 1997 by a group of federal judges who challenged Congress's failure for several years to implement cost of living adjustments for judges that it had previously approved. The Supreme Court declined to take the case, but Justice Breyer, joined by Justices Scalia and Kennedy, issued a dissent suggesting that the Court had declined the case out of embarrassment.

SECTION 2. The judicial Power shall extend to all Cases,[200]

200. The list that follows in this part of Article III includes all matters over which the federal courts have jurisdiction. Notice that the list is divided into two distinct groups: one depending on the substance of the legal question raised, the other depending on the character of the parties. As Chief Justice Marshall wrote in *Cohens v. Virginia*: "In one description of cases, the jurisdiction of the Court is founded entirely on the character of the parties; and the nature of the controversy is not contemplated by the constitution. The character of the parties is every thing, the nature of the case nothing. In the other description of cases, the jurisdiction is founded entirely on the character of the case, and the parties are not contemplated by the constitution. In these, the nature of the case is every thing, the character of the parties nothing." Federal jurisdiction is not necessarily exclusive; most of the time a litigant can bring the same suit in a state court as well. The state cause of action was explicitly protected by the Judiciary Act of 1789, although the Judiciary Act also lets a defendant "remove" a case to federal from state court if it could originally have been brought there.

in Law and Equity,[201]

---

201. Law and equity are two distinct legal traditions. Despite some overlap, they are concerned with different issues and offer different remedies. To give an oversimplified example: To collect a debt one would go to law; to obtain an injunction, to equity. In England and in America at the time of the Revolution, cases in law and cases in equity were handled in different courts. The failure of Congress to create separate federal courts to handle law and equity did not mean that these legal systems were merged but rather that a single federal district court might sit as a law court, an equity court, or an admiralty court—following separate procedures and applying a separate body of law—depending on the case being tried. States with divided court systems began to unify them in the nineteenth century, though a handful of states retain separate equity courts to this day. Law and equity practice in the federal courts was consolidated in 1938, when the modern federal rules of civil procedure were promulgated. Some distinctions between law and equity retain significant consequences for modern litigants. The most visible for constitutional purposes stems from the Seventh Amendment, which guarantees the right to a jury trial "in suits at law" where the value in controversy is more than $20, which, to the founders, meant twenty Spanish milled dollars, or considerably more than is currently meant by twenty one-dollar Federal Reserve notes. Equity proceedings do not involve juries. The need to determine the scope of the Seventh Amendment obliges modern federal courts to decide whether a given claim to relief is legal or equitable, a question that grows increasingly difficult as the everyday distinctions between the legal systems, once familiar to lawyers, judges, and newspapermen, recede further into the past.

arising under this Constitution,[202] the Laws of the United States,[203] and Treaties made, or which shall be made, under their Authority;[204] to all Cases affecting Ambassadors, other public Ministers and Consuls;[205]—to all Cases of admiralty and maritime Jurisdiction;[206]—to Controversies to which the United States shall be a Party;[207]—to Controversies[208] between two or more States;[209]—between a State and Citizens of another State;[210]—between Citizens of different States,[211]

---

202. "To all cases arising under this Constitution, because the meaning, construction, and operation of a compact ought always to be ascertained by all the parties, or by authority derived only from one of them," Chief Justice Jay wrote in 1793 in *Chisholm v. Georgia*.

203. "To all cases arising under the laws of the United States, because, as such laws, constitutionally made, are obligatory on each State, the measure of obligation and obedience ought not to be decided and fixed by the party from whom they are due, but by a tribunal deriving authority from both the parties," Jay wrote in *Chisholm*.

204. "To all cases arising under treaties made by their authority; because, as treaties are compacts made by, and obligatory on, the whole nation, their operation ought not to be affected or regulated by the local laws or courts of a part of the nation," Jay wrote in *Chisholm*.

205. "To all cases affecting Ambassadors, or other public Ministers and Consuls, because, as these are officers of foreign nations whom this nation are bound to protect and treat according to the laws of nations, cases affecting them ought only to be cognizable by national authority," Jay wrote in *Chisholm*. It was to this clause that a Romanian vice consul in Cleveland, Ohio, turned in hopes of preventing his wife from winning a divorce. When his wife filed against him, the consul, John Popovici, argued that, because he was a foreign minister, the state courts of Ohio lacked jurisdiction. Unconvinced, Ohio ordered him to pay alimony. Popovici appealed to the Supreme Court, where he found no friend in Justice Holmes, who,

in *Popovici v. Agler*, handed down an opinion in 1930, affirmed the Ohio order, and noted that Popovici's estranged wife, Helen, was an American citizen and that "her position certainly is not less to be considered than her husband's." More to the constitutional point, Holmes wrote that the ten words of this constitutional clause "do not of themselves and without more exclude the jurisdiction of the State. . . . Therefore they do not affect the present case if it be true as has been unquestioned for three-quarters of a century that the Courts of the United States have no jurisdiction over divorce. If when the Constitution was adopted the common understanding was that the domestic relations of husband and wife and parent and child were matters reserved to the States, there is no difficulty in construing the instrument accordingly and not much in dealing with the statutes. 'Suits against consuls and vice-consuls' must be taken to refer to ordinary civil proceedings and not to include what formerly would have belonged to the ecclesiastical Courts."

206. "To all cases of Admiralty and Maritime jurisdiction, because, as the seas are the joint property of nations, whose right and privileges relative thereto are regulated by the law of nations and treaties, such cases necessarily belong to national jurisdiction," Jay wrote in *Chisholm*.

207. "To controversies to which the United States shall be a party, because, in cases in which the whole people are interested, it would not be equal or wise to let any one State decide and measure out the justice due to others," Jay wrote in *Chisholm*.

208. The words "cases" and "controversies" have been the cause of much meditation. Wrote Chief Justice Warren in *Flast v. Cohen*:

> The judicial power of federal courts is constitutionally restricted to "cases" and "controversies." As is so often the situation in constitutional adjudication, those two words have an iceberg quality, containing beneath their surface simplicity submerged complexities which go to the very heart of our constitutional form of government. Embodied in the words "cases" and "controversies" are two com-

plementary but somewhat different limitations. In part, those words limit the business of federal courts to questions presented in an adversary context and in a form historically viewed as capable of resolution through the judicial process. And in part those words define the role assigned to the judiciary in a tripartite allocation of power to assure that the federal courts will not intrude into areas committed to the other branches of government. Justiciability is the term of art employed to give expression to this dual limitation placed upon federal courts by the 'case and controversy' doctrine.

Justiciability is itself a concept of uncertain meaning and scope. Its reach is illustrated by the various grounds upon which questions sought to be adjudicated in federal courts have been held not to be justiciable. Thus, no justiciable controversy is presented when the parties seek adjudication of only a political question, when the parties are asking for an advisory opinion, when the question sought to be adjudicated has been mooted by subsequent developments, and when there is no standing to maintain the action.

209. "To controversies between two or more States, because domestic tranquillity requires that the contentions of States should be peaceably terminated by a common judicatory, and, because, in a free country, justice ought not to depend on the will of either of the litigants," Jay wrote in *Chisholm*. The great school of constitutional law in respect of this clause is the Mississippi River, which, because of the insouciance with which it steals land, has been called the Great Thief. As the river jumps its beds and absconds, the Supreme Court is occasionally called in to deal with the mayhem.

In a 1974 case between Arkansas and Mississippi, the issue was an erstwhile portion of riverbed called Luna Bar. While the Court, in *Mississippi v. Arkansas*, ruled for the Magnolia State, Justice Douglas, the naturalist on the Court, sided with Arkansas and criticized the majority for ignoring three tree stumps that matched the trees in the Natural State. Douglas wrote that locals "had located great trees that once grew there, the age of the trees going back before 1800. Luna Bar therefore was not recently created nor was it created within the last 100 years."

In the 1893 case *Iowa v. Illinois*, the issue was the "true line" in a navigable river that marks a boundary between states and that, the Court explained, is the middle of the main channel of the river. The Court had more to say on the matter in 1918 in *Arkansas v. Tennessee*, where it brought in the rule of the thalweg, which is the lowest part of a valley or river stream where the water moves most quickly.

When Chicago reversed the direction of the current in the Chicago River, Missouri would eventually sue, claiming that Illinois was responsible for dumping "1,500 tons of poisonous filth daily into the Mississippi," as the Court's opinion described the complaint. Missouri claimed that its neighbor was responsible for inflicting St. Louis with bouts of typhoid fever. The Court ruled for Illinois, with Justice Holmes writing: "There is nothing which can be detected by the unassisted senses—no visible increase of filth, no new smell. On the contrary, it is proved that the great volume of pure water from Lake Michigan which is mixed with the sewage at the start has improved the Illinois River in these respects to a noticeable extent."

210. "To controversies between a State and citizens of another State, because in case a State (that is, all the citizens of it) has demands against some citizens of another State, it is better that she should prosecute their demands in a national court than in a court of the State to which those citizens belong, the danger of irritation and criminations arising from apprehensions and suspicions of partiality being thereby obviated. Because, in cases where some citizens of one State have demands against all the citizens of another State, the cause of liberty and the rights of men forbid that the latter should be the sole judges of the justice due to the latter, and true Republican government requires that free and equal citizens should have free, fair, and equal justice," Jay wrote in *Chisholm*. The Eleventh Amend-

ment was created to deal with Jay's ruling in *Chisolm*, establishing sovereign immunity of the individual states from actions launched in federal court by citizens of another state.

211. This was one of the phrases on which Chief Justice Taney, in the Supreme Court's most shameful opinion, relied in 1857 in denying Dred Scott his freedom and closed the federal courts to his plea. Scott, born into slavery at Virginia in 1799, sued for his freedom on the grounds that his owner, an Army surgeon, had moved him to the free soil of the Wisconsin Territory and Illinois. Legal precedent suggested that a slave owner, in bringing slaves to reside with him on free soil, had legally set them free. This doctrine of "once free, always free" was recognized in Missouri, where Scott sued for his freedom. The case is captioned *Scott v. Sandford*, after the brother of the widow of the Army surgeon, whose last name was Sanford. With Scott of Missouri suing Sanford of New York, the case seemed to meet the jurisdictional requirements of the federal courts.

Taney framed the case this way: "Can a negro, whose ancestors were imported into this country, and sold as slaves, become a member of the political community formed and brought into existence by the Constitution of the United States, and as such become entitled to all the rights, and privileges, and immunities, guaranteed by that instrument to the citizen? One of which rights is the privilege of suing in a court of the United States in the cases specified in the Constitution." He continued a little later: "The only matter in issue before the court, therefore, is, whether the descendants of such slaves, when they shall be emancipated, or who are born of parents who had become free before their birth, are citizens of a State, in the sense in which the word citizen is used in the Constitution of the United States. . . . Does the Constitution of the United States act upon him whenever he shall be made free under the laws of a State, and raised there to the rank of a citizen, and immediately clothe him with all the privileges of a citizen in every other State, and in its own courts?" He continued: "The court think the affirmative of these propositions cannot be maintained. And if it cannot, the plaintiff in error could not be a citizen of the State of Missouri, within the

meaning of the Constitution of the United States, and, consequently, was not entitled to sue in its courts." Forty-nine months
later the Civil War began.

—between Citizens of the same State claiming Lands under Grants of different States,[212]

212. "To controversies between citizens of the same State, claiming lands under grants of different States, because, as the rights of
the two States to grant the land are drawn into question, neither of
the two States ought to decide the controversy," Jay wrote in
Chisholm.

This gave the courts power to settle controversies between the
states that had, under the Articles of Confederation, rested with the
Congress, which seemed not up to the task. In what was to become
Vermont, the Green Mountain Boys, who possessed grants from
New Hampshire, repulsed surveyors sent by New York, which also
claimed the region. The surveyors were tried for trespass and
whipped. In northern Pennsylvania, frontiersmen from Connecticut
and Pennsylvania feuded for decades in what is known as the Penna-
mite and Yankee War, which produced the first and only controversy
between states that a federal court would hear under the Articles.

The Articles had failed to establish a judiciary. So Congress instructed the two states to decide upon a panel of judges who would
hear the case—an arbitration. The resulting court, which sat for
forty-two days, decided for Pennsylvania, although the decision
failed to end the hostilities, which dragged on until 1799. Hampton
Lawrence Carson, a historian of the Supreme Court, writes: "The
decision, which was the only one rendered in controversies between
States, under the Articles of Confederation" also happens to be "the
first settlement of a controversy between States by the decree of a
Court established by the United States."

Justice Henry Baldwin wrote that the power to settle controversies between states—as embodied both in this clause about competing land grants and in the clause before it regarding suits between states—is entrusted entirely to the judiciary, not to Congress, which has no active authority save to ratify compacts reached by the states. He called the results "most clear and satisfactory" and stressed that compacts between the states are "an exercise of their reserved powers" that are "neither given, or in any way abridged" by the Constitution.

and between a State, or the Citizens thereof, and foreign States, Citizens or Subjects.[213, 214]

213."To controversies between a State or the citizens thereof and foreign states, citizens or subjects, because, as every nation is responsible for the conduct of its citizens towards other nations, all questions touching the justice due to foreign nations or people ought to be ascertained by, and depend on, national authority," Jay wrote in *Chisholm*.

In *Fathers of the Constitution*, Max Farrand quotes Commissioner Thieriot of France as disparaging the American courts and as reporting: "It appears that the court of France wished to set up a jurisdiction of its own on this continent for all matters involving French subjects." Farrand says Congress authorized Ambassador Benjamin Franklin to negotiate a consular convention, ratified a few years later, according to which the citizens of the United States and the subjects of the French king, when in the other's country, should be tried by their respective consuls or vice consuls. In submitting it to Congress, Farrand writes, John Jay "clearly pointed out that it was reciprocal in name rather than in substance, as there were few or no Americans in France but an increasing number of Frenchmen in the United States."

214. While lengthy, the list excludes some disputes, ensuring that the judiciary will not settle questions of an administrative nature. Congress had passed an act instructing federal judges to provide hearings to wounded Revolutionary War veterans who sought to receive pensions. This caused an outcry from the circuit courts. In letters to the president, the circuit courts of North Carolina, New York, and Pennsylvania, on which sat five of the six justices of the Supreme Court, objected that Congress could not instruct the courts to hear disputes that do not fall under the types described in this clause. The courts also objected to the fact that both the secretary of war and Congress would have been able to overrule the determinations of the courts that heard the veterans' claims; in other words, even had a circuit court heard a veteran's case and judged that he should be added to the pension list, Congress or the war secretary could have simply ignored the judgment.

In all Cases affecting Ambassadors, other public Ministers and Consuls, and those in which a State shall be Party, the supreme Court shall have original Jurisdiction.[215]

215. On this phrase turned the most famous case in American history, *Marbury v. Madison.* Or, as Akhil Amar puts it in his biography of the Constitution: "The most celebrated constitutional-law case ever decided pivoted on one of the Constitution's most recondite provisions." On its face the language simply explains that in two categories of cases—those involving foreign diplomats and those involving states—the matter goes directly to the Supreme Court. The legal question at the center of *Marbury* was whether Congress could expand the Supreme Court's original jurisdiction to other categories. Congress had done so with the Judiciary Act of 1789, which authorized the Supreme Court to directly issue "writs of mandamus," orders commanding government officials to perform specific duties.

This clause was tested more than a decade later, when a financier named William Marbury petitioned the Supreme Court to order Secretary of State James Madison, to deliver to him a commission—a piece of paper—that would authorize him to take up a judgeship to which he'd been appointed by the previous president. In the last days of his administration John Adams had sought to install forty-two men as justices of the peace (minor judges) in the District of Columbia. The openings were created by a bill that Adams signed in February 1801, with less than a week left in his term. In short, Adams was trying to pack as many Federalists and other politically connected figures into the federal government as he could before his party relinquished control of the government for—as it would turn out—ever.

One of them was Marbury. But Marbury's commission sat on the desk of Adams's secretary of state, John Marshall, and had not reached the intended recipient by the time Adams's term ended. In the new administration, President Jefferson ordered *his* secretary of state, James Madison, not to send out the remaining commissions. Marbury, wanting the job, brought an action in the Supreme Court seeking a writ of mandamus that would command Madison to give to him his commission. At the crux of *Marbury v. Madison* is that Marbury sought his writ from not a lower court but the Supreme Court. He was asking the high court to act in its original jurisdiction, as the Judiciary Act of 1789, but not the Constitution, set forth.

By then Marshall, who as secretary of state hadn't finished sending out the commissions, also held the position of chief justice of the United States. He found that Congress did not have the authority to expand the Court's original jurisdiction to suits such as Marbury's; Marshall read the Constitution to permit the Court to exercise original jurisdiction over only cases involving states and those involving ambassadors and the like. And so he struck down that provision of the Judiciary Act.

It was the first time the Court struck down a law, and Marshall did it with phrasing that rings down through the centuries: "The constitution is either a superior, paramount law, unchangeable by ordinary means, or it is on a level with ordinary legislative acts, and like other acts, is alterable when the legislature shall please to alter it. If the former part of the alternative be true, then a legislative act contrary to the constitution is not law: if the latter part be true, then written constitutions are absurd attempts, on the part of the people, to limit a power in its own nature illimitable. Certainly all those who have framed written constitutions contemplate them as forming the fundamental and paramount law of the nation, and consequently the theory of every such government must be, that an act of the legislature repugnant to the constitution is void."

In all the other Cases before mentioned, the supreme Court shall have appellate Jurisdiction, both as to Law and Fact,[216]

216. "The scariest chase I ever saw since *The French Connection,*" is how, during oral arguments, Justice Scalia characterized an event at the center of a 2007 case called *Scott v. Harris,* in which a dashboard camera drew the Court into exercising its authority, under this clause, to review a trial court's findings of fact as well as law. The case centered on a high-speed chase in Georgia. The fleeing driver, Victor Harris, was left paralyzed after a sheriff's deputy rammed his car, causing Harris to lose control and crash. Harris sued the deputy, Timothy Scott, alleging that excessive force was used. The episode was captured on Scott's dashboard camera, and the video footage clearly made an impression on the justices. The Supreme Court was "entering the YouTube Era," the *New York Times* reporter at the high court, Adam Liptak, later observed. A footnote to the Court's decision ruling against the paralyzed driver, written by Scalia, contains a link to a page on the Supreme Court's website at which the video can be viewed.

At least one justice, John Paul Stevens, was made uncomfortable by this role, as he indicated in a dissent. "Relying on a *de novo* review of a videotape of a portion of a nighttime chase on a lightly traveled road in Georgia where no pedestrians or other 'bystanders' were present, buttressed by uninformed speculation about the possible consequences of discontinuing the chase, eight of the jurors on this Court reach a verdict that differs from the views of the judges on both the District Court and the Court of Appeals who are surely more familiar with the hazards of driving on Georgia roads than we are. The Court's justification for this unprecedented departure from our well-settled standard of review of factual determinations made by a district court and affirmed by a court of appeals is based on its mistaken view that the Court of Appeals' description of the facts was 'blatantly contradicted by the record' and that respondent's version of the events was 'so utterly discredited by the record that no reasonable jury could have believed him.'"

with such Exceptions, and under such Regulations as the Congress shall make.[217]

217. The term "nuclear option" can be applied to Congress's authority to make such exceptions and regulations. At least in theory, it gives Congress the power to prevent the Supreme Court from hearing certain types of cases. It is argued, a lawyer in the Justice Department once wrote about this clause, "that divesting the Supreme Court of jurisdiction over a particular class of cases would undermine the constitutional role of the Court as the ultimate arbiter of constitutional questions. The Constitution, however, does not accord such a role to the Court. The authority of the Court to interpret the Constitution derives from the necessity of its doing so in the course of discharging its judicial responsibility to decide those cases and controversies properly presented to it." This description of the authority of the Supreme Court echoes the language of Justice William Rufus Day in *Muskrat* (page 152). The Justice Department lawyer who wrote it, John Roberts, later acceded as chief justice of the United States.

In 2006 Congress acted under this power to try to strip the federal courts of jurisdiction to hear habeas corpus cases filed by detainees at Guantanamo. It passed the Military Commissions Act, which said: "No court, justice, or judge shall have jurisdiction to hear or consider an application for a writ of habeas corpus filed by or on behalf of an alien detained by the United States who has been determined by the United States to have been properly detained as an enemy combatant or is awaiting such determination." In place of habeas, the act allowed for the U.S. Court of Appeals for the District of Columbia Circuit to make a very narrow review of the military's findings as to the circumstances in favor of each detainee's continued detention. The Court, in *Boumediene v. Bush*, found the maneuver unconstitutional because the Congress had failed to suspend habeas formally under the suspension clause of Article I.

The question, as the Court saw it, was not really one of Congress's power to set the jurisdiction of the federal courts, but of the strength of the habeas right. Congress saw it differently. The Supreme Court 150 years earlier had deferred to an act of Congress that stripped the high court of jurisdiction to hear a certain class of habeas appeals from the South, then under the military rule of the Reconstruction. The ruling, *Ex Parte McCardle*, involved William McCardle, a man Roberts described in his Justice Department memo on appellate jurisdiction as "an unreconstructed Mississippi newspaper editor."

McCardle had been arrested for writing editorials opposing Reconstruction, and he lodged a habeas petition that reached the Supreme Court. After the Court heard McCardle's case but before it had issued a decision, Congress stripped the Supreme Court of jurisdiction over habeas cases brought under the Habeas Corpus Act of 1867, as McCardle's had been. There is a view that the Court should have rebuffed the demarche by Congress because it had stepped into an active, specific case. But instead the justices allowed the Reconstruction lawmakers to step in against the unreconstructed editor: "We are not at liberty to inquire into the motives of the legislature. We can only examine into its power under the Constitution, and the power to make exceptions to the appellate jurisdiction of this court is given by express words."

In recent years Congress has considered a number of jurisdiction-stripping bills. The Marriage Protection Act, most recently introduced in 2007, would have stripped all federal courts of jurisdiction to hear appeals arising out of the 1996 Defense of Marriage Act, which says states don't have to recognize same-gender marriages from other states. The proposed Public Prayer Protection Act of 2007 would have denied the federal courts, including the Supreme Court, jurisdiction in respect of "any matter that relates to the alleged establishment of religion involving an entity of the Federal Government or a State or local government, or an officer or agent of the Federal Government or a State or local government, acting in an official capacity, concerning the expression of public prayer by that entity, officer, or agent."

The Trial of all Crimes,[218] except in Cases of Impeachment,[219]

218. The failure of Article III to guarantee a trial by jury in civil cases was repaired via the Seventh Amendment in the Bill of Rights. The thinking in Philadelphia was that juries should not sit in all civil cases. "Admiralty, chancery, and probate matters were not universally jury-triable," Akhil Amar has noted. "Many of the civil cases apt to be brought in federal courts would arise under state-law rules of tort, contract, property, and the like; perhaps these courts should pay some regard to state procedural rules concerning when juries should sit." Noting that Anti-Federalists "accused the Federalists of undermining the good old jury" by not requiring juries in civil cases, Amar writes: "Had Article III imposed a rigid mandate for all federal civil cases in all states at all times, such inflexibility might, ironically enough, have symbolized disrespect for local diversity—for the very states' rights Anti-Federalists claimed to embrace." One framer, James Wilson, in his State House Speech of October 6, 1787, explained in these words:

"The cases open to a jury, differed in the different states; it was therefore impracticable, on that ground, to have made a general rule." The
Constitutional Convention, he concluded, "found the task too
difficult for them; and they left the business as it stands." All the more
dramatic, then, was the decision of the First Congress to include in
the Seventh Amendment not only a right to a trial by jury in common
law cases involving more than $20, but also to prohibit the second-
guessing of findings of fact by juries except according to the procedures of common law.

219. Which are to be tried by the Senate.

shall be by Jury;[220]

220. The right to a jury trial is rarely invoked in federal court,
with most defendants opting to plead guilty—sometimes to lesser
charges or sometimes to the same charges for which they would otherwise be tried. In 2005, for instance, of the 78,042 defendants who
were convicted, some 74,226, or more than 95 percent, pleaded out,
according to the Justice Department's statistics bureau.

For much of the nation's history, twelve jurors were required.
This was settled through the ordeal of a cattle rustler in Utah who
was indicted as that territory was about to become a state. A certain
Thompson was charged in 1895 with stealing a single calf from
Heber Wilson. Twelve jurors convicted, but a new trial was granted
for reasons not stated in the Supreme Court's summary of the case.
The territory had become a state by the time of Thompson's second
trial, which was conducted under Utah's new constitution. It provided that in noncapital cases involving serious crimes "a jury shall
consist of eight jurors." Convicted again, the tenacious Thompson,
though he hadn't raised the objections at trial, appealed on the
grounds that he deserved a trial by twelve jurors.

In deciding that Thompson was entitled to a third trial, the
Supreme Court noted "that the word 'jury' and the words 'trial by

jury' were placed in the Constitution of the United States with reference to the meaning affixed to them in the law as it was in this country and in England at the time of the adoption of that instrument, and that when Thompson committed the offense of grand larceny in the Territory of Utah—which was under the complete jurisdiction of the United States for all purposes of government and legislation—the supreme law of the land required that he should be tried by a jury composed of not less than twelve persons. And such was the requirement of the statutes of Utah while it was a territory."

All this, however, was thrown into a cocked hat in the 1970s, when the Supreme Court decided that centuries of received wisdom was wrong. In the 1970 case of *Williams v. Florida*, the Court found that twelve was a historical accident and unworthy of constitutional codification. Justice White wrote: "Lord Coke's explanation that the '*number of twelve* is much respected in *holy writ*, as 12 *apostles*, 12 *stones*, 12 *tribes*, etc.,' is typical. In short, while, sometime in the 14th century, the size of the jury at common law came to be fixed generally at 12, that particular feature of the jury system appears to have been a historical accident, unrelated to the great purposes which gave rise to the jury in the first place." His opinion concluded that a twelve-member jury is "unnecessary to effect the purposes of the jury system and wholly without significance 'except to mystics.'"

The Supreme Court has also diluted the notion that a jury must return a unanimous verdict. In twin cases in 1972, *Johnson v. Louisiana* and *Apodaca v. Oregon*, the Court ruled that the Fourteenth Amendment did not prevent state criminal justice systems from convicting defendants when only ten jurors out of twelve voted guilty (in the case of Oregon) or nine jurors out of twelve (in the case of Louisiana). The cases were decided 5 to 4. Justice Powell, who made up one of the majority, held that while state criminal courts could convict on nonunanimous verdicts, unanimity was still a constitutional requirement in federal criminal cases. The point he made, as it was characterized by the dissent, was that the Fourteenth Amendment's due process clause, when applied against the states, provided for a "watered-down" version of the rights that the Constitution secured for defendants in federal court. Those 1972 cases were the last time the Supreme Court took up the unanimity question. So the notion that a citizen can be convicted in federal court only upon a unanimous verdict is hanging by a thread.

and such Trial shall be held in the State where the said Crimes shall have been committed;²²¹ but when not committed within any State,²²² the Trial shall be at such Place or Places as the Congress may by Law have directed.²²³

---

221. Two editors of the *Indianapolis News* were saved by this clause when President Theodore Roosevelt had them indicted in Washington, D.C., for criminal libel for publishing an editorial that looked into a suspected scandal in the financing of the Panama Canal. John Langdon Heaton, whose employer, Joseph Pulitzer, was among a number of newspapermen charged in the wake of Roosevelt's apoplexy, told the story in his book *The Story of a Page.* Citing this Article III safeguard, a judge in Indiana, A. B. Anderson, refused to send the Indiana editors to Washington. According to an October 13, 1909, dispatch in the *New York Times,* he declared that: "If the history of liberty means anything: if the Constitution means anything, then the prosecuting authority should not have the power to select the tribunal, if there be more than one to select from, at the capital of the Nation, nor should the Government have the power to drag citizens from distant States there for trial."

This constitutional requirement that trials take place near the alleged crime was not just a technical point to the founders. The issue it addressed was an enumerated grievance in the Declaration of Independence. One of the king's transgressions was to try colonists back in England, or, in the language of the Declaration, "For transporting us beyond Seas to be tried for pretended offences." Yet even the guarantee of a trial in the U.S. courthouse in the state capital wasn't always satisfactory. The so-called whiskey rebels in western Pennsylvania complained that tax violations had to be settled in the U.S. District Court at Philadelphia, which required "a trip that caused major hardship and actually deprived westerners of recourse to the courts."

Protections against such abuse were strengthened in the Sixth Amendment, which requires not only that the trial be held in the same state as the alleged crime, but that the jury be chosen from within the same district where the crime is charged to have occurred.

222. George Paschal, in his 1868 annotation of the Constitution, wrote that this "may be defined to be offenses committed in the District of Columbia, in forts or arsenals to which jurisdiction has been ceded by the States; in the territories of the United States; in the Indian Country; upon the high seas, and everywhere, when against the law of nations."

223. Paschal relates that the "offenses committed in the District of Columbia have always been tried in the District, under the 'exclusive legislation;' those in the organized territories have been tried there by the local courts of the territories; those committed by whites, or by Indians against whites (to a limited extent), have been tried in the States to whose federal courts jurisdiction had been committed by the laws to regulate trade and intercourse with the Indian tribes; those committed in forts and arsenals, over which the jurisdiction had been ceded by the States, have been tried in the United States District or Circuit Courts in that State; those upon the high seas in the State where the vessel first arrives."

SECTION 3. Treason[224] against the United States shall consist only in levying War against them, or in adhering to their Enemies, giving them Aid and Comfort.[225]

224. The only crime defined in the Constitution. Or, to put it another way, being the most heinous of all crimes, it is the only crime the founders did not trust Congress to define or for which they did not trust prosecutors to take a confession. This clause, in the practical

sense, protected seditious speech—but, at least in theory, not all speech, in that it is possible to imagine a speech or speeches being introduced as overt acts evidencing the treason of adhering to an enemy; an alleged adherent of al Qaeda, Adam Gadahn, was indicted for treason in 2006 in connection with videotapes he allegedly made in support of our enemies.

225. This phrasing picks two of the three definitions contained in the English Statute of Treason enacted in 1350. But, as the annotators of the Library of Congress edition of the Constitution note, the framers "conspicuously omitted the phrase defining as treason the 'compass[ing] or imagin[ing] the death of our lord the King.'" In America's first treason case, Chief Justice Marshall established a strict standard for the term "levying war." The case involved two of Aaron Burr's confederates, Erick Bollman and Samuel Swartwout, who were let off even though they had clearly conspired with the former vice president to subvert by force the new Republic. "To conspire to levy war and actually to levy war, are distinct offenses," Marshall wrote in *Ex Parte Bollman and Swartwout*. "The first must be brought into open action by the assemblage of men for a purpose treasonable in itself, or the fact of levying war cannot have been committed . . . the actual enlistment of men, to serve against the government, does not amount to levying war." But, Marshall warned, it was not necessary to appear in arms against the country to commit treason. Once war is levied, "all those who perform any part, however minute, or however remote from the scene of action, and who are actually leagued in the general conspiracy, are to be considered as traitors."

No Person shall be convicted of Treason unless on the Testimony of two Witnesses to the same overt Act, or on Confession in open Court.[226]

226. This was one of the reasons Vice President Burr escaped the gallows. Marshall, sitting at Richmond, Virginia, held the prosecu-

tion to the task of producing two witnesses to the same overt act. Burr had organized the assemblage on Blennerhassett's Island secretly, so that no witness could be produced. Treason cases have been relatively rare because of the hurdles erected by the framers and because a presidential pardon was granted in 1868 to all who, among other crimes, levied the Civil War against the Union. Convictions were obtained in the Whiskey Rebellion, with fighting against federal revenue collection deemed traitorous, but participation in forcible resistance to the fugitive slave law was not determined to be treason.

The Supreme Court rarely wrestled with treason until World War II, out of which grew three cases of note. In the case of Anthony Cramer, the two-witness rule was strengthened. The Supreme Court sustained its first conviction of treason in the case of Hans Max Haupt, who housed a traitorous son and provided him with a car. Tomoya Kawakita was a citizen of America by birth and of Japan by imperial law, as his parents were Japanese. "While a minor," the Court wrote, "he took the oath of allegiance to the United States; went to Japan for a visit on an American passport; and was prevented by the outbreak of war from returning to this country. During the war, he reached his majority in Japan; changed his registration from American to Japanese, showed sympathy with Japan and hostility to the United States; served as a civilian employee of a private corporation producing war materials for Japan; and brutally abused American prisoners of war who were forced to work there. After Japan's surrender, he registered as an American citizen; swore that he was an American citizen and had not done various acts amounting to expatriation; and returned to this country on an American passport." The Supreme Court sustained the conviction.

The Library of Congress annotators note that the "difficulties created by the Burr case have been obviated to a considerable extent through the punishment of acts ordinarily treasonable in nature under a different label." Julius and Ethel Rosenberg were convicted of espionage—an example of what Chief Justice Marshall was referring to when he wrote in *Ex Parte Bollman*: "Crimes so atrocious as those which have for their object the subversion by violence of those laws and those institutions which have been ordained in order to secure the peace and happiness of society, are not to escape punishment because they have not ripened into treason. The wisdom of the legislature is competent to provide for the case."

The Congress shall have Power to declare the Punishment of Treason,[227] but no Attainder[228] of Treason shall work Corruption of Blood,[229] or Forfeiture except during the Life of the Person attainted.[230]

———

227. Those guilty of treason shall "suffer death," Congress declared in 1790. The act also sets the penalty for misprision of (i.e., failing to report) treason at no more than seven years. At the time, traitors against the Crown risked worse, as Joseph Story notes in his *Commentaries*: "The punishment of high treason by the common law, as stated by Mr. Justice Blackstone, is as follows: 1. That the offender be drawn to the gallows, and not be carried or walk, though usually (by connivance at length ripened into law) a sledge or hurdle is allowed, to preserve the offender from the extreme torment of being dragged on the ground or pavement. 2. That he be hanged by the neck, and cut down alive. 3. That his entrails be taken out and burned, while he is yet alive. 4. That his head be cut off. 5. That his body be divided into four parts. 6. That his head and quarters be at the king's disposal. These refinements in cruelty (which if now practised would be disgraceful to the character of the age) were, in former times, literally and studiously executed; and indicate at once a savage and ferocious spirit, and a degrading subserviency to royal resentments, real or supposed. It was wise to place the punishment solely in the discretion of congress; and the punishment has been since declared, to be simply death by hanging; thus inflicting death in a manner becoming the humanity of a civilized society." Death is

no longer the mandatory punishment for a conviction of treason. The punishment now ranges from between five years in prison to death, as well as an incapacity to hold any office in the U.S.

In 2006 the United States, for the first time in more than a half a century, filed treason charges. The accused was a California man, Adam Yahiye Gadahn, who allegedly appeared in propaganda videos for al Qaeda. As of July 2009, he hadn't been captured.

228. "Attainder means, in its original application, the staining or corruption of the blood of a criminal who was in the contemplation of law dead. He then became '*attinctus*—stained, blackened, attainted,'" William Whiting, solicitor of the War Department during the Civil War, and later a congressman.

229. In England, corruption of blood was what the heirs of a traitor might expect if, say, their father was tortured and executed. As a legal matter, the traitor's bloodline simply ended. His heirs were in effect orphaned of any privileges that they might have expected. As Joseph Story recounts in *Commentaries*: "It is well known, that corruption of blood, and forfeiture of the estate of the offender followed, as a necessary consequence at the common law, upon every attainder of treason. By corruption of blood all inheritable qualities are destroyed; so, that an attainted person can neither inherit lands, nor other hereditaments from his ancestors, nor retain those, he is already in possession of, nor transmit them to any heir. And this destruction of all inheritable qualities is so complete, that it obstructs all descents to his posterity, whenever they are obliged to derive a title through him to any estate of a remoter ancestor. So, that if a father commits treason, and is attainted, and suffers death, and then the grandfather dies, his grandson cannot inherit any estate from his grandfather; for he must claim through his father, who could convey to him no inheritable blood. Thus the innocent are made the victims of a guilt, in which they did not, and perhaps could not, participate; and the sin is visited upon remote generations."

230. Of the treason clause, Madison wrote in 43 *Federalist*: "As treason may be committed against the United States, the authority of

the United States ought to be enabled to punish it. But as newfangled and artificial treasons, have been the great engines, by which violent factions, the natural offspring of free Governments, have usually wrecked their alternate malignity on each other, the Convention have with great judgment opposed a barrier to this peculiar danger, by inserting a constitutional definition of the crime, fixing the proof necessary for conviction of it, and restraining the Congress, even in punishing it, from extending the consequences of guilt beyond the person of its author."

Something of a controversy erupted during the Civil War when the Congress sought to add to the penalties for treason. In 1862 it passed a war measure under which certain classes of secessionists, including Confederate army and naval officers as well as officers of Confederate states or the federal Confederate government, would be stripped of their land and other property. President Lincoln expressed reservations. In a draft of a message to the House of Representatives, the president suggested that the Constitution permitted seizure of property only for the life of the Confederate officer. In other words, the phrase "except during the life of the person attainted" was to be a limit on how long the penalty might last. The Congress adjusted the language to address the president's point, though contemporaries, including the solicitor of his own War Department, William Whiting, believed Lincoln's fears were off the mark. According to Whiting, the phrase "except during the life of the person attainted" meant simply that any forfeiture proceedings had to be initiated while the traitor was still alive. His land could neither be taken from his heirs after his execution, nor, in the case of the Civil War, his death on the battlefield.

ARTICLE IV.

SECTION I. Full Faith and Credit shall be given in each State to the public Acts, Records, and judicial Proceedings of every other State.[231]

---

231. "The very purpose of the full-faith and credit clause," the Supreme Court said in one important case, "was to alter the status of the several states as independent foreign sovereignties, each free to ignore obligations created under the laws or by the judicial proceedings of the others, and to make them integral parts of a single nation throughout which a remedy upon a just obligation might be demanded as of right, irrespective of the state of its origin." The case, *Milwaukee County v. M. E. White Co.*, established that full faith and credit must be given between states in tax judgments.

This clause is one of the constitutional grounds on which the contest over same-gender marriage is taking place. Proponents argue that the clause demands each state, regardless of its own marriage laws, recognize the same-sex marriages performed in other states; that all states must recognize same-sex marriages performed in the four states that permit them—Massachusetts, Connecticut, Iowa, and Vermont. Congress has struck for a different shore, passing the Defense of Marriage Act in 1996 (please see the following footnote).

Even before gay marriage became a topic of debate, marriage law and the full faith and credit clause were actively dating. Historian Lawrence Friedman of Stanford University has called the clause a detour "around strict divorce laws in the United States." While different states have different standards for granting divorce, under the full faith and credit clause "a valid divorce in an 'easy' state could be recognized in all other states." A number of states—such as Indiana and the two Dakotas—experimented with easy divorce in the nineteenth century, he has noted, adding: "In the twentieth century, the main divorce mill was Nevada. This was a barren desert state, with few resources, few people, and even fewer scruples. Easy divorce was good business; so was quick, easy marriage. . . . By the middle of the twentieth century, Nevada was easily the divorce champion of America. Its divorce rate for 'residents' was more than fifty times the rate in New York (the state most stingy with divorce)."

And the Congress may by general Laws prescribe the Manner in which such Acts, Records and Proceedings shall be proved, and the Effect thereof.[232]

232. It was on these two words—"Effect thereof"—that Congress relied in passing, in 1996, the Defense of Marriage Act, which establishes that no state shall be required "to give effect to" any law or court order of another state "respecting a relationship between persons of the same sex that is treated as a marriage under the laws of such other State."

President Clinton, before signing the measure, declared: "I have long opposed governmental recognition of same-gender marriages and this legislation is consistent with that position. The Act confirms the right of each state to determine its own policy with respect to same gender marriage and clarifies for purposes of federal law the operative meaning of the terms 'marriage' and 'spouse.'" But whether the law would survive scrutiny before the high court is a question.

Constitutional scholar Laurence Tribe of Harvard University has argued that Congress lacks the power to tell the states they are free from the strictures of Article IV. "The Constitution delegates to the United States no power to create categorical exceptions to the Full Faith and Credit Clause. To be sure, the clause does empower Congress to enact 'general laws' to 'prescribe the manner in which such acts, records and proceedings shall be proved, and the effect thereof.' But that is a far cry from power to decree that official state acts offensive to a majority in Congress need not even be recognized by states that happen to share Congress's view."

Tribe called claims that "a law inviting states to give no effect to certain acts of other states is a general law prescribing the 'effect' of such acts" a "play on words, not a legal argument." The full faith and credit clause, he wrote, "cannot be read as a fount of authority for Congress to set asunder the states that this clause so solemnly brought together." In a Florida decision handed down in 2005, a federal judge took a different view, dismissing the efforts of two women, Nancy Wilson and Paula Schoenwether, to have their marriage in Massachusetts recognized in the Sunshine State. The judge, James Moody of United States District Court at Tampa, wrote that "rigid and literal interpretation of the Full Faith and Credit Clause" espoused by the couple "would create a license for a single State to create national policy."

SECTION 2. The Citizens of each State shall be entitled to all Privileges and Immunities of Citizens in the several States.[233]

233. This clause extends the privileges and immunities to the citizens of each state—a broader reach than the Articles of Confederation, which extended privileges and immunities to only the "free white inhabitants" of each state and excepted "paupers, vagabonds, and fugitives from justice." The definitive case was brought by a Pennsylvanian, Edward Corfield, whose oystering boat, the *Hiram*, had been seized in New Jersey in an action brought by one Coryell, who charged that not only was the *Hiram* collecting oysters out of season but also was violating a New Jersey law that allowed only New Jersey residents to go after the state's oysters. In 1823 Justice Bushrod Washington, who heard the case while riding circuit, ruled in *Corfield v. Coryell* against the Pennsylvanian in a famous formulation:

> The inquiry is, what are the privileges and immunities of citizens in the several states? We feel no hesitation in

confining these expressions to those privileges and immunities which are, in their nature, fundamental; which
belong, of right, to the citizens of all free governments;
and which have, at all times, been enjoyed by the citizens of the several states which compose this Union,
from the time of their becoming free, independent, and
sovereign. What these fundamental principles are, it
would perhaps be more tedious than difficult to enumerate. They may, however, be all comprehended under
the following general heads: Protection by the government; the enjoyment of life and liberty, with the right to
acquire and possess property of every kind, and to pursue and obtain happiness and safety; subject nevertheless to such restraints as the government may justly
prescribe for the general good of the whole. The right of
a citizen of one state to pass through, or to reside in any
other state, for purposes of trade, agriculture, profes-
sional pursuits, or otherwise; to claim the benefit of the
writ of habeas corpus; to institute and maintain actions
of any kind in the courts of the state; to take, hold and
dispose of property, either real or personal; and an exemption from higher taxes or impositions than are paid
by the other citizens of the state; may be mentioned as
some of the particular privileges and immunities of citizens, which are clearly embraced by the general description of privileges deemed to be fundamental: to which
may be added, the elective franchise, as regulated and
established by the laws or constitution of the state in
which it is to be exercised.

Justice Washington distinguished between the claims of New Jersey residents and out-of-staters to New Jersey's oysters. Where state
property was at issue, the state could favor its own residents, he
ruled. On that principle public universities can charge higher tuition

to out-of-state residents. The Supreme Court could have used this clause as a basis to lay forth a fundamental set of rights for all citizens. Instead, the Court viewed this merely as an antidiscrimination provision to protect those far from home. One of the privileges of national citizenship that Justice Washington failed to enumerate in the *Corfield* decision can be found in Article III—the right to sue a citizen of another state in federal court.

The question of privileges and immunities also figured in a controversy that arose around a law called the Negro Seamen Act. The law had been passed by South Carolina, which feared that free African American or British sailors coming ashore in South Carolina ports would inspire a desire for freedom among South Carolina's slaves. The law authorized the arrest of black seamen who came ashore in the Palmetto State and required the vessel's captain to reimburse costs of their detention until sailing. Failure to pay would result in the seamen being sold into slavery. Objections from England and Massachusetts ignited controversy and brought the matter to the desk of President Jackson's attorney general, who issued a memorandum that free black citizens of a state like Massachusetts were not "citizens" in the sense of Article IV, because if they were, a state like Georgia would have to give them the privileges and immunities of its own citizens.

The attorney general who wrote the memo was Roger Taney, who would later accede as chief justice. A professor at Boston University law school, Andrew Kull, has described the Taney memo as a "prequel" and a "dress rehearsal" for part of the *Dred Scott* case, in which Taney, writing for the majority, penned the question notoriously: "Can a negro whose ancestors were imported into this country and sold as slaves become a member of the political community formed and brought into existence by the Constitution of the United States, and as such become entitled to all the rights, and privileges, and immunities, guaranteed by that instrument to the citizen, one of which rights is the privilege of suing in a court of the United States in the cases specified in the Constitution?" The court, answering the question in the negative, put the country on a course for civil war.

A Person charged in any State with Treason, Felony, or other Crime, who shall flee from Justice, and be found in another State, shall on Demand of the executive Authority of the State from which he fled, be delivered up, to be removed to the State having Jurisdiction of the Crime.[234]

---

234. In 1859 Willis Lago, a free black man living in Ohio, was indicted in Kentucky for helping a slave to escape. The governor of Ohio, William Dennison Jr., refused to extradite Lago on the principle that helping free a slave, while perhaps illegal in Kentucky, was no crime in Ohio. Kentucky sued for a court order instructing Dennison to produce Lago. Chief Justice Taney ruled that Dennison was wrong—that the laws of Kentucky were at issue, not the laws of Ohio. But Taney said the Court could not order the governor in this matter, that it was up to him and him alone to see that extradition occurred. "Though the decision gave considerable dissatisfaction to the slave States, it was rendered at a date too close to the verge of war to have any effect on the development of the slavery issue." The decision was handed down on the last day of the Court's session, March 14, 1861. Secession had already begun. It would be more than 125 years later, in 1987, that Justice Thurgood Marshall, writing for a unanimous bench in *Puerto Rico v. Branstad*, would overturn the second part of *Dennison* and establish that a federal court can in fact order a state governor to extradite a wanted man.

No Person held to Service or Labour in one State, under the Laws
thereof, escaping into another, shall, in Consequence of any Law or
Regulation therein, be discharged from such Service or Labour, but
shall be delivered up on Claim of the Party to whom such Service or
Labour may be due.[235]

235. The fugitive slave clause is one of the blots on the founding
document. One can imagine Congress reacting to this clause by
erecting hurdles to slave catchers sent up from southern states. But
Congress, first with the Fugitive Slave Act of 1793, put the force of
the federal government on the side of slave states by making aiding
in the escape of a slave a crime punishable by a $500 fine, as well as
by making federal judges available to decide whether a black person
found on free soil was in fact a runaway slave. It was upheld in the
most notorious case involving this clause, *Prigg v. Pennsylvania*,
which dealt with a slave catcher named Edward Prigg, who had kid-
napped a black woman, Margaret Morgan, from Pennsylvania and
brought her to Maryland on behalf of a woman who claimed her as a
slave. Although born to slaves, Morgan had lived her whole life free.
Prigg was indicted in Pennsylvania on kidnapping charges, and the
Supreme Court heard the matter after the slave catcher was convicted. Writing for the Court, Justice Story not only overturned
Prigg's conviction but also struck down a Pennsylvania personal liberty law intended to provide some protections to black residents facing seizure by slave catchers.

In 1850, as part of the compromise of that year, Congress passed
a new fugitive slave act that, among other provisions, compelled federal marshals to arrest alleged fugitive slaves and prevented accused
runaways from testifying on their own behalf. In an extraordinary
case involving a fugitive slave, Joshua Glover, and an editor of an
abolitionist newspaper in Milwaukee, Sherman Booth, the Wisconsin Supreme Court declared the 1850 law unconstitutional. A professor of law at Yale, Robert Cover, captured the drama this way:

> In the Sherman Booth affair the long string of failures was finally broken with a single, crowning, if fleeting, achievement. The elements were typical, the result unique. The slave Glover was apprehended in Racine by a federal marshal pursuant to a warrant. Upon Glover's arrest, the slave owner, Garland, and the federal marshal were arrested by the sheriff for assault and battery upon Glover. While they went off to jail, Glover was rescued by a mob. Sherman Booth and John Rycraft were then apprehended for prosecution as aiders and abettors in the rescue of Glover. . . . Booth was ordered discharged on the writ [of habeas corpus] by Judge A. D. Smith of the Wisconsin Supreme Court, sitting alone during vacation. Smith upheld virtually all of the arguments that had been made against the Fugitive Slave Acts for the past two decades. He held the Act of 1850 unconstitutional on the ground that the Article IV conferred on Congress no power to legislate with respect to fugitives; on the ground that the Act of 1850 denied to the fugitive a right to a trial by jury.

While the Wisconsin Supreme Court would affirm when its other members returned, the decision would eventually be overturned by the Supreme Court, only to be defied by Wisconsin in a long struggle that was finally eclipsed by the Civil War.

SECTION 3. New States may be admitted[236] by the Congress into this Union;[237]

---

236. Admission is final. No procedure obtains in the Constitution by which states can be released from the union, that is, secede. The contrary constitutional claim was rejected at Appomattox. In 2009 a controversy arose when Governor Rick Perry of Texas seemed to

suggest that the Lone Star State could secede. According to an Associated Press dispatch cited on the website of the *Austin-American-Statesman*, Perry said: "We've got a great union. There's absolutely no reason to dissolve it. But if Washington continues to thumb their nose at the American people, you know, who knows what might come out of that. But Texas is a very unique place, and we're a pretty independent lot to boot." As to whether Texas could be broken up into other states, please see footnote 238.

237. President Jefferson, in acquiring the Louisiana Territory and bringing the foreign subjects of New Orleans and elsewhere into the fold of the new nation, calculated that he was acting beyond the strictures of the Constitution. To his friend in the Senate, John Breckenridge of Kentucky, Jefferson wrote: "The Constitution has made no provision for our holding foreign territory, still less for incorporating foreign nations into our Union. The Executive in seizing the fugitive occurrence which so much advances the good of their country, have done an act beyond the Constitution." Historian Garry Wills writes: "The Constitution gave Congress the power to form new states—but those were envisaged as coming from western territories already claimed by the federal government. Inhabitants of that land were not considered the subjects of foreign governments—none, at least, that Congress recognized as valid." Wills writes that Jefferson's plan, which he relayed to Congress via Breckenridge, was for the inhabitants of the lands of the Louisiana Purchase to be, as Wills puts it, "governed by executive authority during a formative period."

but no new State shall be formed or erected within the Jurisdiction
of any other State; nor any State be formed by the Junction of two or
more States, or Parts of States, without the Consent of the Legislatures of the States concerned as well as of the Congress.[238]

---

238. These are the requirements that New York City would have
to satisfy were it to attempt to become the fifty-first state, a scheme
that has been championed by the likes of Norman Mailer, now deceased, and Leon Panetta, now director of central intelligence.
When Panetta was an aide to Mayor John Lindsay, he prepared a
memo explaining that to become a state, New York City would need
to elect delegates to a constitutional convention, submit the resulting
constitution to the people for approval, gain approval from the legislature, and gain the approval of a majority of Congress.

West Virginia was created out of the Unionist parts of Virginia
that refused to secede. Its founders viewed themselves as restoring the
government of Virginia rather than seceding and forming a break-
away state. Yet one of the new government's first acts, in May 1862,
while acting as the government of Virginia, was to give itself permission to form a state so as to satisfy this Article IV requirement.

President Lincoln had no difficulty dispersing the legal clouds
when he recommended congressional recognition and approval of
the new state: "It is said that the admission of West Virginia is secession, and tolerated only because it is our secession. Well, if we call it
by that name, there is still difference enough between secession
against the Constitution and secession in favor the Constitution. I
believe the admission of West Virginia into the Union is expedient."

In April 2009, it was pointed out—in the context of Governor
Rick Perry's comments to the effect that Texas has a right to
secede—that under the terms of its admission to the United States
Texas could be broken up into five separate states.

This was a reference to the Joint Resolution of the Congress of
Texas of June 23, 1845, which gave the consent of the then-existing
government of Texas to its annexation to the United States. The

resolution was subject to a number of conditions, one of which held that "new States of convenient size, not exceeding four in number, in addition to said State of Texas, and having sufficient population, may hereafter, by the consent of said State, be formed out of the territory thereof, which shall be entitled to admission under the provision of the Federal constitution. And such States as may be formed out of that portion of said territory lying south of thirty-six degrees thirty minutes north latitude, commonly known as the Missouri compromise line, shall be admitted into the Union, with or without Slavery, as the people of each State asking admission may desire. And in such State or States as shall be formed out of said territory north of said Missouri compromise line, slavery or involuntary servitude (except for crime) shall be prohibited. And whereas, by said terms, the consent of the existing Government of Texas is required."

The Congress shall have Power to dispose of and make all needful Rules and Regulations respecting the Territory[239]

239. This delegation of authority helped frame the battle over the expansion of slavery. While the founders met at Philadelphia, the Continental Congress banned slavery in the newly organized Northwest Territory. It would take Congress until 1820, with the Missouri Compromise, to decide the boundaries of slavery within the Louisiana Territory. The Mexican-American War and the Kansas-Nebraska Act reopened the question of the westward growth of slavery. The stakes were enormous, for as territories matured into states, the boundaries of slavery would decide the future of slavery. This fragile balance between slave territory and free soil was undone by the Supreme Court's decision in its most notorious case, *Dred Scott*.

Much of *Dred Scott* turned on the diversity clause of Article III, which is discussed previously in footnote 211 on page 165, and the privileges and immunities clause in this Article, which is discussed in footnote 233 beginning on page 185. Chief Justice Taney, writing for a 7 to 2 majority, also focused on the territory clause, holding that Congress lacked the power to ban slavery in the territories without violating the Fifth Amendment rights of slaveholders: "An act of Congress which deprives a citizen of the United States of his liberty or property, merely because he came himself or brought his property into a particular Territory of the United States, and who had committed no offence against the laws, could hardly be dignified with the name of due process of law."

It was under this language that Congress claimed the power to prohibit polygamy in the Utah Territory and hounded the Mormon Church. Congress, which passed the Morrill Anti-Bigamy Act of 1862, asserted that it had the power to ban the practice of bigamy in "a territory of the United States or other place over which the United States have exclusive jurisdiction." Congress followed with several other acts aimed against polygamists, including an 1887 law that tried to unincorporate the Church of Jesus Christ of Latter-Day Saints and tasked the U.S. attorney general with going to court to "wind up the affairs" of the church and seize its property. A description of Congress's antibigamy legislation is found in *Mormon Church v. United States*, in which Justice Bradley, writing for the Court, left Congress's power to legislate in the territories nearly unlimited.

or other Property[240] belonging to the United States; and nothing in this Constitution shall be so construed as to Prejudice any Claims of the United States, or of any particular State.

---

240. Three free-roaming burros prompted a showdown between New Mexico and the federal government over this clause. A rancher, Kelley Stephenson, was watering his herd on federal land when he asked the New Mexico Livestock Board to rid him of a band of wild burros that were "molesting his cattle," as the Supreme Court decision in the matter would later put it. The state obliged him and

rounded up some nineteen burros and sold them off at auction. But the Bureau of Land Management instructed New Mexico to recover the burros from their new owners and place them back on federal property. New Mexico proved as stubborn as a mule, challenging in federal court the constitutionality of the Wild Free-Roaming Horses and Burros Act, which maintained that "all unbranded and unclaimed horses and burros on public lands of the United States" were to be left alone on account of their being "an integral part of the natural system of the public lands." The Supreme Court zeroed in on the word "needful" and whether it applied to an act protecting burros. Arguing that this protected only federal land, not the burros on it, New Mexico claimed that the burro law was more regulation than this clause, with its reference to property, would permit. The Supreme Court sided with the federal government and the historic burros, part of a population of animals that, a Senate report cited by the Court concluded, "have been cruelly captured and slain, and their carcasses used in the production of pet food and fertilizer. They have been used for target practice and harassed for 'sport' and profit."

Section 4. The United States shall guarantee to every State in this Union a Republican Form of Government,[241] **and shall protect each of them against Invasion; and on Application of the Legislature, or of the Executive (when the Legislature cannot be convened), against domestic Violence.**

---

241. This clause was first tested in the 1840s during the civil strife in Rhode Island known as the Dorr War. The state held fast not to any constitution—it hadn't ratified one—but to its colonial charter of 1663, which restricted suffrage to freeholders, meaning landowners or their eldest sons. This irked the growing manufacturing and working class, and in 1841 the state's two factions—the suffragists and, as those who supported the established government under the colonial charter were variously called, the Freeholders or Charterites—drew

up competing constitutions, which were submitted separately to voters for ratification. The suffragists set up a government and elected as governor, a Harvard man turned revolutionary, Thomas Dorr—a move in direct opposition to Samuel Ward King, who was more widely recognized as holding that position. Dorr raised a small army and made to attack the arsenal at Providence, though his military campaign lost steam when his artillery wouldn't fire.

Both Dorr and King petitioned for the support of President John Tyler, who wrote in respect to this clause: "This is the first occasion, so far as the government of a state and its people are concerned, on which it has become necessary to consider of the propriety of exercising these high and most important constitutional and legal functions." Tyler refused to send troops but said he wouldn't shrink from doing so if needed. He suggested, moreover, that he would side against Dorr, because, come a fight, "the executive could not look into real or supposed defects of the existing government." Instead, Tyler wrote: "It will be my duty, on the contrary, to respect the requisitions of that government which has been recognized as the existing government of the state through all time past, until I shall be advised, in regular manner, that it has been altered and abolished, and another substituted in its place, by legal and peaceable proceedings, adopted and pursued by the authorities and people of the state."

If King found support in Washington, Dorr found support in New York as he traveled up and down the East Coast pleading his cause. Tammany Hall recognized him as the true governor, and several military companies in the city even volunteered to escort him back to Providence (an offer that Dorr declined). Returning to Rhode Island in 1843, Dorr was arrested, convicted of the state crime of treason, and sentenced to life in prison, but was released on order of the state legislature in 1845. Eventually a militia loyal to King searched the home of a Dorr supporter, who then sued, claiming that because King's government was unlawfully in power the search was an illegal entry. The Supreme Court said it wasn't for the courts to decide which of Rhode Island's governments was the legitimate one in 1849. Wrote Chief Justice Taney: "Under this article of the Constitution it rests with Congress to decide what government is the established one in a State."

President Andrew Johnson cited this clause when, at the outset of Reconstruction, he appointed a military governor in North Carolina and laid out the process by which that state would be brought back into the Union. His proclamation began: "Whereas the 4th section of the Constitution of the United States declares that the United States shall guarantee to every State in the Union a republican form of government, and shall protect each of them against invasion and domestic violence; and whereas the President of the United States is, by the Constitution, made Commander-in-chief of the army and navy, as well as chief civil executive officer of the United States, and is bound by solemn oath faithfully to execute the office of President of the United States, and to take care that the laws be faithfully executed; and whereas the rebellion, which has been waged by a portion of the people of the United States against the properly constituted authorities of the government thereof, in the most violent and revolting form, but whose organized and armed forces have now been almost entirely overcome, has, in its revolutionary progress, deprived the people of the State of North Carolina of all civil government; and whereas it becomes necessary and proper to carry out and enforce the obligations of the United States to the people of North Carolina, in securing them in the enjoyment of a republican form of government."

Several years later, in the 1869 case *Texas v. White*, Chief Justice Salmon Chase would explain that the effort to secede placed two burdens on the Union. "The first was that of suppressing the rebellion. The next was that of reestablishing the broken relations of the State with the Union. The first of these duties having been performed, the next necessarily engaged the attention of the National government. The authority for the performance of the first had been found in the power to suppress insurrection and carry on war; for the performance of the second, authority was derived from the obligation of the United States to guarantee to every State in the Union a republican form of government."

Chase made it clear that the guarantee clause protected the political rights of former slaves. "Slaves, in the insurgent States, with certain local exceptions, had been declared free by the Proclamation of Emancipation, and whatever questions might be made as to the effect of that act under the Constitution, it was clear from the beginning that its practical operation in connection with legislative acts of like tendency must be complete enfranchisement."

Madison had foreseen as much in 43 *Federalist*: "In a confederacy founded on republican principles, and composed of republican members, the superintending government ought clearly to possess authority to defend the system against aristocratic or monarchical innovations." He continued later: "As long therefore as the existing republican forms are continued by the States, they are guaranteed by the Federal Constitution. Whenever the States may chuse to substitute other republican forms, they have a right to do so, and to claim the federal guaranty for the latter. The only restriction imposed on them is, that they shall not exchange republican for anti-republican Constitutions; a restriction which it is presumed will hardly be considered as a grievance."

ARTICLE V.

The Congress, whenever two thirds of both Houses shall deem it necessary,[242] shall propose Amendments to this Constitution,[243]

242. More than 10,000 proposals for amending the Constitution have been introduced in Congress, according to remarks made by Representative Charles Canady of Florida, chairman of the Constitution subcommittee, during a 1999 hearing. Of those, only thirty-three have been referred to the states for ratification. There have been twenty-seven amendments to the Constitution.

243. Wrote Madison in 49 *Federalist*: "A constitutional road to the decision of the people, ought to be marked out, and kept open, for certain great and extraordinary occasions." The Anti-Federalists

didn't see the procedures laid out here as being reserved for rare occasions. Said George Mason of Virginia: "The plan now to be formed will certainly be defective, as the Confederation has been found on trial to be. Amendments therefore will be necessary, and it will be better to provide for them, in an easy, regular and Constitutional way than to trust to chance and violence."

Nelson Lund, a professor at the Virginia law school named after George Mason, has made the point that since 1791 "Congress has never approved a constitutional amendment that decreased its own power in any significant way. Indeed, since the Bill of Rights was adopted, Congress has not even approved any amendments—with the possible exception of the Twenty-First—that reinforced the original plan for a Federal legislature of limited and enumerated powers."

or, on the Application of the Legislatures of two thirds of the several States, shall call a Convention for proposing Amendments,[244]

244. There has never been such a convention. The provision for it came at the behest of Mason, who said he believed that the states, and not just their representatives in the national government, should be able to propose amendments. According to the Convention records, he worried that otherwise "no amendments of the proper kind would ever be obtained by the people, if the Government should become oppressive, as he verily believed would be the case." By the mid-1980s, state legislatures had submitted more than four hundred petitions for constitutional conventions.

Congress has never acted on these petitions. Article V doesn't specify whether the obligation of Congress to call a convention is triggered only when two-thirds of the states seek a convention to address a specific proposal, such as in the case of the more than thirty states that have sought the introduction of a balanced budget amendment. Or must Congress call a convention whenever at least thirty-four of the states have sought a convention on any topic, even if no two states want to amend the same constitutional provision?

Lund, testifying during the 1999 House Constitution subcommittee hearing, suggested "one possibility" is that "Congress has for some time been in violation of its legal duty to call a constitutional convention." He noted: "Some 45 States at one time or another have applied for a constitutional convention in language that does not expressly restrict the application to a convention for the 'sole' or 'exclusive' purpose of considering some limited range of proposals, such as a balanced budget amendment. There is a legal argument, at least colorable and perhaps stronger than that, that this fact implies that Congress is and has been for some time constitutionally obliged to call an Article V convention."

In 1985 a Congressional Research Service report discussed the questions abounding. Could the scope of a constitutional convention be limited? Or could a convention called to weigh a balanced budget amendment decide, when assembled to propose for ratification, say, the repeal of the First Amendment? Or, even more radically, could some future constitutional convention propose an entirely new Constitution for ratification, much as the founders themselves had done when assembled in Philadelphia? Congress has taken a stab at addressing some of these questions, most notably when the Senate passed the Federal Constitutional Convention Procedures Act of 1973.

which, in either Case, shall be valid to all Intents and Purposes, as Part of this Constitution, when ratified by the Legislatures of three fourths of the several States,[245]

---

245. Once a state has decided to adopt an amendment, can it backtrack prior to the amendment's ratification and withdraw its vote? Far from being hypothetical, this is a crucial question, as amendments can float around for centuries before being ratified by

the requisite three-quarters of states. The issue arose most recently in the mid-1970s with the Equal Rights Amendment, when four states that had voted for ratification would later rescind. When Secretary of State William Seward announced in 1868 that the requisite three-quarters of the states—twenty-eight in number—had ratified the Fourteenth Amendment, he noted in his official report that two of those ratifying, Ohio and New Jersey, had subsequently professed to withdraw their ratification. In addition, two states that initially rejected the amendment had ratified it, under new Reconstruction governments. Congress, counting both New Jersey and Ohio, as well as the states that had first rejected but later adopted the proposal, judged that the necessary number of states had ratified the Fourteenth Amendment. In reciting these facts in a 1939 case, *Coleman v. Miller*, the Supreme Court expressed satisfaction that it was a political question that ought to rest with the Congress.

In respect of whether an amendment must be ratified within a given number of years, the Supreme Court in 1939 considered whether the proposed Child Labor Amendment—sent to the states for ratification in 1924—had expired by dint of the failure of three-quarters of the states to ratify it promptly. It concluded in *Coleman v. Miller* that it was a political question to be addressed by the Congress. The Twenty-seventh Amendment was accepted as ratified more than two centuries after it was first proposed.

Congress can include a self-destruct clause in a proposed amendment to hold that the states must ratify it within a set number of years, the Supreme Court has decided. This happened in 1921 in *Dillon v. Gloss*. The court brushed aside a challenge to the Eighteenth Amendment over a clause that had required ratification within seven years. A more troubling question is whether Congress, after circulating to the states a petition with such a time limit, can later extend that time limit. Such is what Congress did in 1979, when it said the proposed Equal Rights Amendment, which had a built-in seven-year time limit for ratification, would stay open for three more years. The Supreme Court was never called in to decide the constitutionality of that move, as the ERA still failed to get the requisite votes.

or by Conventions in three fourths thereof, as the one or the other
Mode of Ratification may be proposed by the Congress;[246]

---

246. It falls to Congress, once it has proposed an amendment, to
decide whether to submit the measure to the statehouses or to state
conventions. Only once, in the case of the repeal of Prohibition,
which would become the Twenty-first Amendment, did it choose
the latter. The states were left to themselves to organize the conventions and set the rules by which they would consider repeal.

A professor who has examined how the states handled the repeal
process, Everett Somerville Brown of the University of Michigan,
reports: "Although a number of bills were introduced in Congress to
provide a uniform method of ratifying the proposed amendment,
none was adopted, and the details were left to the states. However,
there was some doubt on this point among the members of state legislatures, even after the proposed amendment had been submitted to
them for ratification. In their laws providing for the conventions no
less than twenty-one states included a section stating that, if Congress should prescribe the manner in which the conventions should
be constituted, the provisions of the state act should be inoperative
and officers of the state were authorized and directed to act in obedience to the act of Congress with the same force and effect as if acting
under a state statute."

New Mexico, however, "championed the cause of state rights in a
declaration that any attempt on the part of Congress to prescribe the
details governing the convention 'shall be null and void in the state
of New Mexico, and all officers of the state, or any subdivision
thereof, are hereby authorized and required to resist to the utmost
any attempt to execute any and all such congressional dictation and
usurpation.'"

Provided that no Amendment which may be made prior to the Year One thousand eight hundred and eight shall in any Manner affect the first and fourth Clauses in the Ninth Section of the first Article;[247] and that no State, without its Consent, shall be deprived of its equal Suffrage in the Senate.[248]

---

247. The first clause of Article I, Section 9 prevents Congress from ending the slave trade until 1808, a compromise the founders accepted after John Rutledge of South Carolina said that he "never could agree to give a power by which the articles relating to slaves might be altered by the States not interested in that property and prejudiced against it." The fourth clause of the same section of Article I mandates that direct taxes be levied in proportion to population. Such a clause would protect slavery by seeming to forbid Congress from levying direct taxes on slaves or from imposing another capitation tax that would disproportionately burden southern states.

248. Further proof of the importance the founders attached to the equal representation of each state in the Senate, which emerges from this article as the sturdiest component of the government. Protection of the Senate was at the insistence of a delegate of Connecticut, Roger Sherman, who saw his opportunity after Rutledge gained special protection for the slave trade. Madison's notes record that Sherman "expressed his fears that three fourths of the States might be brought to do things fatal to particular States, as abolishing them altogether or depriving them of their equality in the Senate. He thought it reasonable that the proviso in favor of the States importing slaves should be extended so as to provide that no State should be affected in its internal police, or deprived of its equality in the Senate."

ARTICLE VI.

All Debts contracted and Engagements entered into, before the Adoption of this Constitution, shall be as valid against the United States under this Constitution, as under the Confederation.[249]

---

249. "Of historical interest only" is how one famed annotator of the Constitution, Edward S. Corwin of Princeton, characterizes this clause. Constitutional cynic Charles Beard, in *An Economic Interpretation of the Constitution of the United States*, sets the scene by noting that under the Articles of Confederation the government "was not paying the interest on its debt and its paper had depreciated until it was selling at from one-sixth to one-twentieth of its par value." The young nation's foreign lenders maintained an interest in the fate of this debt, but Beard estimates that some $60 million of the roughly $70 million in paper reflecting this debt "lay in the hands of American citizens in the spring of 1787." Given the way the market was discounting the paper, Beard estimates, "at least $40,000,000 gain came to holders of securities through the adoption of the Constitution and the sound financial system which it made possible."

Beard sees this as a central incentive for the nation's moneyed men to push for ratification. Here he is writing about the ratification date in Massachusetts: "Continental paper bought at two and three shillings in the pound was bound to rise rapidly with the establishment of the federal government. No one knew this better than the members of the federal Convention from Massachusetts and their immediate friends and adherents in Boston. . . . Meanwhile, it may be said with safety that the communities in which personality was relatively more powerful favored the ratification of the Constitution, and that in these communities large quantities of public securities were held. Moreover, there was undoubtedly a vital connection between the movement in support of the Constitution and public security holding, or to speak concretely, among the leading men in Massachusetts who labored to bring about the ratification was a large number of public creditors. For example, Boston had twelve representatives in the state-ratifying convention, all of whom voted in favor of the Constitution. Of these twelve men the following were holders of public securities: Samuel Adams James Bowdoin, Sr. Thomas Dawes, Jr. Christopher Gore John Coffin Jones William Phillips Thomas Russell John Winthrop. In other words, at least eight of the twelve men representing the chief financial centre of the state were personally interested in the fate of the new Constitution."

This Constitution, and the Laws of the United States which shall be made in Pursuance thereof; and all Treaties made, or which shall be made,[250] **under the Authority of the United States, shall be the supreme Law of the Land;**[251] **and the Judges in every State shall be bound thereby, any Thing in the Constitution or Laws of any State to the Contrary notwithstanding.**[252]

250. The place of treaties in the hierarchy laid forth in this clause was at issue in the 2008 case of a Mexican man who was sentenced to die in Texas for the murder and rape there of two teenage girls. The U.N. court in The Hague had found an error in the Texas prosecution of José Ernesto Medellin: He and some fifty other Mexicans on death row in the United States had never been informed of their right, under the Vienna Convention on Consular Relations, to seek assistance from the Mexican consulate. The Senate had ratified the treaty granting this right in 1969. But in the Medellin case, neither the treaty nor the ruling from the U.N. court nor even an order from President Bush instructing Texas to comply was enough to force the state of Texas to give Medellin a new hearing for habeas corpus. The Supreme Court, in *Medellin v. Texas*, found that mere ratification by the Senate was insufficient to give the treaty supremacy over the Lone Star State. In the case of the Vienna Conventions, the Court decided, Congress would have had to adopt federal law implementing it before it could supersede Texas

law. And, in an opinion by Chief Justice Roberts, the Court curtly brushed aside the protestations of the president, saying his constitutional authority is "to execute the laws, not make them."

Congress had provided the implementing law in one famous case establishing the supremacy of treaty law. The case was brought against a U.S. game warden by Missouri, which asserted ownership within its borders of migratory birds. Justice Oliver Wendell Holmes deemed the logic flighty and sketched the case for overarching treaty power. "The whole foundation of the State's rights is the presence within their jurisdiction of birds that yesterday had not arrived, tomorrow may be in another State, and, in a week, a thousand miles away," he wrote. He called the issue "a national interest of very nearly the first magnitude," adding, "but for the treaty and the statute, there soon might be no birds for any powers to deal with. We see nothing in the Constitution that compels the Government to sit by while a food supply is cut off and the protectors of our forests and our crops are destroyed. It is not sufficient to rely upon the States."

251. Chief Justice Marshall cited this clause in *McCulloch v. Maryland* (1819), in which the Supreme Court told Maryland it lacked authority to tax the Bank of the United States: "The states have no power, by taxation or otherwise, to retard, impede, burden, or in any manner control, the operations of the constitutional laws enacted by congress to carry into execution the powers vested in the general government. This is, we think, the unavoidable consequence of that supremacy which the constitution has declared." In recent decades, though, the Supreme Court has enacted an important new barrier to protect state sovereignty from federal policies. The Rehnquist Court established an "anticommandeering" principle by which federal laws cannot require state officials to enforce federal regulations. It was by this principle that the Supreme Court struck down a provision of the Brady Bill that sought to require local sheriffs to conduct background checks on prospective firearm purchasers, if the state wasn't already conducting those checks (27 states were and 23 weren't).

Wrote Justice Scalia in the case, called *Printz v. United States* (after Jay Printz of Montana, one of two sheriffs who brought the challenge): "The Federal Government may neither issue directives requiring the States to address particular problems, nor command the States' officers, or those of their political subdivisions, to administer or enforce a federal regulatory program. It matters not whether policymaking is involved, and no case-by-case weighing of the burdens or benefits is necessary; such commands are fundamentally incompatible with our constitutional system of dual sovereignty."

252. This requirement enlists state judges to enforce the Constitution. State judges feel this responsibility day in, day out when hearing criminal cases, as defendants routinely raise constitutional claims under the Fourth, Fifth, Sixth, and Fourteenth Amendments. This also explains why inferior federal courts aren't an integral part of the constitutional structure and aren't provided for in the Constitution. The founders deputized state judges to decide constitutional claims. At the moment of ratification, this clause ensured that, in theory, there were local officials in place in every county to enforce the new constitutional order, even at the expense of local laws. Sometimes this has led to the discovery of superior constitutional understanding at the state level, such as when, in the decade before the Civil War, the Supreme Court was prepared to protect the federal slave-catching regime only to have the Supreme Court of Wisconsin recognize and declare that the Fugitive Slave Act was unconstitutional (please see p. 189).

The Senators and Representatives before mentioned, and the Members of the several State Legislatures, and all executive and judicial Officers, both of the United States and of the several States, shall be bound by Oath or Affirmation, to support this Constitution;[253] but no religious Test shall ever be required as a Qualification to any Office or public Trust under the United States.[254]

253. What happens if a governor swears an oath to support and defend a state constitution that a litigant asserts is in conflict with

the Constitution of the United States that this clause requires him to support? This is the predicament in which Governor Schwarzenegger of California found himself when a same-gender couple, Kristin Perry and Sandra Steir, went into federal district court to charge that a recently ratified provision of the California constitution limiting marriage to heterosexual couples violated the federal constitution. The governor had sworn the California oath—to "support and defend the Constitution of the United States and the Constitution of the State of California." In the case that became known as *Perry v. Schwarzenegger*, the governor chose to abandon his oath to defend his state's fundamental law, leaving the defense of California's constitution to private litigants. Had Perry and Steir lost their case in district court, it's possible to imagine a move to impeach the governor. In the event, the federal district court ruled the marriage provision of California's constitution to be a violation of the equal rights provision of the federal document, vindicating the governor's gamble, at least while the appeals process runs its course.

254. The most emphatic statement in the Constitution: "no . . . ever . . . any." Myriad religious tests obtained in the colonies and in the newly independent states. But nearly a century after the Fourteenth Amendment extended coverage of constitutional rights to the states, the governor of Maryland appointed an atheist named Roy Torcaso to be a notary public. Torcaso was asked to swear belief in God and refused. He then sued to gain his commission. Justice Hugo Black wrote the opinion for the Supreme Court: "There is, and can be, no dispute about the purpose or effect of the Maryland Declaration of Rights requirement before us—it sets up a religious test which was designed to, and, if valid, does, bar every person who refuses to declare a belief in God from holding a public 'office of profit or trust' in Maryland. The power and authority of the State of Maryland thus is put on the side of one particular sort of believers— those who are willing to say they believe in 'the existence of God.' It is true that there is much historical precedent for such laws. Indeed, it was largely to escape religious test oaths and declarations that a great many of the early colonists left Europe and came here hoping

to worship in their own way. It soon developed, however, that many of those who had fled to escape religious test oaths turned out to be perfectly willing, when they had the power to do so, to force dissenters from their faith to take test oaths in conformity with that faith. This brought on a host of laws in the New Colonies imposing burdens and disabilities of various kinds upon varied beliefs depending largely upon what group happened to be politically strong enough to legislate in favor of its own beliefs. The effect of all this was the formal or practical 'establishment' of particular religious faiths in most of the Colonies, with consequent burdens imposed on the free exercise of the faiths of nonfavored believers." Black told the story of "wise and farseeing men in the Colonies" who, he said, "spoke out against test oaths and all the philosophy of intolerance behind them." He wrote of George Calvert, the first Lord Baltimore, who helped establish the colony of Maryland and who, as a Catholic, had refused to take the Oath of Supremacy in England at the cost of resigning from high governmental office. Black wrote that in upholding Maryland's religious test for public office, the state's Supreme Court said that Torcaso was "not compelled to believe or disbelieve" because he was "not compelled to hold office." Wrote Black: "The fact, however, that a person is not compelled to hold public office cannot possibly be an excuse for barring him from office by state-imposed criteria forbidden by the Constitution." In ruling for Torcaso, the Court discussed this prohibition of a religious test but relied in deciding the case on the First Amendment establishment clause.

ARTICLE VII.

The Ratification of the Conventions[255] of nine[256] States,

---

255. As opposed to the legislatures. Quoth one of the founding fathers, Rufus King of Massachusetts: "The Legislatures also being to lose power, will be most likely to raise objections. The people having

already parted with the necessary powers it is immaterial to them, by which Government they are possessed, provided they be well employed." The founders believed that the enactment of such a fundamental compact as a Constitution required more than a legislative vote in the statehouse; it required ratification by the people, or representatives chosen by them for this single task. The founders were looking to situate their Constitution on firmer ground than the Articles of Confederation. Madison, writing about himself in the third person, said in his notes that he "thought this provision essential. The articles of Confedn. themselves were defective in this respect, resting in many of the States on the Legislative sanction only. . . . He thought it indispensable that the new Constitution should be ratified . . . by the supreme authority of the people themselves."

George Mason gave what was perhaps the most impassioned explanation in Philadelphia of the necessity of conventions. Madison noted: "Col. Mason considered a reference of the plan to the authority of the people as one of the most important and essential of the Resolutions. The Legislatures have no power to ratify it. They are the mere creatures of the State Constitutions, and cannot be greater than their creators. And he knew of no power in any of the Constitutions, he knew there was no power in some of them, that could be competent to this object. Whither then must we resort? To the people with whom all power remains that has not been given up in the Constitutions derived from them. It was of great moment he observed that this doctrine should be cherished as the basis of free Government. Another strong reason was that admitting the Legislatures to have a competent authority, it would be wrong to refer the plan to them, because succeeding Legislatures having equal authority could undo the acts of their predecessors; and the National Govt. would stand in each State on the weak and tottering foundation of an Act of Assembly."

256. This is no magic number. In early drafts of this clause in Philadelphia, the number of states needed was simply left blank. On August 30, the delegates debated as to whether as few as seven states or a unanimous thirteen were required for the Constitution to go

into effect. A more complicated proposal came from Gouverneur Morris, who, according to Madison's notes, proposed that "the blank ought to be filled in a twofold way, so as to provide for the event of the ratifying States being contiguous which would render a smaller number sufficient, and the event of their being dispersed, which wd require a greater number for the introduction of the Government." For his part, Madison suggested the number should be as many states as was necessary to warrant at least thirty-three House seats— a majority of the population by the count laid out in Article I—as long as at least seven states ratified.

The important thing about the number nine is that it is less than thirteen. The delegates weren't about to let a single antisocial state— likely Rhode Island, which hadn't even sent a delegate—sink the enterprise. Madison's notes summarize what Pierce Butler of South Carolina said: "Mr. Butler was in favor of 'nine.' He revolted at the idea, that one or two States should restrain the rest from consulting their safety." Or, as Madison would write in 43 *Federalist*: "To have required the unanimous ratification of the thirteen States, would have subjected the essential interests of the whole to the caprice or corruption of a single member. It would have marked a want of foresight in the Convention, which our own experience would have rendered inexcusable."

By the time the First Congress met in New York in the spring of 1789 (both houses attained a quorum by the first week of April), two states were still out on their own as independent entities. North Carolina wouldn't ratify until November of that year; Rhode Island not until May 1790. Had these states not ratified, what would have occurred? In 43 *Federalist*, Madison took up the question of what would happen to any that decided to stay out in the cold. He promises nothing: "It is one of those cases which must be left to provide for itself. In general it may be observed, that although no political relation can subsist between the assenting and dissenting States, yet the moral relations will remain uncancelled. The claims of justice, both on one side and on the other, will be in force, and must be fulfilled; the rights of humanity must in all cases be duly and mutually respected; whilst

considerations of a common interest, and above all the remembrance
of the endearing scenes which are past, and the anticipation of a
speedy triumph over the obstacles to re-union, will, it is hoped, not
urge in vain MODERATION on one side, and PRUDENCE on
the other."

**shall be sufficient²⁵⁷ for the Establishment of this Constitution be-
tween the States so ratifying the Same.**

257. The Federalists and their opponents disagreed over the
scope of the proposed conventions. The Federalists demanded that
the conventions take an up-or-down vote on the proposed Constitution, and they would brook no changes or conditions. This infuriated the Anti-Federalists, who insisted on a Bill of Rights. What
right had the Federalists to set the terms of the debate? Here is 5
Federal Farmer: "The members of the convention met without
knowing the sentiments of one man in ten thousand in these states
respecting the new ground taken. Their doings are but the first attempts in the most important scene ever opened. Though each individual in the state conventions will not, probably, be so respectable
as each individual in the federal convention, yet as the state conventions will probably consist of fifteen hundred or two thousand men
of abilities, and versed in the science of government, collected from
all parts of the community and from all orders of men, it must be acknowledged that the weight of respectability will be in them. In
them will be collected the solid sense and the real political character
of the country. Being revisers of the subject, they will possess peculiar advantages. To say that these conventions ought not to attempt,
coolly and deliberately, the revision of the system, or that they cannot amend it, is very foolish or very assuming."

The Federalists had strategic reasons for opposing giving the conventions leeway to introduce amendments. Professor Rakove considered the problem in *Original Meanings*: "Who would propose a

suitable set of amendments? How could consensus be reached among a sufficient number of states—presumably nine—acting separately? If five states ratified the Constitution unamended, would that preclude the adoption of amendments by the other eight? Would a second federal convention be needed to attain consensus on the revisions? If so, who would call and elect it? And would its decisions not have to be referred to the states in their turn? Once begun, how could this cycle of deliberation and revision ever end?" In the event, the Federalists ended up controlling the conventions. Out of this dispute Madison emerged in the First Congress to propose the most famous set of laws since Sinai, the Bill of Rights.

BILL OF RIGHTS[258]

258. "Why declare that things shall not be done which there is no power to do?" asks Hamilton in 84 *Federalist,* which sketches his argument against the Bill of Rights. Hamilton's judgment looks doubtful, in light of how often the Bill of Rights has had to be invoked over the centuries to stymie the government. Madison answered Hamilton's famous question when he introduced the Bill of Rights in the First Congress. A Virginia representative who had coauthored the *Federalist* with Hamilton, Madison said he wished "that those who have been friendly to the adoption of this constitution may have the opportunity of proving to those who were opposed to it that they were as sincerely devoted to liberty and a republican government, as those who charged them with wishing the adoption of this constitution in order to lay the foundation of an aristocracy or despotism."

And so the Bill of Rights came into being. It is a restriction on the Congress that did not, at least until 1868, lay a finger on the states. The original Constitution limited the authority of the states only in what a Boston University law professor, Andrew Kull, has characterized as "tangential" ways, particularly the privileges and immunities clause. The states were brought under the Bill of Rights only by the Fourteenth Amendment. A constitutional process of incorporation, which has been fought case by case, has involved everything from abortion to libel law to religious establishment, and continues to this day over such matters as, say, gun control.

AMENDMENT I.

Congress shall make no law[259]

---

259. A prohibition on the Congress. This is the most important point to be made in respect of the First Amendment. It affects the Congress only. And pointedly not the states.

respecting an establishment of religion,[260]

---

260. Why did the founders choose this precise wording? Does it mean that Congress will not establish a church? Clearly. But what about the states, to which this amendment didn't apply at the time it was written—a time when churches were established by the governments of a number of states? If there were already churches formally established at the state level, did this phrase mean, to the founders, that Congress would not regulate, or even disestablish, them? In other words, does it mean the opposite of what many twentieth-century commentators have taken it to mean?

One scholar who examined the question, Joseph Snee, concluded that the state ratifying conventions "feared, not only federal interference with individual religious freedom, but also federal interference with state establishments or quasi-establishments then existing. To them, there was a danger of such interference with state sovereignty by affirmative federal action to establish a national religion, or by negative action disestablishing state establishments."

And what about Jefferson? His famous phrase about a "wall of sep-aration between Church & State" was made in a letter to the Dan-bury Baptist Association, an opponent of the Congregational Church that was established in Connecticut. Jefferson's letter of January 1, 1802, contained this sentence: "Believing with you that religion is a matter which lies solely between Man & his God, that he owes ac-count to none other for his faith or his worship, that the legitimate powers of government reach actions only, & not opinions, I contem-plate with sovereign reverence that act of the whole American people which declared that their legislature should 'make no law respecting an establishment of religion, or prohibiting the free exercise thereof,' thus building a wall of separation between Church & State."

A posting on beliefnet.com suggests that the use of the phrase "their legislature" makes it clear that Jefferson was speaking only of the national Congress. The idea that the framers of the First Amendment intended a wall of separation is disputed by Columbia Law School Professor Philip Hamburger. He suggests that the constitutional de-mands of dissenters—the opponents of the established churches—"typically had little to do with a separation of church and state."

Neither the establishment clause nor the First Amendment, how-ever, contains any prohibition of any kind on the church or any other institution or facet of religion. The establishment of churches continued for years after the First Amendment went into the Con-stitution. The Congregational Church in Connecticut was not dis-established until 1818. And whether the clause was designed to separate church and state or protect the establishment of churches by the states, the passage of the Fourteenth Amendment, which brought the Bill of Rights into force at the state level, emerges as a dramatic reorientation.

The most important modern Supreme Court decision in respect of this clause was handed down in 1971 in a case involving a lawyer for the American Civil Liberties Union, Alton J. Lemon, who as the father of a student at a school in Pennsylvania challenged a state statute under which public schools reimbursed church-affiliated schools for offering teaching help with secular subjects. The

Supreme Court, in *Lemon v. Kurtzman*, found the law in Pennsylvania, and a similar law in Rhode Island, to be unconstitutional. Chief Justice Burger, writing for the majority, pointedly distanced the Court from Jefferson's formulation about a "wall of separation." He said the Court's "prior holdings do not call for total separation between church and state" and went on to assert that "total separation is not possible in an absolute sense." He cited as "necessary and permissible contacts" the example of fire inspections, building and zoning regulations, and state requirements under compulsory school-attendance laws. But the Court said that "judicial caveats against entanglement must recognize that the line of separation, far from being a 'wall,' is a blurred, indistinct, and variable barrier depending on all the circumstances of a particular relationship."

The Court said that "every analysis in this area must begin with consideration of the cumulative criteria developed by the Court over many years," and that "three such tests" could be "gleaned from our cases." The tests: a statute "must have a secular legislative purpose"; its "principal or primary effect must be one that neither advances nor inhibits religion"; and it must not foster "an excessive government entanglement with religion." The three-part hurdle came to be known as the "Lemon test." It was cited by the Court in, among other cases, a lawsuit involving Lamb's Chapel, an evangelical church that had been turned down in its application to use the premises of the Center Moriches Union Free School District after school hours to show films. The Court, in a unanimous decision, granted Lamb's Chapel access to after-hours space that other groups were also permitted to use. It did so on free speech grounds, but also noted that permitting Lamb's Chapel access wouldn't have been an establishment of religion under the Lemon test.

This irked Justice Scalia, who wrote: "Like some ghoul in a late night horror movie that repeatedly sits up in its grave and shuffles abroad, after being repeatedly killed and buried, *Lemon* stalks our Establishment Clause jurisprudence once again, frightening the little children and school attorneys of Center Moriches Union Free School District." He noted that over the years "no fewer than five of the currently sitting Justices have, in their own opinions, personally driven pencils through the creature's heart . . . and a sixth has joined an opinion doing so." He wrote that the "secret of the *Lemon* test's survival" was that "it is so easy to kill. It is there to scare us (and our audience) when we wish it to do so, but we can command it to return to the tomb at will." He said he agreed with the "long list of constitutional scholars who have criticized *Lemon* and bemoaned the strange Establishment Clause geometry of crooked lines and wavering shapes its intermittent use has produced." Scalia was also irked by the Court's statement that Lamb's Chapel's proposed use of the school's facilities was constitutional because, among other things, it would not, in the Court's view, signal endorsement of religion in general.

"What a strange notion," Scalia remonstrated, "that a Constitution which *itself* gives 'religion in general' preferential treatment (I refer to the Free Exercise Clause) forbids endorsement of religion in general." He ridiculed the attorney general of New York for suggesting that "religious advocacy . . . serves the community only in the eyes of its adherents and yields a benefit only to those who already believe." Wrote Scalia: "That was *not* the view of those who adopted our Constitution, who believed that the public virtues inculcated by religion are a public good." He noted that the very Congress that drafted this amendment enacted the Northwest Territory Ordinance, Article 3 of which, Scalia pointed out, provides: "Religion, morality, and knowledge, *being necessary to good government and the happiness of mankind*, schools and the means of education shall forever be encouraged."

or prohibiting the free exercise thereof;[261]

261. The free exercise clause. Its first big test, over the question of polygamy, came in a case that was sought by the Mormon Church in an attempt to secure a finding that an antibigamy law in Utah, the Morrill Anti-Bigamy Act, was unconstitutional. A church employee,

George Reynolds, was charged and convicted under the law. In 1878 the Supreme Court sustained his conviction with these words:

> In our opinion, the statute immediately under consideration is within the legislative power of Congress. It is constitutional and valid as prescribing a rule of action for all those residing in the Territories, and in places over which the United States have exclusive control. This being so, the only question which remains is whether those who make polygamy a part of their religion are excepted from the operation of the statute. If they are, then those who do not make polygamy a part of their religious belief may be found guilty and punished, while those who do, must be acquitted and go free. This would be introducing a new element into criminal law. Laws are made for the government of actions, and while they cannot interfere with mere religious belief and opinions, they may with practices. Suppose one believed that human sacrifices were a necessary part of religious worship; would it be seriously contended that the civil government under which he lived could not interfere to prevent a sacrifice? Or if a wife religiously believed it was her duty to burn herself upon the funeral pile of her dead husband; would it be beyond the power of the civil government to prevent her carrying her belief into practice?
>
> So here, as a law of the organization of society under the exclusive dominion of the United States, it is provided that plural marriages shall not be allowed. Can a man excuse his practices to the contrary because of his religious belief? To permit this would be to make the professed doctrines of religious belief superior to the law of the land, and, in effect, to permit every citizen to become a law unto himself. Government could exist only in name under such circumstances.

The precedent set in *Reynolds v. United States* would stand relatively undisturbed for nearly a century, until free-exercise jurisprudence took a turn in 1963, after a textile worker in South Carolina, Adell Sherbert, a Seventh-Day Adventist, was denied unemployment benefits because she had refused to work on Saturdays. Justice Brennan wrote the decision for the 7 to 2 majority of the high court, concluding that the state lacked a "compelling interest" in overriding Sherbert's rights to the free exercise of religion. This turned the free exercise clause into an equal-protection clause, guarding against laws intentionally antagonistic to religion. The application of the free exercise clause was narrowed in 1990, when the Court brushed aside a claim by a Native American, Alfred Smith, who had asserted that the use of peyote was a part of his religious observance. The court held the Oregon law constitutional, as the law applied neutrally to all in Oregon and was not specifically aimed at religious activity.

or abridging the freedom of speech, or of the press;[262]

262. One of the most intriguing questions about this clause is why the founders wrote separately about the freedom of, on the one hand, speech, and, on the other, the press. The question arose in a case called *Houchins v. KQED* (1978), which was brought after a prisoner being held in the jail at Alameda County, California, committed suicide. A broadcaster, KQED, and local branches of the National Association for the Advancement of Colored People sued to gain access to the lockup. Sheriff Houchins took the matter to the Supreme Court and won a ruling that said, in essence, that the press doesn't have a right superior to a member of the general public. Justice Potter Stewart concurred in a separate opinion, in which he included this cautionary note: "That the First Amendment speaks separately of freedom of speech and freedom of the press is no constitutional accident, but an acknowledgment of the critical role played by the

press in American society. The Constitution requires sensitivity to that role, and to the special needs of the press in performing it effectively. A person touring Santa Rita jail can grasp its reality with his own eyes and ears. But if a television reporter is to convey the jail's sights and sounds to those who cannot personally visit the place, he must use cameras and sound equipment. In short, terms of access that are reasonably imposed on individual members of the public may, if they impede effective reporting without sufficient justification, be unreasonable as applied to journalists who are there to convey to the general public what the visitors see."

Justice Oliver Wendell Holmes's famous formulation about falsely shouting fire in a theater was made in *Schenck v. United States* (1919). Charles Schenck, general secretary of the Socialist Party, had been put in the dock for mailing to conscripts leaflets encouraging them to resist the draft during World War I. The Supreme Court came down against him. Here's how Holmes put it: "We admit that in many places and in ordinary times the defendants in saying all that was said in the circular would have been within their constitutional rights. But the character of every act depends upon the circumstances in which it is done. . . . The most stringent protection of free speech would not protect a man in falsely shouting fire in a theatre and causing a panic. . . . The question in every case is whether the words used are used in such circumstances and are of such a nature as to create a clear and present danger that they will bring about the substantive evils that Congress has a right to prevent. It is a question of proximity and degree. When a nation is at war many things that might be said in time of peace are such a hindrance to its effort that their utterance will not be endured so long as men fight and that no Court could regard them as protected by any constitutional right."

It's but one example of courts examining "time, manner, and place" in speech cases. The courts have distinguished between content-based laws, which receive strict scrutiny, and content-neutral laws, which receive a lower level of scrutiny. One criterion is whether the area is private or public. If it is public, questions then arise as to whether it is a traditional public forum, such as a park or street, or is otherwise dedicated to speech purposes—a theater, say—or whether it is public property devoted to some other use. In *International Society for Krishna Consciousness, Inc. v. Lee* (1992), airports, for example, have been held to be private and may limit speech; so have shopping malls in *Hudgens v. National Labor Relations Board* (1976). Schools were addressed in a case involving a fifteen-year-old named John Tinker, his thirteen-year-old sister, Mary Beth, and a sixteen-year-old classmate Christopher Eckhardt, who wore black armbands to school as a silent protest of the Vietnam War. In *Tinker v. Des Moines School District* (1969), the Supreme Court decided that a school board rule banning the armbands violated the students' freedom of speech under the First Amendment. Justice Abe Fortas wrote that the school policy sought to prevent "a silent, passive expression of opinion." Justice Hugo Black, often thought of as a First Amendment fundamentalist, dissented, chiding the Court for deciding "which school disciplinary regulations are 'reasonable.'"

The most important showdown over press freedom in American history—the attempt by President John Adams and the Federalist-controlled Congress to suppress Vice President Jefferson's pro-French Republicans as France readied a war against America—illuminated nothing so much as the limits of the Constitution in protecting press freedom. Congress passed four laws as part of its attempt, including the Sedition Act of 1798. Gordon T. Belt, in a summary published by the First Amendment Center, reckons that most scholars cite "25 arrests and at least 17 verifiable indictments," of which fourteen were under the Sedition Act and three were under common law. Benjamin Bache, the proprietor of the *Aurora* in Philadelphia and the most prominent of the press figures, was arrested under common law for seditious libel. He died of yellow fever while out on bail. No challenge was mounted in the Supreme Court against the Sedition Act or three other measures passed at the time, for the Court was controlled by Federalist judges. It fell to the state legislatures, and the Virginia and

Kentucky legislatures stepped up, passing resolutions declaring the Alien and Sedition Acts unconstitutional. The crisis ended when Jefferson was elected president, though the Enemy Alien Act is still part of the United States Code.

The idea of truth as a defense against libel began to form in pre-constitutional America, erupting in the summer of 1735 in the trial of John Peter Zenger. The printer of the *Weekley Journal* was in the dock for libeling Governor Crosby. He was defended by Andrew Hamilton, who—as the story is narrated in an account by Doug Linder of the University of Missouri–Kansas City—announced that his client "would not contest having printed and published the allegedly libelous materials . . . and that 'therefore I shall save Mr. Attorney the trouble of examining his witnesses to that point.'" The prosecutor, caught by surprise, sent his witnesses home and declared: "As Mr. Hamilton has confessed the printing and publishing of these libels, I think the Jury must find a verdict for the king. For supposing they were true, the law says that they are not the less libelous for that. Nay, indeed the law says their being true is an aggravation of the crime." In what has been called a "jury nullification," Zenger was acquitted.

That prior restraint on the press—enjoining initial publication before an offense has been committed—is unconstitutional was established in the case of the Minnesota racist Jay Near, whose *Saturday Press* operated against Jews and Catholics as well as African Americans, and whose agitation against the mayor of Minneapolis was met with an injunction against further publication that was twice sustained by the Supreme Court of Minnesota before landing at the Supreme Court of the United States. The Court's opinion was handed down in 1931 by Chief Justice Hughes, who wrote: "The fact that for approximately one hundred and fifty years there has been almost an entire absence of attempts to impose previous restraints upon publications relating to the malfeasance of public officers is significant of the deep-seated conviction that such restraints would violate constitutional right. Public officers, whose character and conduct remain open to debate and free discussion in the press, find their remedies for false accusations in actions under libel laws providing for redress and punishment, and not in proceedings to restrain the publication of newspapers and periodicals."

The Court, however, was divided, with four justices dissenting with a warning that the Court had declared "Minnesota and every other state powerless to restrain by injunction the business of publishing and circulating among the people malicious, scandalous, and defamatory periodicals that in due course of judicial procedure has been adjudged to be a public nuisance. It gives to freedom of the press a meaning and a scope not heretofore recognized, and construes 'liberty' in the due process clause of the Fourteenth Amendment to put upon the states a federal restriction that is without precedent." The principle sketched by the majority held and was reaffirmed in 1971, when the Supreme Court rebuffed an effort by the Nixon administration to block both the *New York Times* and the *Washington Post* from publishing the government's history of decision making in the Vietnam War, known as the *Pentagon Papers.*

The Supreme Court's decision was sketched in several concurring opinions. Justice Hugo Black wrote: "I believe that every moment's continuance of the injunctions against these newspapers amounts to a flagrant, indefensible, and continuing violation of the First Amendment." Not all the justices agreed. In a dissent joined by Chief Justice Burger and Justice Blackmun, Justice Harlan reached all the way back to President Washington's rebuff of Congress's attempts to learn the secrets of the negotiations over the Jay Treaty to suggest that the Court had been rushed to a decision that gave too short a shrift to the president's constitutional authority in respect of foreign affairs.

In the modern era, the defining case involving libel centered on an advertisement in the *New York Times.* The case was brought by a commissioner of Montgomery, Alabama, L. B. Sullivan, who argued that he'd been defamed by an advertisement the *Times* had published for an organization raising funds to defend Martin Luther King Jr. The court found unanimously for the newspaper in a decision that lifted an enormous burden from the press. In an opinion by Justice Brennan, the Court warned that a "rule compelling the critic of official conduct to guarantee the truth of all his factual assertions" on "pain of libel judgments virtually unlimited in amount" could lead to "self-censorship." It said that allowing the "defense of truth" but putting the burden on the defendant "does not mean that only false speech will be deterred." Wrote Brennan: "Under such a rule, would-be critics of official conduct may be deterred from voicing their criticism, even though it is believed to be true and even though it is, in fact, true, because of doubt whether it can be proved in court or fear of the expense of having to do so." He said such a rule "dampens the vigor and limits the variety of public debate," and declared: "The constitutional guarantees require, we think, a federal rule that prohibits a public official from recovering damages for a defamatory falsehood relating to his official conduct unless he proves that the statement was made with 'actual malice'—that is, with knowledge that it was false or with reckless disregard of whether it was false or not."

In January 2010, the Supreme Court decided one of its most controversial free speech cases, *Citizens United v. Federal Election Commission*. It involved a nonprofit corporation that, during the 2008 presidential election campaign, sought to distribute via pay-per-view television a film critical of one of the Democratic candidates, Senator Hillary Clinton. Citizens United feared that its financial outlays to air, distribute, and advertise the film during the election season might subject it to both civil and criminal sanctions under a ban on corporate-funded independent expenditures in the Bipartisan Campaign Reform Act, known as McCain-Feingold. So it asked the federal courts to protect its plan.

In the lower court, it lost, but eventually a sharply divided Supreme Court ruled that Citizens United was within its rights. Its opinion established that for-profit and nonprofit corporations and labor unions could spend money independently to participate in the political debate. It included such flashes of constitutional fundamentalism as this sentence: "The First Amendment does not permit laws that force speakers to retain a campaign finance attorney, conduct demographic marketing research, or seek declaratory rulings before discussing the most salient political issues of our day."

The court noted that McCain-Feingold contained an "outright ban" on certain speech "backed by criminal sanctions" and observed that the law "makes it a felony for all corporations—including nonprofit advocacy corporations—either to expressly advocate the election or defeat of candidates or to broadcast electioneering communications within 30 days of a primary election and 60 days of a general election." It went on to observe that under the law the following acts "would all be felonies"—

> [t]he Sierra Club runs an ad, within the crucial phase of 60 days before the general election, that exhorts the public to disapprove of a Congressman who favors logging in national forests; the National Rifle Association publishes a book urging the public to vote for the challenger because the incumbent U.S. Senator supports a handgun ban; and the American Civil Liberties Union creates a Web site telling the public to vote for a Presidential candidate in light of that candidate's defense of free speech.

It called such prohibitions "classic examples of censorship" and went on to rule unconstitutional most of McCain-Feingold's restrictions on independent corporate expenditures. The ruling infuriated the Court's minority, lead by Justice Stevens, who, in a dissent, declared that "[a]t bottom" the Court's opinion was "a rejection of the common sense of the American people, who have recognized a need to prevent corporations from undermining self-government since the founding, and who have fought against the distinctive corrupting potential of corporate electioneering since the days of Theodore Roosevelt." One of the Nine, however, felt the ruling did not go far enough because the court upheld certain of McCain-Feingold's disclosure requirements. Wrote Justice Thomas: "Congress may not abridge the 'right to anonymous speech' based on the 'simple interest in providing voters with additional relevant information.'"

or the right of the people peaceably to assemble,[263] **and to petition the Government for a redress of grievances.**[264]

---

263. "The most alarming Process that ever appeared in a British Government" is how Thomas Jefferson described a proclamation issued by General Gage in Massachusetts "declaring it Treason for the Inhabitants of that Province to assemble themselves to consider of their Grievances and form Associations for their common Conduct on the Occasion."

264. "In every stage of these Oppressions," said the Declaration of Independence, "we have Petitioned for Redress in the most humble terms: Our repeated Petitions have been answered only by repeated injury."

"'Petitioning,'" according to the First Amendment Center, "has come to signify any nonviolent, legal means of encouraging or disapproving government action, whether directed to the judicial, executive or legislative branch. Lobbying, letter-writing, e-mail campaigns, testifying before tribunals, filing lawsuits, supporting referenda, collecting signatures for ballot initiatives, peaceful protests and picketing: all public articulation of issues, complaints and interests designed to spur government action qualifies under the petition clause, even if the activities partake of other First Amendment freedoms." An article on the center's website focuses on *United Mine Workers of America v. Illinois State Bar Association*, in which the Supreme Court in 1967 cited the right to petition in permitting the union to employ a lawyer to represent its members. It also cites *NAACP v. Button*, a 1963 case in which the Supreme Court, marking this clause, overruled Virginia and allowed the civil rights organization to solicit plaintiffs, saying: "Litigation may well be the sole practical avenue open to a minority to petition for a redress of grievances."

In 1952 Justices Black and Douglas tried to convince their colleagues on the Supreme Court that this clause was broad enough to protect one Joseph Beauharnais, who was arrested for passing out leaflets. The leaflet contained the text of a petition calling for Chicago to institute segregation. This allegedly violated a statute that prohibited the distribution of racist literature in public places. He was soliciting signatures as well. His conviction was upheld by the Supreme Courts of Illinois. It was also upheld by the Supreme Court in Washington, but Black and Douglas dissented, arguing that no one disputed that "both Beauharnais and his group were making a genuine effort to petition their elective representatives." Asked they: "How does the court justify its holding today that states can punish people for exercising the vital freedoms intended to be safeguarded from suppression by the First Amendment?"

AMENDMENT II.

A well regulated Militia, being necessary[265] to the security of a free State, the right of the people to keep and bear Arms, shall not be infringed.[266]

---

265. That a well-regulated militia is the only institution that the founders went so far as to characterize in the Constitution as "necessary" to the security of a free state has been remarked on by a number of commentators, including Edwin Vieira Jr. Certainly the founders, in enacting this amendment, were concerned with the danger of tyranny. Elbridge Gerry said: "This declaration of rights, I take it, is intended to secure the people against the mal-administration of the Government; if we could suppose that, in all cases, the rights of the people would be attended to, the occasion for guards of this kind would be removed. . . . What, sir, is the use of a militia? It is to prevent the establishment of a standing army, the bane of liberty."

266. A "relic of the American Revolution" is how, in the summer of 2001, the *Boston Globe* characterized the way this amendment had been viewed by the courts. It was reporting on the declaration by a new U.S. attorney general, John Ashcroft, that it was the government's policy that the right to keep and bear arms was vested not in the militia but in the people. For several years the debate grew in intensity. Then Ashcroft's view was roundly vindicated in two dramatic Supreme Court cases, one in 2008 and the other in 2010, both of which confirmed Ashcroft's view and established that the right being vouchsafed here belongs to the people.

The first of the two cases was *District of Columbia v. Heller*, involving a retired security guard who was denied a permit to keep an assembled handgun at home. The Court, in a 5 to 4 decision, ruled unconstitutional a District law forbidding the keeping of such a gun at home. The opinion, by Justice Scalia, relied in part on a grammatical deconstruction of the amendment. Here is how Scalia made the point: "The Second Amendment is naturally divided into two parts:

its prefatory clause and its operative clause. The former does not limit the latter grammatically, but rather announces a purpose. The Amendment could be rephrased, 'Because a well regulated Militia is necessary to the security of a free State, the right of the people to keep and bear Arms shall not be infringed.'"

The Court ordered the District of Columbia to permit Heller to register his handgun and issue him a license to carry it in his home. It pointedly did not rule out any regulation of arms. It stated its awareness of "the problem of handgun violence in this country" and asserted that it took "seriously the concerns" of those "who believe that prohibition of handgun ownership is a solution." It said the Constitution "leaves the District of Columbia a variety of tools for combating that problem, including some measures regulating handguns," but said the Constitution "takes certain policy choices off the table." It said that it had no doubt that "some think that the Second Amendment is outmoded in a society where our standing army is the pride of our Nation, where well-trained police forces provide personal security, and where gun violence is a serious problem." It called such views "perhaps debatable." What "is not debatable is that it is not the role of this Court to pronounce the Second Amendment extinct."

Heller involved a gun law in the District of Columbia, which is directly under the jurisdiction of Congress. It left open the question of whether the Second Amendment applied to the states. That question was dealt with by the Court in 2010, in *McDonald v. Chicago*, which held that the states, too, had to bow to the Second Amendment. The decision was an important step in the process known as incorporation, in which the Bill of Rights was, after the passage of the Fourteenth Amendment, deemed to apply not only to the Congress but also to the states. The court's decisions in *Heller* and *McDonald*, like the school desegregation ruling *Brown v. Board of Education*, presage a long period of litigation to define and implement the constitutional principles laid down by the Court. The intensity of the struggle over the amendment suggests that "the right of the citizens to keep and bear arms" is widely seen as, in the words of Justice Story, "the palladium of the liberties of a republic."

AMENDMENT III.

No Soldier shall, in time of peace be quartered in any house, without the consent of the Owner, nor in time of war, but in a manner to be prescribed by law.[267]

267. This amendment was one of the bases on which the Court, in *Griswold v. Connecticut*, overturned Connecticut's law in respect of certain aspects of birth control. The idea that birth control was what the founders had in mind when they wrote the amendment has been mocked by a number of commentators. But Justice Douglas, writing for the Court, decided the matter this way: "Various guarantees create zones of privacy. The right of association contained in the penumbra of the First Amendment is one, as we have seen. The Third Amendment in its prohibition against the quartering of soldiers 'in any house' in time of peace without the consent of the owner is another facet of that privacy. The Fourth Amendment explicitly affirms the 'right of the people to be secure in their persons, houses, papers, and effects, against unreasonable searches and seizures.' The Fifth Amendment in its Self-Incrimination Clause enables the citizen to create a zone of privacy which government may not force him to surrender to his detriment. The Ninth Amendment provides: 'The enumeration in the Constitution, of certain rights, shall not be construed to deny or disparage others retained by the people.'" *Griswold*'s reliance on the First, Third, Fourth, Fifth, and Ninth Amendments was ridiculed by Justices Black and Stewart, the latter of whom noted: "No soldier has been quartered in any house."

The actual record from the founding period suggests the authors of the Constitution were concerned with one of the grievances that had been raised against George III in the Declaration of Independence, which complained of the keeping "among us, in times of peace, Standing Armies, without the Consent of our legislatures" and of "quartering large bodies of armed troops among us." Colonial New

York had resisted the first Quartering Act, of 1765, which allowed Redcoats to stay in private homes. The second Quartering Act, issued in 1774, was greeted as one of the so-called Intolerable Acts. "The billeting of soldiers upon the citizens of a state, has been generally found burthensome to the people, and so far as this article may prevent that evil it may be deemed valuable; but it certainly adds nothing to the national security." Joseph Story wrote: "[The] plain object is to secure the perfect enjoyment of that great right of the common law, that a man's house shall be his own castle, privileged against all civil and military intrusion. The billetting of soldiers in time of peace upon the people has been a common resort of arbitrary princes, and is full of inconvenience and peril."

This amendment has seldom been adjudicated in the federal courts, as the practice of quartering troops in homes was brought to a halt with the triumph of the Revolution. But the amendment figured in one case, *Engblom v. Carey*, which was dealt with in 1982 by the judges who ride the Second U.S. Appeals Circuit. It involved a strike of corrections officers at the Mid-Orange Correctional Facility in Warwick, New York. Governor Hugh Carey called out the National Guard, and several of its members stayed in the homes of the striking guards, who brought suit under this amendment. The circuit court did not rule out a claim for protection under the Third Amendment, but Judge Irving Kaufman, in a dissent, said the Court majority's "willingness seriously to entertain a 'quartering of troops' claim" in the prison strike "holds us up to derision."

AMENDMENT IV.

The right of the people to be secure in their persons, houses, papers, and effects, against unreasonable searches and seizures, shall not be violated, and no Warrants shall issue, but upon probable cause, supported by Oath or affirmation, and particularly describing the place to be searched, and the persons or things to be seized.[268]

---

268. A "conspiracy of amazing magnitude," as it was characterized by Chief Justice Taft, was at the center of one of the first cases to test how the advance of technology would be treated under this amendment. The case involved a bootlegger, Roy Olmstead, on whose operations federal agents placed a wiretap. Taft described it this way: "Small wires were inserted along the ordinary telephone wires from the residences of four of the petitioners and those leading from the chief office. The insertions were made without trespass upon any property of the defendants. They were made in the basement of the large office building. The taps from house lines were made in the streets near the houses." He reasoned: "By the invention of the telephone fifty years ago and its application for the purpose of extending communications, one can talk with another at a far distant place. The language of the Amendment cannot be extended and expanded to include telephone wires reaching to the whole world from the defendant's house or office. The intervening wires are not part of his house or office any more than are the highways along which they are stretched."

Things have come a long way since *Olmstead v. United States*. Witness the furor that erupted after September 11, 2001, when America's intelligence services, in a time of war, tracked telephone numbers in the United States that had been connected to telephones being used by terrorists overseas. The big step to the current state of the law was taken in a 1967 case involving a gambler named Charles Katz, whose telephone conversation in a telephone booth was monitored by the FBI. Justice Potter Stewart, writing in *Katz v. United States*, said the

Court had concluded that the underpinnings of *Olmstead* "have been so eroded by our subsequent decisions" that the "doctrine there enunciated can no longer be regarded as controlling." The government's activities "in electronically listening to and recording" the gambler's words "violated the privacy upon which he justifiably relied while using the telephone booth, and thus constituted a 'search and seizure' within the meaning of the Fourth Amendment."

In recent decades, the Court has suggested that it would permit a cocaine-sniffing canine to case the luggage of a suspected drug trafficker. In *United States v. Place*, the Court decided that the Fourth Amendment rights of Raymond J. Place, who was traveling to New York from Miami, had been violated, but for reasons other than the dog that sniffed the cocaine. "Despite the fact that the sniff tells the authorities something about the contents of the luggage," wrote Justice O'Connor for the Court, "the information obtained is limited. This limited disclosure also ensures that the owner of the property is not subjected to the embarrassment and inconvenience entailed in less discriminate and more intrusive investigative methods. In these respects, the canine sniff is *sui generis*. We are aware of no other investigative procedure that is so limited both in the manner in which the information is obtained and in the content of the information revealed by the procedure. Therefore, we conclude that the particular course of investigation that the agents intended to pursue here—exposure of respondent's luggage, which was located in a public place, to a trained canine—did not constitute a 'search' within the meaning of the Fourth Amendment."

The use of thermal imaging equipment was deemed by the Court to be a search under the Fourth Amendment. The case involved an Oregon man, Danny Lee Kyllo, whose garage was the source of a large amount of heat detected by federal agents. They speculated it was emanating from heat lamps such as those used to grow marijuana. The Supreme Court, in a case on which supposedly conservative members such as Justice Thomas and supposedly liberal members such as Justice Ginsberg agreed, declared, in an opinion by Justice Scalia, that not only does the Fourth Amendment draw "a firm line at the entrance to the house," as it had said in an earlier case, but the line "must be not only firm but also bright—which requires clear specification of those methods of surveillance that require a warrant."

Controversy over where to draw the line of the Fourth Amendment during a time when foreign terrorist organizations are targeting the United States has intensified since the attacks of September 11, 2001, and the passage of the Uniting and Strengthening America by Providing Appropriate Tools Required to Intercept and Obstruct Terrorism Act, known as the USA PATRIOT Act.

AMENDMENT V.

No person shall be held to answer for a capital, or otherwise infamous crime,[269] unless on a presentment or indictment of a Grand Jury,[270] except in cases arising in the land or naval forces, or in the Militia, when in actual service in time of War or public danger;

---

269. A felony.

270. From Joseph Story: "The grand jury may consist of any number, not less than twelve, nor more than twenty-three; and twelve at least must concur in every accusation. They sit in secret, and examine the evidence laid before them by themselves. A presentment, properly speaking, is an accusation made *ex mero motu* by a grand jury of an offence upon their own observation and knowledge, or upon evidence before them, and without any bill of indictment laid before them at the suit of the government. An indictment is a written accusation of an offence preferred to, and presented, upon oath, as true, by a grand jury at the suit of the government. Upon a presentment the proper officer of the court must frame an indictment, before the party accused can be put to answer it. But an indictment is usually in the first instance framed by the officers of the government, and laid before the grand jury. When the grand jury have heard the evidence, if they are of opinion, that the indictment is groundless, or not sup-

ported by evidence, they used formerly to endorse on the back of the bill, 'ignoramus,' or we know nothing of it, whence the bill was said to be *ignored*. But now they assert in plain English, 'not a true bill,' or which is a better way, 'not found;' and then the party is entitled to be discharged, if in custody, without farther answer. But a fresh bill may be preferred against him by another grand jury. If the grand jury are satisfied of the truth of the accusation, then they write on the back of the bill, 'a true bill' (or anciently, '*billa vera*'). The bill is then said to be found, and is publicly returned into court; the party stands indicted, and may then be required to answer the matters charged against him."

From Bruce T. Olson's preface to the 1973 edition of *The Grand Jury*, by George J. Edwards: "While, to many people's way of thinking, citizen participation in government in general, and criminal justice in particular, has been poorly provided for, the grand jury surely stands as an example of classical attempts to involve citizens in the administration of criminal justice. In theory, after all, the grand jury is a publicly constituted panel of a community's citizens whose job it is to act as an impartial overseer of the criminal justice apparatus." Yet the grand jury has proved but a weak check on prosecutors. All that is needed to indict is a majority of the grand jurors. "Any prosecutor who wanted to, could indict a ham sandwich," goes the famous saying, which a former chief justice of the Court of Appeals in New York State, Sol Wachtler, writes that he coined in an interview in 1985 with the television journalist Marcia Kramer.

nor shall any person be subject for the same offence to be twice put in jeopardy of life or limb;[271] nor shall be compelled in any criminal case to be a witness against himself,[272] nor be deprived of life, liberty, or property, without due process of law;[273]

271. This prevents prosecutors from appealing acquittals or making a second attempt to convict an individual found not guilty. Yet it

is not always a bar to repeated prosecutions for the same act. In 1992, after four Los Angeles police officers were acquitted in the beating of Rodney King, federal prosecutors charged the four with the crime of violating King's civil rights. The original thinking behind this kind of second prosecution in civil rights law is that a white person charged with a racially motivated crime was not, when put before a jury in the era of Jim Crow, necessarily in actual jeopardy. But more generally the practice of bringing federal charges where state prosecutors have failed to win convictions was allowed in a 1922 case involving violations of Prohibition. In *United States v. Lanza* the Supreme Court said double jeopardy was no bar to a state and the federal governments each pursuing its own case against a defendant. Wrote Chief Justice Taft:

> We have here two sovereignties, deriving power from different sources, capable of dealing with the same subject matter within the same territory. Each may, without interference by the other, enact laws to secure prohibition, with the limitation that no legislation can give validity to acts prohibited by the amendment. Each government, in determining what shall be an offense against its peace and dignity, is exercising its own sovereignty, not that of the other.
>
> It follows that an act denounced as a crime by both national and state sovereignties is an offense against the peace and dignity of both, and may be punished by each. The Fifth Amendment, like all the other guaranties in the first eight amendments, applies only to proceedings by the federal government and the double jeopardy therein forbidden is a second prosecution under authority of the federal government after a first trial for the same offense under the same authority.

272. Ernesto Miranda was arrested at his home on March 13, 1963, at Phoenix, Arizona, as the circumstances were summarized by

the chief justice of the United States, Earl Warren, in one of the most famous Supreme Court cases of all time. Miranda was taken to a police station, where he was identified by what Warren called "the complaining witness" as having committed rape. "The police then took him to 'Interrogation Room No. 2' of the detective bureau. There he was questioned by two police officers. The officers admitted at trial that Miranda was not advised that he had a right to have an attorney present. Two hours later, the officers emerged from the interrogation room with a written confession signed by Miranda. At the top of the statement was a typed paragraph stating that the confession was made voluntarily, without threats or promises of immunity and 'with full knowledge of my legal rights, understanding any statement I make may be used against me.'"

Wrote Warren:

> At his trial before a jury, the written confession was admitted into evidence over the objection of defense counsel, and the officers testified to the prior oral confession made by Miranda during the interrogation. Miranda was found guilty of kidnapping and rape. He was sentenced to 20 to 30 years' imprisonment on each count, the sentences to run concurrently. On appeal, the Supreme Court of Arizona held that Miranda's constitutional rights were not violated in obtaining the confession, and affirmed the conviction. In reaching its decision, the court emphasized heavily the fact that Miranda did not specifically request counsel.
>
> We reverse. From the testimony of the officers and by the admission of respondent, it is clear that Miranda was not in any way apprised of his right to consult with an attorney and to have one present during the interrogation, nor was his right not to be compelled to incriminate himself effectively protected in any other manner. Without these warnings, the statements were inadmissible. The mere fact that he signed a statement which contained a

typed-in clause stating that he had "full knowledge" of his "legal rights" does not approach the knowing and intelligent waiver required to relinquish constitutional rights.

273. Due process is one of the big constitutional concepts—and is based on language that goes back centuries before the Constitution was written. The idea comes from the Magna Charta, which declared that "no freemen shall be taken or imprisoned or disseised or exiled or in any way destroyed, nor will we go upon him nor send upon him, except by the lawful judgment of his peers or by the law of the land." The actual phrase "due process of law" first appeared later in a 1354 statutory reconfirmation of the English charter.

During the process of ratification of the Constitution, seven states made recommendations for additional amendments. New York specified the use of this wording, which it took from the Bill of Rights in its own state constitution and on which Madison relied when drafting the federal version. According to legal scholar Bernard Siegan, Madison's decision to use this phrasing was likely purposeful: "The use of the words 'due process' instead of 'law of the land' may also be attributable to Madison's desire for more clarity in meaning. The words 'law of the land' may misleadingly suggest the inclusion of a greater number of laws than do the words 'due process,' although English law regarded the meaning of the two phrases as the same."

Due process has had a checkered career in the courts. Chief Justice Taney actually cited the phrase as one of the grounds for denying freedom to Dred Scott. He reckoned that the individual acting as Scott's owner, John F. A. Sanford, would be deprived of his property in an unconstitutional way simply by having brought the property to a free state. Wrote Taney: "And an act of Congress which deprives a citizen of the United States of his liberty or property merely because he came himself or brought his property into a particular Territory of the United States, and who had committed no offence against the laws, could hardly be dignified with the name of due process of law." Taney's reasoning was eviscerated in an opinion by Justice Curtis, but he was one of only two dissenters.

With ratification of the Fourteenth Amendment, which applies the due process language in the Bill of Rights to the states, a new phase of due process jurisdiction began. This is discussed further at page 259. The process of incorporation has not been uniform. At one point, Justice Oliver Wendell Holmes brushed aside a due process claim involving one Charles Moyer, who early in the twentieth century had rushed to Telluride, Colorado, and was arrested in a miner's strike, by writing, in *Moyer v. Peabody*: "Of course, the plaintiff's position is that he has been deprived of his liberty without due process of law. But it is familiar that what is due process of law depends on circumstances. It varies with the subject matter and the necessities of the situation."

For decades the Fourteenth Amendment, which applied the Bill of Rights to the states—was used by the Supreme Court to deal with substantive aspects of legislation. Were efforts to regulate business, say, depriving businesses or their owners of due process? The Court said they were in a famous case involving a New York baker named Lochner, and the period in which the due process clause was used to protect Americans against overly zealous regulation came to be known, after this humble kneader of bread, as the Lochner era. It is discussed in a footnote to the Fourteenth Amendment at page 260.

nor shall private property be taken for public use, without just compensation.[274]

274. One of the things that Susette Kelo prized about her house in the Fort Trumbull area of New London, Connecticut, the Supreme Court said, was the water view. Her neighbor, Wilhelmina Dery, was born in her house in 1918 and had lived there her entire life, the Court added, noting that her husband, Charles, had lived in the house since they married some sixty years before the Court ruled. "In all," the Court said, "the nine petitioners own 15 properties in Fort Trumbull. . . . Ten of the parcels are occupied by the owner or a

family member; the other five are held as investment properties. There is no allegation that any of these properties is blighted or otherwise in poor condition; rather, they were condemned only because they happen to be located in the development area." Yet the Court, in a 5 to 4 decision in *Kelo v. New London,* ruled against the homeowners in 2005 in a dispute that, more than two hundred years after the Fifth Amendment was written, could yet upend the law in respect of takings.

The issue in *Kelo* was the definition of public use—whether the New London Development Corporation's intention to use the land to bring private businesses, including a major pharmaceutical company, to the area was the kind of use contemplated in the Fifth Amendment. The majority deferred to the political institutions at the local and state levels, including the Supreme Court of Connecticut. The minority, for whom Justice O'Connor wrote the opinion, issued a warning: "Any property may now be taken for the benefit of another private party, but the fallout from this decision will not be random. The beneficiaries are likely to be those citizens with disproportionate influence and power in the political process, including large corporations and development firms. As for the victims, the government now has license to transfer property from those with fewer resources to those with more. The Founders cannot have intended this perverse result."

Grand Central Terminal in New York City emerged at the center of a famous case on the question of whether designation of a property as a landmark was a taking. In 1978 the railroad that owned the terminal, Penn Central Transportation Co., took its case to the Supreme Court, only to be dismissed in a 6 to 3 decision in which the Court concluded that the landmarking did not involve a "taking," and that the "restrictions imposed are substantially related to the promotion of the general welfare." Justice Rehnquist issued a dissent noting that of more than a million buildings and structures in New York City, only four hundred had been singled out as official landmarks. "The owner of a building might initially be pleased that his property has been chosen by a distinguished committee of architects, historians, and city planners for such a singular distinction. But he may well discover, as appellant Penn Central Transportation Co. did here, that the landmark designation imposes upon him a substantial cost, with little or no offsetting benefit except for the honor of the designation." He said the question in the case was whether the "cost associated with the city of New York's desire to preserve a limited number of 'landmarks' within its borders must be borne by all of its taxpayers, or whether it can, instead, be imposed entirely on the owners of the individual properties."

In 1984 the Supreme Court made it clear that it was, except in rare circumstances, loath to second-guess local authorities in takings disputes. The case involved a land reform that Hawaii's legislature had enacted to reduce, as the Court put it, "the perceived social and economic evils of a land oligopoly traceable to the early high chiefs of the Hawaiian Islands." The reform involved what the Court called "a land condemnation scheme whereby title in real property is taken from lessors and transferred to lessees in order to reduce the concentration of land ownership." The Court, without a dissent, decided Hawaii's law was constitutional. "This Court," it declared, "will not substitute its judgment for a legislature's judgment as to what constitutes 'public use' unless the use is palpably without reasonable foundation."

Unlike other controversial takings decisions, *Kelo* ignited some political backlash, with legislatures in 43 states—including Connecticut—moving to restrict the use of eminent domain to benefit private parties. Within a year of the Court's decision, some twenty-five states were estimated by CBS News to have passed reforms aimed at curbing abuse of eminent domain.

AMENDMENT VI.

In all criminal prosecutions, the accused shall enjoy the right to a speedy and public trial,[275] by an impartial jury of the State and district wherein the crime shall have been committed, which district shall have been previously ascertained by law, and to be informed of the nature and cause of the accusation; to be confronted with the witnesses against him;[276] to have compulsory process for obtaining witnesses in his favor, and to have the Assistance of Counsel for his defence.[277]

---

275. This was one of the clauses under which a Special Forces captain, Jeffrey MacDonald, in one of the most sensational murder cases in American history, sought to escape prosecution for slaying his wife and two daughters in 1970 at Fort Bragg, North Carolina. MacDonald was first indicted in 1975 by the military, but charges were dropped. A long investigation ensued, and MacDonald was recharged. He sought throughout to avoid prosecution under the speedy-trial clause. He was convicted for the killings in 1979 and given three consecutive life sentences. He again pressed the speedy-trial defense, and his conviction was overturned by the riders of the Fourth U.S. Appeals Circuit. The Supreme Court reinstated the conviction, rejecting the Sixth Amendment claims over a lengthy dissent by Justice Thurgood Marshall detailing the length of the investigation, which at one point involved the submission of a report totaling thirteen volumes.

276. This language was closely scrutinized as states enacted laws that excused children alleged to be victims of sexual assault from confronting the persons against whom they were testifying. This was done either by the use of closed-circuit television or by placing a screen between the child and the individual the child was accusing. In a 1988 case, the Supreme Court, in an opinion by Justice Scalia, ruled that the use of a screen violated the defendant's right under this

clause. The opinion, *Coy v. Iowa*, quoted Shakespeare's Richard II: "Then call them to our presence—face to face, and frowning brow to brow, ourselves will hear the accuser and the accused freely speak." But in 1990, in *Maryland v. Craig*, the Supreme Court upheld a Maryland conviction that was based on testimony by an accusing child whose testimony was piped into the courtroom via closed-circuit television.

277. "Petitioner was charged in a Florida state court with having broken and entered a poolroom with intent to commit a misdemeanor. This offense is a felony under Florida law. Appearing in court without funds and without a lawyer, petitioner asked the court to appoint counsel for him, whereupon the following colloquy took place:

> The COURT: Mr. Gideon, I am sorry, but I cannot appoint Counsel to represent you in this case. Under the laws of the State of Florida, the only time the Court can appoint Counsel to represent a Defendant is when that person is charged with a capital offense. I am sorry, but I will have to deny your request to appoint Counsel to defend you in this case.
>
> The DEFENDANT: The United States Supreme Court says I am entitled to be represented by Counsel.

So begins the Supreme Court's own narration of one of the most astounding cases in the history of law, brought against the secretary of the Florida Division of Corrections, Louie L. Wainwright, via a handwritten pauper's petition sent to the Supreme Court by a prisoner named Clarence Earl Gideon. The plaintiff was asking, though he did not say so, the Supreme Court to overturn its precedent in *Betts v. Brady*, in which a petition had also been filed from prison by a convict who had requested and been denied counsel in a trial for robbery. In *Betts*, the Court reprised the practices of the various states in providing counsel to indigent defendants and concluded "that, in the great majority of the States, it has been the considered judgment of the people, their representatives, and their courts that appointment of counsel is not a fundamental right, essential to a fair trial."

Come *Gideon*, Justice Black confronted *Betts* head-on. "Treating due process as 'a concept less rigid and more fluid than those envisaged in other specific and particular provisions of the Bill of Rights,' the Court held that refusal to appoint counsel under the particular facts and circumstances in the *Betts* case was not so 'offensive to the common and fundamental ideas of fairness' as to amount to a denial of due process. Since the facts and circumstances of the two cases are so nearly indistinguishable, we think the *Betts v. Brady* holding, if left standing, would require us to reject Gideon's claim that the Constitution guarantees him the assistance of counsel. Upon full reconsideration, we conclude that *Betts v. Brady* should be overruled."

Wrote Black: "We accept *Betts v. Brady*'s assumption, based as it was on our prior cases, that a provision of the Bill of Rights which is 'fundamental and essential to a fair trial' is made obligatory upon the States by the Fourteenth Amendment. We think the Court in *Betts* was wrong, however, in concluding that the Sixth Amendment's guarantee of counsel is not one of these fundamental rights." Granted a new trial by the Supreme Court, Gideon retained counsel and was found to have been not guilty.

AMENDMENT VII.

In Suits at common law, where the value in controversy shall exceed twenty dollars,[278] the right of trial by jury shall be preserved, and no fact tried by a jury, shall be otherwise re-examined in any Court of the United States, than according to the rules of the common law.

---

278. This is the second of two mentions of "dollars" in the Constitution. By a dollar the founders meant a Spanish milled dollar, which came to be established by law, in the Coinage Act of 1792, as "three hundred and seventy-one grains and four sixteenth parts of a

grain of pure, or four hundred and sixteen grains of standard silver" (please see this volume's footnotes to Article I, Section 8). In other words, at current exchange rates, a Federal Reserve one-dollar note today is worth about 8.6 percent of what the founders meant by a dollar. Or to put it another way, the founders intended jury trials to be held where the value in controversy shall exceed, in very rough numbers of modern Federal Reserve notes, $230.

AMENDMENT VIII.

Excessive bail[279] shall not be required,[280]

---

279. In other words, reasonable bail is a right.

280. Controversy arose over this right in the case of Bernard Madoff, who pleaded guilty to operating the largest Ponzi scheme ever prosecuted. Following his arrest in 2008, a court refused to hold him in prison, assenting to a $10 million bail agreement that allowed him to stay in the luxury of his penthouse. The agreement remained in place even after it was disclosed that, while out on bail, he disposed of some of his assets by mailing jewelry valued at more than $1 million to friends and family. The bail sparked outrage in the press. But, with few exceptions other than cases where the defendant poses a flight risk or a threat to society, bail is a right. Due process, moreover, prohibits the use of bail as a way of punishing the defendant before he is found guilty, or the demand of impossibly high bail for particularly egregious offenses. In *Stack v. Boyle*, in which twelve Communists were charged with conspiring to violate the Smith Act, the Supreme Court, in 1951, ruled that the $50,000 bail set for each defendant was excessive under the Eighth Amendment.

From the Judiciary Act of 1789 to the latest federal rules of criminal procedure, the Supreme Court said, "federal law has unequivocally provided that a person arrested for a noncapital offense shall be admitted to bail." It added: "This traditional right to freedom before conviction permits the unhampered preparation of a defense, and serves to prevent the infliction of punishment prior to conviction." The 1789 law itself provided that "upon all arrests in criminal cases, bail shall be admitted, except where the punishment may be death, in which cases it shall not be admitted but by the supreme or a circuit court, or by a justice of the supreme court, or a judge of a district court, who shall exercise their discretion therein, regarding the nature and circumstances of the offence, and of the evidence, and the usages of law."

The first major bail reforms since 1789 were passed by Congress in 1966, mandating bail for most persons arrested save in capital cases. The reforms were met with controversy in the District of Columbia, where federal law governs most cases and the 1966 reforms resulted in the release of violent offenders; in 1984, additional reforms tightened procedures for persons who might be a danger to the community.

nor excessive fines imposed, nor cruel and unusual punishments inflicted.[281]

281. This prohibition is at issue in a constitutional contest over the death penalty. In *Kennedy v. Louisiana*, the question was whether capital punishment for the nonhomicidal offense of raping a child was unconstitutional. The nine, in a 5 to 4 decision, concluded that it would be unconstitutional to execute Patrick Kennedy for raping his eight-year-old stepdaughter. Writing for the majority, Justice Kennedy explained that such a penalty would violate the "evolving standards of decency" by which the phrase "cruel and unusual" is applied. No sooner was the decision handed down, however, than controversy erupted over which branch is better equipped to decide evolving standards of decency—the judiciary or the legislature or, for that matter, the executive branch. Both major candidates for president in the season that *Kennedy v. Louisiana* was decided, Barack Obama and John McCain, came out strongly against the ruling.

In an unusual denouement to the case, it was disclosed—by Linda Greenhouse of the *New York Times*, in a final scoop before retiring from the newspaper's Supreme Court beat—that a factual error lay at the core of the Court's decision. In determining that societal standards precluded the death penalty for child rape, Kennedy noted that execution was sanctioned as a punishment for child rape in six states, whereas the federal government and the thirty other death penalty states did not authorize death as an appropriate punishment for child rapists. But a civilian defense lawyer almost immediately posted a weblog entry pointing out that the federal government had recently authorized the death penalty in cases where the rape of a child is committed by a member of the military; Congress had amended the Uniform Code of Military Justice to that effect in 2006. In other words, both the Senate and House believed that the crime could warrant death, a blow to Kennedy's assertions that Americans do not approve of executing prisoners for crimes in which no life is taken. The Justice Department acknowledged having erred in failing to inform the Court about the new law.

The Supreme Court denied a petition for a rehearing on the grounds that the military penalty did not change its conclusions. Justice Scalia joined in denying the rehearing, but criticized the Court's original decision. "I am voting against the petition for rehearing because the views of the American people on the death penalty for child rape were, to tell the truth, irrelevant to the majority's decision in this case. The majority opinion, after an unpersuasive attempt to show that a consensus against the penalty existed, in the end came down to this: 'The Constitution contemplates that in the end our own judgment will be brought to bear on the question of the acceptability of the death penalty under the Eighth Amendment.' . . . Of course the Constitution contemplates no such thing; the proposed Eighth Amendment would have been laughed to scorn if it had read 'no criminal penalty shall be imposed which the Supreme Court deems unacceptable.' But that is what the majority opinion said, and there is no reason to believe that absence of a national consensus would provoke second thoughts."

AMENDMENT IX.

The enumeration in the Constitution, of certain rights, shall not be construed to deny or disparage others retained by the people.[282]

---

282. "The great residuum" is how Madison (in 1789) character-ized all powers that are not granted by the Constitution and are re-tained by the people. But the Supreme Court famously preferred the word "penumbra," which merriam-webster.com defines as "a space of partial illumination (as in an eclipse) between the perfect shadow on all sides and the full light," or, among other definitions, "a body of rights held to be guaranteed by implication in a civil constitution." The word sprang into the national debate when an executive of Planned Parenthood, Estelle Griswold, challenged Connecticut over her contraception clinic. In *Griswold v. Connecticut*, Justice Douglas considered the Ninth Amendment to be one of several penumbras that make up "zones of privacy." Justice Goldberg wrote at length about the Ninth Amendment in a concurring opinion: "To hold that a right so basic and fundamental and so deep-rooted in our society as the right of privacy in marriage may be infringed because that right is not guaranteed in so many words by the first eight amendments to the Constitution is to ignore the Ninth Amendment and to give it no effect whatsoever."

Goldberg cited Joseph Story, who stated that the Ninth Amend-ment "was manifestly introduced to prevent any perverse or ingen-ious misapplication of the well-known maxim, that an affirmation in particular cases implies a negation in all others," as well as the re-verse, "that a negation in particular cases implies an affirmation in all others." But Justice Black, dissenting in *Griswold*, noted that the Constitution nowhere expressly spells out a right to privacy: "I like my privacy as well as the next one, but I am nevertheless compelled to admit that government has a right to invade it unless prohibited by some specific constitutional provision."

Griswold was a watershed in Ninth Amendment jurisprudence. One academic, Russell Caplan, has written that the Ninth Amendment had been "mostly a source of intermittent curiosity" until *Griswold* "catapulted" it "into respectability." In *Roe v. Wade*, Justice Blackmun reprised how the district court had decided that the choice of whether to have children was a fundamental right protected by the Ninth Amendment. He argued for the privacy right by relying on other grounds but clung to the Ninth Amendment just in case: "This right of privacy, whether it be founded in the Fourteenth Amendment's concept of personal liberty and restrictions upon state action, as we feel it is, or, as the District Court determined, in the Ninth Amendment's reservation of rights to the people, is broad enough to encompass a woman's decision whether or not to terminate her pregnancy."

Douglas, in his concurrence in *Roe*, wrote that the Ninth Amendment did not conceive of "federally enforceable rights," but rather meant that the people retain "customary, traditional, and time-honored rights, amenities, privileges and immunities that come within the sweep of 'the Blessings of Liberty'" from the Preamble. Judge Bork, during his fractious confirmation hearings in 1987, said he viewed the Ninth as "an amendment that says 'Congress shall make no' and then there is an inkblot, and you can't read the rest of it, and that is the only copy you have."

AMENDMENT X.

The powers not delegated to the United States by the Constitution, nor prohibited by it to the States, are reserved to the States respectively, or to the people.[283]

---

283. The Articles of Confederation contained the word "expressly" in its formulation: "Each state retains its sovereignty, freedom, and independence, and every Power, Jurisdiction and right,

which is not by this confederation expressly delegated to the United States, in Congress assembled." But during constitutional debates, Madison opposed attempts in the House of Representatives to strengthen state power by likewise including the word "expressly" in the amendment. The proposal would have prevented the federal government from claiming implied capacities. In *United States v. Sprague* (1931), the Court declared that the amendment "added nothing to the instrument as originally ratified," and in *United States v. Darby* (1941) it dismissed the Tenth Amendment as stating "but a truism."

In recent years the Tenth has gained respect. In *New York v. United States*, the state of New York sued the federal government over an attempt to direct the state in its disposal of radioactive waste. The government tried to threaten the state, mandating that it would have to take title to the radioactive waste if it did not properly dispose of it. Justice O'Connor, writing for the Court in 1992, adopted an anticommandeering principle and held that states could not be compelled "to enact or administer a federal regulatory program." Citing the Tenth Amendment, O'Connor added, "States are not mere political subdivisions of the United States. State governments are neither regional offices nor administrative agencies of the Federal Government. The positions occupied by state officials appear nowhere on the Federal Government's most detailed organizational chart."

Just as *New York v. United States* limited federal encroachment on state legislatures, *Printz v. United States* sought to curb federal interference with state executive branches. The chief law enforcement officer in Maryland's Ravalli County, Jay Printz, and in Arizona's Graham County, Richard Mack, sued the government for forcing state and local executive branch members to follow a federal regulation. The case involved a gun control measure, the Brady Bill, named for the former presidential aide shot by a would-be assassin of President Reagan. The Brady Bill required local and state police authorities to conduct background checks on those wishing to purchase firearms. Writing for the 5 to 4 majority, Justice Scalia said he found no support for this in the *Federalist Papers* or in early Congresses. He held that the part of the Brady Bill that directs state and local officers to follow a federal regulation in conducting background checks violated the Tenth Amendment. "The power of the Federal Government," he wrote, "would be augmented immeasurably if it were able to impress into its service—and at no cost to itself—the police officers of the 50 States."

AMENDMENT XI.

[Proposed 1794; Ratified 1798]

The Judicial power of the United States shall not be construed to extend to any suit in law or equity, commenced or prosecuted against one of the United States by Citizens of another State, or by Citizens or Subjects of any Foreign State.[284]

---

284. It was the reaction to a lawsuit, *Chisholm v. Georgia,* that startled the Congress into passing the Eleventh Amendment. The case involved a South Carolina resident, Alexander Chisholm, who was entrusted with the estate of another South Carolinian, Robert Farquhar, who had died. Chisholm sued the state of Georgia to compensate Farquhar for the debt he incurred in helping Georgia during the Revolutionary War. The state of Georgia failed to show up for the trial, as it believed that federal courts lacked jurisdiction. With each of the four justices in the majority writing separate opinions, the Court sided with Chisholm. They relied on Article III, which allowed judicial power over controversies "between a State and Citizens of another State." Chief Justice Jay wrote that although he believed citizens of one state could sue another state, there might be exceptions. He was "far from being prepared to say, that an individual may sue a state on bills of credit issued before the constitution was established, and which were issued and received on the faith of the state, and at a time when no ideas or expectations of judicial interposition were entertained or contemplated."

Justice Blair, also in the majority, queried whether there was "sufficient ground from which to conclude, that the jurisdiction of this court reaches the case where a state is plaintiff, but not where it is defendant?" He inquired, "In this latter case, should any man be asked, whether it was not a controversy between a state and citizen of another state, must not the answer be in the affirmative?" He further wrote, "A dispute between A. and B. is surely a dispute between B. and A. Both cases, I have no doubt, were intended; and probably, the state was first named, in respect to the dignity of a state." The sole dissenting voice was Justice Iredell, whose view was eventually vindicated. He concluded that there were neither new nor old laws "that in any manner authorize the present suit, either by precedent or by analogy. The consequence of which, in my opinion, clearly is, that the suit in question cannot be maintained, nor, of course, the motion made upon it be complied with." Alarmed over the decision, Congress rushed through the Eleventh Amendment.

AMENDMENT XII.

[Proposed 1803; Ratified 1804]

The Electors shall meet in their respective states, and vote by ballot for President and Vice-President, one of whom, at least, shall not be an inhabitant of the same state with themselves;[285] they shall name in their ballots the person voted for as President, and in distinct ballots the person voted for as Vice-President, and they shall make distinct lists of all persons voted for as President, and of all persons voted for as Vice-President, and of the number of votes for each, which lists they shall sign and certify, and transmit sealed to the seat of the government of the United States, directed to the President of the Senate;—The President of the Senate shall, in the presence of the Senate and House of Representatives, open all the certificates and the votes shall then be counted;—The person having the greatest number of votes for President, shall be the President, if such number be a majority of the whole number of

Electors appointed; and if no person have such majority, then from the persons having the highest numbers not exceeding three on the list of those voted for as President, the House of Representatives shall choose immediately, by ballot, the President. But in choosing the President, the votes shall be taken by states, the representation from each state having one vote; a quorum for this purpose shall consist of a member or members from two-thirds of the states, and a majority of all the states shall be necessary to a choice. And if the House of Representatives shall not choose a President whenever the right of choice shall devolve upon them, before the fourth day of March next following, then the Vice-President shall act as President, as in the case of the death or other constitutional disability of the President.—The person having the greatest number of votes as Vice-President, shall be the Vice-President, if such number be a majority of the whole number of Electors appointed, and if no person have a majority, then from the two highest numbers on the list, the Senate shall choose the Vice-President; a quorum for the purpose shall consist of two-thirds of the whole number of Senators, and a majority of the whole number shall be necessary to a choice. But no person constitutionally ineligible to the office of President shall be eligible to that of Vice-President of the United States.

---

285. To avoid any confrontation with this clause, in 2000 Richard Cheney changed his voter registration to Wyoming, the state in which he was born and which he represented in Congress, from Texas, in which he worked as chief executive officer of Halliburton. Three Texans sued, claiming that, for the purposes of this amendment, Cheney was a Texan, making it, because George W. Bush was also a Texan, unconstitutional for Texas electors to cast votes in the presidential election for the Bush-Cheney ticket. The United States District Court for the Northern District of Texas decided, in *Jones v. Bush*, in favor of the future President Bush, concluding that the three Texans who filed the case did not have standing to sue because they

"failed to demonstrate a specific and individualized injury from the impending alleged violation of the Twelfth Amendment" and also were "unable to show personal injury through harm done to non-defendant candidates." The Twelfth Amendment replaced the original electoral procedure outlined in Article II, Section 1, Clause 3 of the Constitution. For a history of the political disaster that led to this amendment's passage, please see footnote 161 on page 122.

AMENDMENT XIII.

[Proposed 1865; Ratified 1865]

1. Neither slavery nor involuntary servitude, except as a punishment for crime whereof the party shall have been duly convicted, shall exist within the United States, or any place subject to their jurisdiction.[286]

2. Congress shall have power to enforce this article by appropriate legislation.[287]

---

286. The Thirteenth Amendment, writes historian Alexander Tsesis, "changed the fundamental structure of U.S. law." He argues that the delegates to the Philadelphia Convention "decided that the Three-Fifths Clause, the Fugitive Slave Clause, and the twenty-year protection on slave importation were more important to drafting an acceptable Constitution than including a Bill of Rights." From the founding of the country, he goes on to say, "slavery's protagonists held a decisive share of power in the highest echelons of national decision making." All the more dramatic was the impact of the Thirteenth Amendment, which, as Tsesis characterizes it, "abolished the political structure that was linked to slavery."

Some, such as Senator Sumner, the radical of Massachusetts, wanted to slip the amendment through on ratification by only the northern states. Tsesis writes that Lincoln, in his last public address, "did not outright disagree with Sumner's perspective but thought 'such a ratification would be questionable and sure to be persistently questioned.' The President therefore favored ratification by three-fourths of all states so that the amendment's authority would be incontrovertible. Lincoln envisioned ratification as part of the process of Southern reconstruction and did not want to alienate states like Louisiana whose legislature had already voted for ratification." That is how it panned out under President Andrew Johnson, who, during Reconstruction, pressed for the abrogation of secessionist ordinances, adoption of new state constitutions, repudiation of war debts, and ratification of the Thirteenth Amendment.

The scope of the Thirteenth Amendment was limited when the Supreme Court consolidated a group of pleadings as the Civil Rights Cases of 1883. The Court seemed to comprehend the potential of the Thirteenth Amendment: "It is true that slavery cannot exist without law, any more than property in lands and goods can exist without law, and, therefore, the Thirteenth Amendment may be regarded as nullifying all State laws which establish or uphold slavery. But it has a reflex character also, establishing and decreeing universal civil and political freedom throughout the United States, and it is assumed that the power vested in Congress to enforce the article by appropriate legislation clothes Congress with power to pass all laws necessary and proper for abolishing all badges and incidents of slavery in the United States." But the Court held, as was summarized in its syllabus, that the Thirteenth Amendment "relates only to slavery and involuntary servitude" and that "the denial of equal accommodations in inns, public conveyances, and places of public amusement (which is forbidden by the sections in question), imposes no badge of slavery or involuntary servitude upon the party." And the Court left the rest to be sorted out under the Fourteenth Amendment.

The decision met with a dissent from Justice Harlan, who concluded with this famous paragraph: "Today it is the colored race which is denied, by corporations and individuals wielding public authority, rights fundamental in their freedom and citizenship. At some future time, it may be that some other race will fall under the ban of race discrimination. If the constitutional amendments be enforced according to the intent with which, as I conceive, they were adopted, there cannot be, in this republic, any class of human beings in practical subjection to another class with power in the latter to dole out to the former just such privileges as they may choose to grant. The supreme law of the land has decreed that no authority shall be exercised in this country upon the basis of discrimination, in respect of civil rights, against freemen and citizens because of their race, color, or previous condition of servitude. To that decree—for the due enforcement of which, by appropriate legislation, Congress has been invested with express power—everyone must bow, whatever may have been, or whatever now are, his individual views as to the wisdom or policy either of the recent changes in the fundamental law or of the legislation which has been enacted to give them effect."

In the event, the Court's error was not to be reversed until after World War II and the rise of the modern civil rights movement. In 1968 the Supreme Court, in deciding a housing discrimination case called *Jones v. Alfred H. Mayer Co.,* declared that the Thirteenth Amendment "authorized Congress to do more than merely dissolve the legal bond by which the Negro slave was held to his master; it gave Congress the power rationally to determine what are the badges and the incidents of slavery and the authority to translate that determination into effective legislation." Mississippi did not ratify the Thirteenth Amendment until 1995, as historian James Edward Bond points out.

287. This was the first grant of power to the Congress to enforce a provision of the Constitution, a grant attributed by Jack Rakove, a professor of history at Stanford University, to a "distrust of the will and capacity of the Supreme Court, an institution still tainted by the memory of the Dred Scott case (1857), to respond judicially to the opposition that emancipation might spark."

AMENDMENT XIV.

[Proposed 1866; Ratified 1868]

Section 1.[288] All persons born or naturalized in the United States and subject to the jurisdiction thereof,[289] are citizens of the United States and of the State wherein they reside.[290]

---

288. Were the amendments musical compositions, the Fourteenth would be the grand symphony in four movements, full of exciting themes, varied movements, and clashing cymbals—but none to rival what would be the first movement, Section 1. It set the stage for the generations-long series of legal cases through which the Bill of Rights is being, step by step, held to protect the rights of the people not only from the United States Congress but also from legislatures of the states.

This legal struggle began with a case involving the regulation of slaughterhouses in New Orleans. When the justices sat down to consider the matter, they were uncharacteristically humbled by the revolutionary implication of Section 1 of the Fourteenth Amendment. "No questions so far-reaching and pervading in their consequences, so profoundly interesting to the people of this country, and so important in their bearing upon the relations of the United States, of the several States to each other, and to the citizens of the States and of the United States, have been before this court during the official life of any of its present members," wrote Justice Miller.

As it turned out, the Supreme Court, in what came to be known as the Slaughterhouse Cases, forbore. It ruled that the Fourteenth Amendment did not preclude New Orleans from policing the slaughterhouses. But late in the nineteenth century and early in the twentieth, it began the process of incorporating the Bill of Rights and extending to the states the privileges and immunities and due process rights vouchsafed in the Constitution. The process is still under way, most pointedly at the moment in court cases involving whether gun control measures infringe on the Second Amendment right to keep and bear arms.

289. Should a foreign diplomat give birth while posted to America, the newborn would not be a citizen by virtue of being born in this country. This principle is mentioned in *Elk v. Wilkins*, on which more is below.

290. This sentence overturns the Supreme Court's decision in *Scott v. Sandford*, but it proved inadequate for John Elk, who moved to Omaha, Nebraska, severed his ties to the Indian tribe of his birth, started paying taxes, and joined the militia. Yet upon seeking to register to vote, he was turned away. Justice Gray, in rejecting Elk's claim, framed the question as "whether an Indian, born a member of one of the Indian tribes within the United States, is, merely by reason of his birth within the United States, and of his afterwards voluntarily separating himself from his tribe and taking up his residence among white citizens, a citizen of the United States, within the meaning of the first section of the Fourteenth Amendment of the Constitution."

Indians, the Court ruled, "although in a geographical sense born in the United States, are no more 'born in the United States and subject to the jurisdiction thereof,' within the meaning of the first section of the Fourteenth Amendment, than the children of subjects of any foreign government born within the domain of that government, or the children born within the United States, of ambassadors or other public ministers of foreign nations." Not until the federal government brokered a treaty with Elk's tribe that contained a provision inviting tribal members to become citizens would Elk have an avenue to citizenship. In a mighty dissent, Justice Harlan, joined by Justice Woods, wrote: "It seems to us that the Fourteenth Amendment, in so far as it was intended to confer national citizenship upon persons of the Indian race, is robbed of its vital force by a construction which excludes from such citizenship those who although born in tribal relations, are within the complete jurisdiction of the United States."

The result was to "shut down the fight for the rights of Indians as citizens. On into the next century a vast number of American Indi-

ans remained in a situation outlined in the 1857 *Dred Scott* decision."
Indians, as a matter of law, were given citizenship in 1924.

**No State shall make or enforce any law which shall abridge the priv-
ileges or immunities of citizens of the United States,**[291]

291. Here is one of the grounds on which the fight over gun control was shot out. The Supreme Court, in *District of Columbia v.
Heller*, recognized in 2008 that the Second Amendment's right to
keep and bear arms belongs to the individual and declared that the
federal government could not abridge that right. But it left open the
question of whether that holding served as a curb on state governments as well. More generally, the question of just what elements of
the Bill of Rights the framers of the Fourteenth intended to extend to
the states with this language has been—and, one can speculate, will
continue to be—fought among litigants, judges, and historians. In
McDonald v. Chicago, the Supreme Court did incorporate the Second
Amendment, limiting the degree to which the states can abridge the
right to keep and bear arms. But it did so using the due process clause
of the Fourteenth Amendment, rather than this clause.

nor shall any State deprive any person of life, liberty,[292, 293] **or property, without due process of law;**[294]

292. One of the most controversial cases in history is often discussed in terms of the word "privacy." But the word "liberty" is the
actual constitutional door through which the Supreme Court, in *Roe
v. Wade*, brought the right of privacy that protects abortions. "This
right of privacy, whether it be founded in the Fourteenth Amendment's concept of personal liberty and restrictions upon state action,

as we feel it is, or, as the District Court determined, in the Ninth Amendment's reservation of rights to the people, is broad enough to encompass a woman's decision whether or not to terminate her pregnancy," wrote Justice Blackmun in the opinion for the Court.

In *Planned Parenthood v. Casey* the Supreme Court in 1992 reiterated the central point of *Roe* in firmer language. Wrote Justice O'Connor: "Constitutional protection of the woman's decision to terminate her pregnancy derives from the Due Process Clause of the Fourteenth Amendment. It declares that no State shall 'deprive any person of life, liberty, or property, without due process of law.' The controlling word in the case before us is 'liberty.' Although a literal reading of the Clause might suggest that it governs only the procedures by which a State may deprive persons of liberty, for at least 105 years . . . the Clause has been understood to contain a substantive component as well, one 'barring certain government actions regardless of the fairness of the procedures used to implement them.'"

Again, from O'Connor: "Our law affords constitutional protection to personal decisions relating to marriage, procreation, contraception, family relationships, child rearing, and education. Our cases recognize 'the right of the individual, married or single, to be free from unwarranted governmental intrusion into matters so fundamentally affecting a person as the decision whether to bear or beget a child.' Our precedents 'have respected the private realm of family life which the state cannot enter.' These matters, involving the most intimate and personal choices a person may make in a lifetime, choices central to personal dignity and autonomy, are central to the liberty protected by the Fourteenth Amendment. At the heart of liberty is the right to define one's own concept of existence, of meaning, of the universe, and of the mystery of human life. Beliefs about these matters could not define the attributes of personhood were they formed under compulsion of the State."

William Rehnquist, then an associate justice, dissented in *Roe v. Wade*: "To reach its result, the Court necessarily has had to find within the scope of the Fourteenth Amendment a right that was apparently completely unknown to the drafters of the Amendment. As early as 1821, the first state law dealing directly with abortion was enacted by the Connecticut Legislature. . . . By the time of the adoption of the Fourteenth Amendment in 1868, there were at least 36 laws enacted by state or territorial legislatures limiting abortion. While many States have amended or updated their laws, 21 of the laws on the books in 1868 remain in effect today. Indeed, the Texas statute struck down today was, as the majority notes, first enacted in 1857, and 'has remained substantially unchanged to the present time.' There apparently was no question concerning the validity of this provision or of any of the other state statutes when the Fourteenth Amendment was adopted. The only conclusion possible from this history is that the drafters did not intend to have the Fourteenth Amendment withdraw from the States the power to legislate with respect to this matter."

293. Joseph Lochner, proprietor of a bakeshop in Utica, New York, employed Aman Schmitter for more hours a week than was allowed under the state's Bakeshop Act. When the case reached the Supreme Court, the justices centered on the word "liberty" in the Fourteenth Amendment to strike down the state's restriction on the liberty to work as much as one wanted. Wrote Justice Rufus Peckham for the Court: "The general right to make a contract in relation to his business is part of the liberty of the individual protected by the 14th Amendment of the Federal Constitution." Added he: "The right to purchase or to sell labor is part of the liberty protected by this amendment." The decision opened what is called the "Lochner era," in which the government's authority to regulate business was held in check, though the Court has been less vigilant in the years since, starting, most notably, with *West Coast Hotel v. Parrish*, permitting the establishment of a minimum wage.

294. It is through the due process clause that the Supreme Court has done much of the incorporation by which the Bill of Rights is applied to the states.

nor deny to any person within its jurisdiction the equal protection of the laws.[295]

---

295. For nearly sixty years, the Supreme Court had been inviting states to segregate the races—despite this clause. The invitation was a case called *Plessy v. Ferguson*, in which the Court upheld a Louisiana law providing for segregated trains and used this amendment to do it. "We think the enforced separation of the races, as applied to the internal commerce of the state, neither abridges the privileges or immunities of the colored man, deprives him of his property without due process of law, nor denies him the equal protection of the laws, within the meaning of the Fourteenth Amendment." Then along came a welder from Topeka, Kansas, who, wanting his eight-year-old daughter to avoid a five-mile bus ride to a segregated school, sought to enroll her in a white school close to their home. When he was refused, Oliver Brown went to court with a new argument under this amendment and etched his name, and that of his daughter, Linda, into history for all time. Wrote Chief Justice Earl Warren in *Brown v. Board of Education*: "The plaintiffs contend that segregated public schools are not 'equal' and cannot be made 'equal,' and that hence they are deprived of the equal protection of the laws." The court, Warren wrote, concluded "that, in the field of public education, the doctrine of 'separate but equal' has no place. Separate educational facilities are inherently unequal. Therefore, we hold that the plaintiffs and others similarly situated for whom the actions have been brought are, by reason of the segregation complained of, deprived of the equal protection of the laws guaranteed by the Fourteenth Amendment. This disposition makes unnecessary any discussion whether such segregation also violates the Due Process Clause of the Fourteenth Amendment."

In recent years, the equal protection clause has been cited by opponents of ameliorating discrimination through affirmative action. Justice Thomas argues that the equal protection clause prevents government officials from divvying up citizens into groups based on race in any respect. When the Supreme Court upheld the race conscious admissions policy of the University of Michigan Law School in 2003, in a case known as *Grutter v. Bollinger,* Thomas dissented: "In my view, there is no basis for a right of public universities to do what would otherwise violate the Equal Protection Clause." He wrote: "The Constitution abhors classifications based on race, not only because those classifications can harm favored races or are based on illegitimate motives, but also because every time the government places citizens on racial registers and makes race relevant to the provision of burdens or benefits, it demeans us all."

SECTION 2. Representatives shall be apportioned among the several States according to their respective numbers, counting the whole number[296] of persons in each State, excluding Indians not taxed. But when the right to vote at any election for the choice of electors for President and Vice President of the United States, Representatives in Congress, the Executive and Judicial officers of a State, or the members of the Legislature thereof, is denied to any of the male[297] inhabitants of such State, being twenty-one years of age, and citizens of the United States, or in any way abridged, except for participation in rebellion, or other crime, the basis of representation therein shall be reduced in the proportion which the number of such male citizens shall bear to the whole number of male citizens twenty-one years of age in such State.[298]

---

296. The three-fifths clause was overwritten by the Civil War. This language redrafts that clause to remove any sanction of slavery.

297. For the first time, gender is written into the Constitution. This mention infuriated many feminists of the time, as it conditioned federal protection of the right to vote in national and state elections on gender.

298. A threat that has yet to be acted upon. It gives Congress a mechanism by which to reduce the House seats of a state should its

black citizens be prevented from voting, but it requires a solid majority in the House to agree to adjust the apportionment. It was tested by Henry L. Saunders of Virginia, who, while running for election to the House of Representatives, filed a suit claiming that Virginia's poll tax was disenfranchising some 60 percent of the state's qualified voters. He demanded that Virginia's delegation be reduced accordingly, under this part of the Fourteenth Amendment. The case made it as high as the Fourth Circuit U.S. Court of Appeals, which in a 1945 decision ruled that the poll tax was constitutional. Of Saunders's demand that Virginia's delegation be cut to four from nine, the Fourth Circuit opined:

> We think that this contention presents a question political in its nature which must be determined by the legislative branch of the government and is not justiciable. It is well known that the elective franchise has been limited or denied to citizens in various States of the union in past years, but no serious attempt has been made by Congress to enforce the mandate of the second section of the Fourteenth Amendment, and it is noteworthy that there are no instances in which the courts have attempted to revise the apportionment of Representatives by Congress.

SECTION 3. No person shall be a Senator or Representative in Congress, or elector of President and Vice President, or hold any office, civil or military, under the United States, or under any State, who, having previously taken an oath, as a member of Congress, or as an officer of the United States, or as a member of any State legislature, or as an executive or judicial officer of any State, to support the Constitution of the United States, shall have engaged in insurrection or rebellion against the same, or given aid or comfort to the enemies thereof. But Congress may by a vote of two-thirds of each House, remove such disability.[299]

299. This ban that prevented former Confederates from holding office provoked a Texas legislative committee to assert that to accept the provision would be "to barter our birthright for the empty shadow of representation offered in these Amendments." More than a century later, Congress made a symbolic gesture of restoring the rights of a Confederate general, Robert E. Lee, and of the president of the Confederacy, Jefferson Davis. President Carter suggested that Davis had been "singled out for punishment" and asserted that reconciliation between North and South was now officially complete.

Section 4. The validity of the public debt of the United States, authorized by law, including debts incurred for payment of pensions and bounties for services in suppressing insurrection or rebellion, shall not be questioned. But neither the United States nor any State shall assume or pay any debt or obligation incurred in aid of insurrection or rebellion against the United States, or any claim for the loss or emancipation of any slave; but all such debts, obligations and claims shall be held illegal and void.[300]

Section 5. The Congress shall have power to enforce, by appropriate legislation, the provisions of this article.[301]

300. This clause ensures that the federal government will never reimburse slaveholders. One subplot of the years after the Civil War involved a spate of cases questioning whether former slave owners remained obliged to pay off whatever debts they owed slave traders, from whom slaves were often purchased via installments. The Supreme Court demanded that such contracts be honored. The case of *Osborn v. Nicholson* concerned an Arkansas man who sold a slave in 1861 and sought what money was still owed from the purchaser. The court ruled that "slavery having been recognized as lawful at the time when and the place where the contract was made, and the contract having been one which at the time when it was made could have been

enforced in the courts of every state of the Union and in the courts of every civilized country elsewhere, the right to sue upon it was not to be considered as taken away by the Thirteenth Amendment."

301. "Immediate opposition" greeted the first draft of this part of the Fourteenth Amendment, according to Justice Kennedy, writing for the Court in an opinion striking down as unconstitutional a law called the Religious Freedom Restoration Act. The first draft had been submitted after the Civil War by the Joint Committee on Reconstruction of the Thirty-ninth Congress. It said: "The Congress shall have power to make all laws which shall be necessary and proper to secure to the citizens of each State all privileges and immunities of citizens in the several States, and to all persons in the several States equal protection in the rights of life, liberty, and property." But, in Justice Kennedy's account, members of Congress from "across the political spectrum" complained that the draft "gave Congress too much legislative power at the expense of the existing constitutional structure." The language that was finally adopted gave Congress power that was, as Justice Kennedy put it, "no longer plenary but remedial." The enforcement power was used by the Congress in 1871 in the Ku Klux Klan Act.

Justice Kennedy's review of the history of the Religious Freedom Restoration Act came in the 1990s in the case of a church at Boerne, Texas. The church had sued after local zoning authorities denied it a permit to expand its building. In throwing out the Religious Freedom Restoration Act, the Court asserted the supremacy of its own authority over that of the Congress, despite any niceties of Section 5 of the Fourteenth Amendment. It put the matter this way: "It is for Congress in the first instance to 'determin[e] whether and what legislation is needed to secure the guarantees of the Fourteenth Amendment,' and its conclusions are entitled to much deference. Congress' discretion is not unlimited, however, and the courts retain the power, as they have since *Marbury* v. *Madison*, to determine if Congress has exceeded its authority under the Constitution." It said that in passing the Religious Freedom Restoration Act Congress had gone too far.

AMENDMENT XV.

[Passed 1869; Ratified 1870]

1. The right of citizens of the United States to vote shall not be denied or abridged by the United States or by any State on account of race, color, or previous condition of servitude.

2. The Congress shall have power to enforce this article by appropriate legislation.[302]

---

302. President Grant greeted the passage of this amendment by announcing that black suffrage was now "out of politics and reconstruction completed." In a special message to Congress following the amendment's ratification, he also called it "a measure of grander importance than any other one act of the kind from the foundation of our free government to the present day." In the cold light of history, however, it proved an inadequate piece of constitutional craftsmanship.

The amendment was passed at the end of an extraordinary period in American history, as African Americans acceded to office in a number of the southern states. They emerged in the majority in several state constitutional conventions and were sent to Congress in numbers once unimagined. The first African American in the Senate was sent by the state of Mississippi. Historian Richard Zuczek has written that for "the period between 1867 and the early 1870s, interracial democracy was an American reality." Republicans advanced the idea of the Fifteenth Amendment, he suggests, because they felt it necessary to secure black voting rights on a more permanent basis.

Several versions of what would become this amendment were considered. One version would have outlawed property, nativity, and literacy requirements for voting; another asserted that all adult male citizens had a universal right to vote. Republicans were motivated by concerns that they would appear hypocritical for allowing restrictions on black suffrage in the North while championing it in the South, and they also wanted to expand their party base. To secure the amendment's passage, they chose the least aggressive version. As a result, the Fifteenth Amendment that was ratified by the states was met with the schemes that disgraced America for another three-quarters of a century. Methods used to disenfranchise African Americans included grandfather clauses, whereby voting rights were restricted for everyone except people who had previously enjoyed the vote (i.e., whites), racial gerrymandering, discrimination in primary elections, poll taxes, and literacy tests. The enfranchisement of which Grant boasted was deferred until modern court decisions used the Fifteenth Amendment to validate the authorities Congress had legislated in the 1960s.

In *South Carolina v. Katzenbach*, the Court in 1966 upheld the Voting Rights Act of 1965, which required the attorney general to preclear changes to voting practices in areas that had a history of discrimination: "The language and purpose of the Fifteenth Amendment, the prior decisions construing its several provisions, and the general doctrines of constitutional interpretation all point to one fundamental principle. As against the reserved powers of the States, Congress may use any rational means to effectuate the constitutional prohibition of racial discrimination in voting." It added, "After enduring nearly a century of widespread resistance to the Fifteenth Amendment, Congress has marshalled an array of potent weapons against the evil, with authority in the Attorney General to employ them effectively."

AMENDMENT XVI.

[Proposed 1909; Ratified 1913]

The Congress shall have power to lay and collect taxes on incomes, from whatever source derived, without apportionment among the several States, and without regard to any census or enumeration.[303]

---

303. Enthusiasts who seek a sense of the intimacy that Supreme Court justices have sought to establish with the founders would be hard put to find a better opinion to study than that issued by Chief Justice Melville Fuller in 1895, in holding certain levies under the Income Tax Act of 1894 to be unconstitutional. The issue was whether taxes on certain kinds of rent and dividends and interest were "direct taxes," and therefore had to be, under Article I, Section 9, apportioned according to the population. The Court's decision in *Pollock v. Farmers' Loan and Trust Co.*, wrote Edward Corwin, "put most of the taxable wealth of the country out of the reach of the National Government," and led to the adoption of this amendment in 1913.

In *Pollock*, the Supreme Court invalidated the income tax law then in place on several grounds, the first of which was that "in imposing a tax on the income or rents of real estate, [it] imposes a tax upon the real estate itself, and in imposing a tax on the interest or other income of bonds or other personal property held for the purposes of income or ordinarily yielding income, [it] imposes a tax upon the personal estate itself; that such tax is a direct tax, and void because imposed without regard to the rule of apportionment, and that, by reason thereof, the whole law is invalidated." The Court reckoned also that the law violated the requirement that all duties, imposts, and excises shall be uniform throughout the United States.

Now read the chief justice on the framers: "The men who framed and adopted that instrument had just emerged from the struggle for independence whose rallying cry had been that 'taxation and representation go together.' The mother country had taught the colonists, in the contests waged to establish that taxes could not be imposed by the sovereign except as they were granted by the representatives of the realm, that self-taxation constituted the main security against oppression." The chief justice quoted Edmund Burke, summarizing his speech "Conciliation with America" this way: "The principle was that the consent of those who were expected to pay it was essential to the validity of any tax."

Then Fuller ruminated on how the states "were about, for all national purposes embraced in the Constitution, to become one, united under the same sovereign authority and governed by the same laws. But as they still retained their jurisdiction over all persons and things within their territorial limits, except where surrendered to the general government or restrained by the Constitution, they were careful to see to it that taxation and representation should go together, so that the sovereignty reserved should not be impaired, and that, when Congress, and especially the House of Representatives, where it was specifically provided that all revenue bills must originate, voted a tax upon property, it should be with the consciousness, and under the responsibility, that, in so doing, the tax so voted would proportionately fall upon the immediate constituents of those who imposed it."

He noted that not only did the states give, via the Constitution, the Congress the power to tax persons and property, but they "surrendered their own power to levy taxes on imports and to regulate commerce," though all thirteen were seaboard states. Then he wrote of the importance of remembering that "the fifty-five members of the constitutional convention were men of great sagacity, fully conversant with governmental problems, deeply conscious of the nature of their task, and profoundly convinced that they were laying the foundations of a vast future empire." He reviewed how they had read and studied history and Europe, and were also familiar with the "modes of taxation pursued in the several States." He quoted Madison, in 46 *Federalist*: "The Federal and state governments are, in fact, but different agents and trustees of the people, constituted with different powers and designated for different purposes."

And he was just getting warmed up. He reprised the colloquies in Philadelphia, quoting Pinckney's and Randolph's plans leading up to the great compromise that he characterized as "resting on the doctrine that the right of representation ought to be conceded to every community on which tax is to be imposed." He then proceeded to the objections to ratification, quoting such Anti-Federalists as Luther Martin, before launching into an essay on the particulars of the debate in several of the individual ratifying conventions. And he then turned to a review of the case law that had started to mount between the ratification of the Constitution and the end of the nineteenth century. It's no wonder that the country concluded that if the Congress was going to make another attempt at an income tax, it would have to amend its basic document.

AMENDMENT XVII.

[Proposed 1912; Ratified 1913]

The Senate of the United States shall be composed of two Senators from each State, elected by the people thereof, for six years; and each Senator shall have one vote. The electors in each State shall have the qualifications requisite for electors of the most numerous branch of the State legislatures.[304]

304. This changed the method of choosing senators, moving the choice out of the state legislatures and giving it directly to the voters, but it left unchanged the fundamental differences between the two houses of the federal legislature. The House of Representatives still represents the people. The Senate still represents the states as incorporated bodies and gives each of them, though they may be of different sizes and populations, an equal vote. The original approach, established in Article I, Section 3, Clause 2, had become problematic in the late nineteenth century, when graft and Reconstruction politics

led to abuses that undermined the idea of the Senate as a representative body. Deadlocks in state legislatures left Senate vacancies unfilled; an Indiana Senate seat, for example, stayed empty for two years due to tensions between the state's more Republican northern region and Democratic southern region. Some Senate elections were also plagued by corruption within the state legislatures. By the time the Seventeenth Amendment was finally passed by a previously reluctant Congress, many states had already attempted to address the problem by holding referendums that determined the legislatures' choices.

A number of figures, however, have concluded that direct election of senators was an error. In 2004, shortly before retiring from the Senate, Georgia Democrat Zell Miller issued a call for the repeal of this amendment, saying that federalism "has become to this generation of leaders some vague philosophy of the past that is dead, dead, dead." He said: "Reformers of the early 1900s killed it dead and cremated the body when they allowed for the direct election of U.S. senators." He argued that direct elections had "allowed Washington's special interests to call the shots, whether it's filling judicial vacancies or issuing regulations. The state governments aided in their own collective suicide by going along with the popular fad of the time." He suggested Congress would not have been able to impose on the states various unfunded mandates were U.S. senators "still chosen by and responsible to the state legislatures." He called the amendment "the death of the careful balance between state and federal governments. As designed by that brilliant and very practical group of Founding Fathers, the two governments would be in competition with each other and neither could abuse or threaten the other." Commentator Bruce Bartlett wrote in the *National Review* that it was "a truth that no senator except a retiring one would dare say."

In Montana, an effort was begun in 2002 to amend the Seventeenth Amendment, with a joint resolution submitted to the Montana house and senate. It begins with a long list of predicates—calling the election of U.S. senators by state legislatures "the political mechanism against congressional encroachment into the sovereignty of the states," asserting that "a Senator's general responsibility is to represent state government and the State Legislature," and noting that "the State Legislature has a role in compelling accountability from United States Senators." Its proposed amendment would not only provide for the state legislatures to choose senators but would preclude Congress from enacting any legislation "affecting the senatorial selection process." The proposed amendment to the Seventeenth Amendment has yet to pass the Montana legislature.

When vacancies happen in the representation of any State in the Senate, the executive authority of such State shall issue writs of election to fill such vacancies: Provided, That the legislature of any State may empower the executive thereof to make temporary appointments until the people fill the vacancies by election as the legislature may direct.[305]

This amendment shall not be so construed as to affect the election or term of any Senator chosen before it becomes valid as part of the Constitution.

---

305. Even while the direct election of senators is coming under renewed criticism, the Seventeenth Amendment's second clause, which enables governors to fill Senate vacancies, is being questioned. This arises largely from the scandal that erupted in December 2008, when the governor of Illinois, Rod Blagojevich, was arrested by the FBI amid allegations that he had sought to sell the Senate seat being vacated by the new president, Barack Obama. After the allegations surfaced but before the governor was impeached, convicted, and removed from office, Blagojevich elevated to the Senate a Democratic politician, Roland Burris. At first the Democratic leadership in the Senate tried to block the appointment but soon acknowledged it lacked standing to do so. Once Burris was seated, it emerged that he had given conflicting testimony in respect of his ties to Blagojevich, and calls were made for his resignation,

including one from the senior senator of Illinois, Richard Durbin. Burris has denied any wrongdoing.

AMENDMENT XVIII.

[Proposed 1917; Ratified 1919; Repealed 1933]

After one year from the ratification of this article the manufacture, sale, or transportation of intoxicating liquors within, the importation thereof into, or the exportation thereof from the United States and all territory subject to the jurisdiction thereof for beverage purposes is hereby prohibited.[306]

The Congress and the several States shall have concurrent power to enforce this article by appropriate legislation.

This article shall be inoperative unless it shall have been ratified as an amendment to the Constitution by the legislatures of the several States, as provided in the Constitution, within seven years from the date of the submission hereof to the States by the Congress.

---

306. This is the only amendment to restrict liberty, a point that has been widely remarked on. Doug Kendall and Hannah McCrea of the Constitutional Accountability Center note that Akhil Amar has observed that the Constitution has "thus far and in general, followed a progressive course." They suggest that the Eighteenth Amendment, in casting a moral judgment on actions important to such a sizable portion of the population, has taken the Constitution more in a conservative direction than any other amendment, and they cite its repeal as a "warning to those who would seek to further amend the Constitution to restrict Americans' individual freedoms."

Was the Eighteenth Amendment unconstitutional? Rhode Island, the one state that failed to ratify the amendment, thought so. The *New York Times* characterized the Ocean State's campaign for liquor as being waged "with the same spirit that kept her out of the Union until she was satisfied that amendments would be passed to the Constitution which would assure her the retention of her State sovereignty." The campaign was led by the state's attorney general, Herbert A. Rice. Reported the *Times*: "The point Rhode Island is trying to make is that she is fighting this question as a matter of State rights; that she is not interested in getting the help of the liquor or brewery interests; that their fight is secondary to hers and is not aligned with hers; that the retention of experts on constitutional or prohibition questions would detract from the inherent principle of the case; that these lawyers would probably base their contentions on arguments which any anti-prohibition organization might produce, and that Rhode Island, above all, wants it understood that it is entirely a State matter and not a prohibition matter which leads her to inaugurate proceedings to prove the Eighteenth Amendment invalid."

Rhode Island's arguments were voiced in the *National Prohibition Cases*, in which the Supreme Court upheld the Eighteenth Amendment. Rhode Island made an eloquent appeal. Rice, according to one historian of Prohibition, David Kyvig, argued that the amendment "invaded the sovereignty of Rhode Island and her people, an invasion not contemplated by the amending clause of the Constitution." Kyvig quotes the attorney general of New Jersey, which had ratified Prohibition, as arguing a similar line to Rhode Island's, stressing "that the Tenth Amendment reserved all unenumerated powers to the states and to the people." He argued that, as Kyvig puts it, the "right to surrender such powers" belonged "exclusively to the people themselves and not their legislative representatives."

According to Kyvig's account, Elihu Root's argument attracted the most attention. The former secretary of war, representing a New Jersey brewer, "asserted that the Eighteenth Amendment was simply unconstitutional." Kyvig quotes Root as warning the nine justices: "If your Honors shall find a way to declare this so-called Amendment to the Federal Constitution valid, then the Government of the United States as it has been known to us and to our forefathers will have ceased to exist. Your Honors will have discovered a new legislative authority hitherto unknown to the Constitution and quite untrammelled by any of its limitations. You will have declared that two-thirds of a quorum of each of the two Houses of the Legislatures of three-fourths of the States, may enact any legislation they please without any reference to the limitations of the Constitution, including the Bill of Rights itself. In that case, Your Honors, John Marshall need never have sat upon that bench." The Court dismissed such arguments in a cryptic opinion that is little remembered.

AMENDMENT XIX.

[Passed 1919; Ratified 1920]

The right of citizens of the United States to vote shall not be denied or abridged by the United States or by any State on account of sex.[307]

Congress shall have power to enforce this article by appropriate legislation.

---

307. Language in the Constitution had previously indicated that women could not be enfranchised or could be disenfranchised. The exception, ironically, was the Fourteenth Amendment, which contained an equal protection clause but confirmed the right to vote only for all "male inhabitants" over the age of twenty-one. In post-Revolutionary New Jersey, some women enjoyed voting rights until 1807. Writes historian D. Grier Stephenson: "From the outset of the Revolutionary War some women who met the property requirement were allowed to vote in New Jersey, apparently at the discretion of local election officials—until 1807 at least. In that year the law was changed to exclude all but 'free, white male citizen[s]' from the polls."

It took more than half a century of advocacy for women to gain suffrage. The movement employed legal challenges, militant protest, and political organizing. The amendment that was ratified in 1920 was the same one that had been introduced in 1878. Although some states had already extended the vote to women, support for a national amendment accelerated in World War I, when women leaned into the war effort and served in government positions left vacant by departing soldiers. President Wilson, who had previously seemed doubtful about the virtues of a women's suffrage amendment, changed his position and backed it as a war measure, which made it politically palatable to lawmakers.

AMENDMENT XX.

[Proposed 1932; Ratified 1933]

The terms of the President and Vice President shall end at noon[308] on the 20th day of January, and the terms of Senators and Representatives at noon on the 3d day of January, of the years in which such terms would have ended if this article had not been ratified; and the terms of their successors shall then begin.

---

308. This establishes when the presidential term ends, but when does it begin—when the previous term ends or when the president takes the constitutional oath that Article II requires the president to swear or affirm before "he enter on the Execution of his Office"? The plain language of these clauses from two parts of the Constitution suggest that a person might be president for a few moments without having the authority to "enter the Execution" of his duties. Amid the pomp and circumstance of Inauguration Day, it is not unusual for participants to diverge from the constitutional calendar. President Obama finished taking his oath at 12:05 PM, five minutes into his presidency. He may already have been president of America before Chief Justice Roberts began to administer the constitutional oath, but he had to take the oath before he was in full possession of constitutional authority. (Please see page 132.)

The Congress shall assemble at least once in every year, and such meeting shall begin at noon on the 3d day of January, unless they shall by law appoint a different day.[309]

If, at the time fixed for the beginning of the term of the President, the President elect shall have died, the Vice President elect shall become President. If a President shall not have been chosen before the time fixed for the beginning of his term, or if the President elect shall have failed to qualify, then the Vice President elect shall act as President until a President shall have qualified; and the Congress may by law provide for the case wherein neither a President elect nor a Vice President elect shall have qualified, declaring who shall then act as President, or the manner in which one who is to act shall be selected, and such person shall act accordingly until a President or Vice President shall have qualified.

The Congress may by law provide for the case of the death of any of the persons from whom the House of Representatives may choose a President whenever the right of choice shall have devolved upon them, and for the case of the death of any of the persons from whom the Senate may choose a Vice President whenever the right of choice shall have devolved upon them.

Sections 1 and 2 shall take effect on the 15th day of October following the ratification of this article.

This article shall be inoperative unless it shall have been ratified as an amendment to the Constitution by the legislatures of three-fourths of the several States within seven years from the date of its submission.

———

309. This shortens the length of the lame duck session, and ensures that it is the newly elected House of Representatives, not the outgoing House, that chooses a president should the electoral

process fail to yield a winner. The Senate Judiciary Committee report on this amendment states:

> If it should happen that in the general election in November in presidential years no candidate for President had received a majority of all the electoral votes, the election of a President would then be thrown into the House of Representatives and the memberships of the House of Representatives called upon to elect a President would be the old Congress and not the new one just elected by the people. It might easily happen that the Members of the House of Representatives, upon whom devolved the solemn duty of electing a Chief Magistrate for 4 years, had themselves been repudiated at the election that had just occurred, and the country would be confronted with the fact that a repudiated House, defeated by the people themselves at the general election, would still have the power to elect a President who would be in control of the country for the next 4 years. It is quite apparent that such a power ought not to exist, and that the people having expressed themselves at the ballot box should through the Representatives then selected, be able to select the President for the ensuing term.

AMENDMENT XXI.

[Proposed 1933; Ratified 1933]

The eighteenth article of amendment to the Constitution of the United States is hereby repealed.

The transportation or importation into any State, Territory, or possession of the United States for delivery or use therein of intoxicating liquors, in violation of the laws thereof, is hereby prohibited.

This article shall be inoperative unless it shall have been ratified as an amendment to the Constitution by conventions in the several States, as provided in the Constitution, within seven years from the date of the submission hereof to the States by the Congress.[310]

---

310. In the classic movie comedy *Smokey and the Bandit* Burt Reynolds stars as the daredevil driver hired to smuggle beer from Texas to Atlanta. But a real-life constitutional struggle between the states and Congress over the power to regulate liquor involved the kind of interstate tariff wars that the commerce clause in Article I was designed to prevent. In 1936 the Supreme Court, in *State Board of Equalization v. Young's Market Co.*, upheld a California law that imposed a $500 annual license fee on those seeking to import beer. The Court wrote: "What the plaintiffs complain of is the refusal to let them import beer without paying for the privilege of importation. Prior to the Twenty-First Amendment, it would obviously have been unconstitutional to have imposed any fee for that privilege. The imposition would have been void not because it resulted in discrimination, but because the fee would be a direct burden on interstate commerce, and the commerce clause confers the right to import merchandise free into any state, except as Congress may otherwise provide. The exaction of a fee for the privilege of importation would

not, before the Twenty-First Amendment, have been permissible even if the state had exacted an equal fee for the privilege of transporting domestic beer from its place of manufacture to the wholesaler's place of business."

In two 1939 cases—one from Missouri, *Joseph S. Finch Co. v. McKittrich*, and one from Michigan, *Indianapolis Brewing Co. v. Liquor Control Comm'n*—the Court upheld retaliatory state laws that prohibited the importation of beer from states whose beer laws discriminated against their brewers. But the Court, like a tippler traipsing along a sidewalk, eventually veered off that line of reasoning, ruling against a Hawaiian tax exemption aimed at propping up the state's locally manufactured alcoholic beverages. Quoth the Court: "The tax exemption is not saved by the Twenty-first Amendment. The exemption violates a central tenet of the Commerce Clause, but is not supported by any clear concern of that Amendment in combating the evils of an unrestricted traffic in liquor. The central purpose of the Amendment was not to empower States to favor local liquor industry by erecting barriers to competition."

The Congress, despite having much of its regulatory power in respect of alcohol stripped away by the Twenty-first Amendment, struck upon the idea of withholding federal highway funds from states that refused to set the minimum drinking age at twenty-one. In *South Dakota v. Dole*, the Supreme Court held that this practice was not "invalidated by the spending power limitation that the conditional grant of federal funds must not be independently barred by other constitutional provisions (the Twenty-first Amendment here). Such limitation is not a prohibition on the indirect achievement of objectives which Congress is not empowered to achieve directly, but, instead, means that the power may not be used to induce the States to engage in activities that would themselves be unconstitutional. Here, if South Dakota were to succumb to Congress' blandishments and raise its drinking age to twenty-one, its action would not violate anyone's constitutional rights. Moreover, the relatively small financial inducement offered by Congress here—resulting from the

State's loss of only 5% of federal funds otherwise obtainable under certain highway grant programs—is not so coercive as to pass the point at which pressure turns into compulsion."

The Twenty-first Amendment is the only one to be ratified by state conventions rather than state legislatures. That requirement was at the insistence of the amendment's "wet" backers. They feared that ratification might be thwarted by state legislatures, where rural districts were overrepresented, rendering them more conservative. Proponents of the convention method argued generally that their plan was more democratic. Historian Everett Somerville Brown quotes the president of the Association Against the Prohibition Amendment, Jouett Shouse, as saying: "It is obvious that the only method whereby popular expression on this proposition, which deals so intimately with the life and habits of the people, could be had is through the convention method of ratification."

AMENDMENT XXII.

[Proposed 1947; Ratified 1951]

No person shall be elected to the office of the President more than twice,[311] and no person who has held the office of President, or acted as President, for more than two years of a term to which some other person was elected President shall be elected to the office of the President more than once. But this Article shall not apply to any person holding the office of President when this Article was proposed by the Congress, and shall not prevent any person who may be holding the office of President, or acting as President, during the term within which this Article becomes operative from holding the office of President or acting as President during the remainder of such term.

This article shall be inoperative unless it shall have been ratified as an amendment to the Constitution by the legislatures of three-fourths of the several States within seven years from the date of its submission to the States by the Congress.

311. Washington stepped down despite the near certainty that he would be reelected. It was not until President Franklin Roosevelt chose to stand for four terms that Congress enacted and the states ratified the Twenty-second Amendment. Nevertheless, the presidential term limit has met with some disapproval. Historians James MacGregor Burns and Susan Dunn, writing in the *New York Times* on January 5, 2006, warned of "second termitis." Citing President Nixon's Watergate, President Reagan's Iran-Contra affair, and President Clinton's impeachment, they asked: "Is there some human failing that affects second-term presidents, like arrogance or sheer fatigue?" The historians suggested that the Twenty-second Amendment was to blame. "A second-term president will, in effect, automatically be fired within four years. Inevitably his influence over Congress, and even his authority over the sprawling executive branch, weaken. His party leadership frays as presidential hopefuls carve out their own constituencies for the next election. Whether the president is trying to tamp down scandal or push legislation, he loses his ability to set the agenda."

Alexander Hamilton laid out the basic case against term limits as early as 72 *Federalist*: "Nothing appears more plausible at first sight, nor more ill-founded upon close inspection, than a scheme which in relation to the present point has had some respectable advocates—I mean that of continuing the chief magistrate in office for a certain time, and then excluding him from it, either for a limited period or forever after." He warned of a "diminution of the inducements to good behavior"; "the temptation to sordid views, to peculation, and, in some instances, to usurpation"; "the depriving the community of the advantage of the experience gained by the chief magistrate in the exercise of his office"; "the banishing men from stations in which, in certain emergencies of the state, their presence might be of the greatest moment to the public interest or safety"; and an "interdiction of stability in the administration."

AMENDMENT XXIII.

[Proposed 1960; Ratified 1961]

1. The District constituting the seat of Government of the United States shall appoint in such manner as the Congress may direct: A number of electors of President and Vice President equal to the whole number of Senators and Representatives in Congress to which the District would be entitled if it were a State, but in no event more than the least populous State; they shall be in addition to those appointed by the States, but they shall be considered, for the purposes of the election of President and Vice President, to be electors appointed by a State; and they shall meet in the District and perform such duties as provided by the twelfth article of amendment.[312]

2. The Congress shall have power to enforce this article by appropriate legislation.

---

312. This amendment, which enables residents of Washington, D.C., to cast votes for president and vice president, is based on the logic that those who pay federal taxes and serve their country in war should be entitled to a vote. It currently grants three electoral votes. The failure of the amendment to give the city a voting member of Congress has set the stage for a constitutional showdown. The District of Columbia's nonvoting delegate to the House of Representatives, Eleanor Holmes Norton, has pushed for a bill that would add a seat in the House so that the city's interests could be represented with a full vote. In February 2009, the Senate passed a bill that would give Washington a voting seat in the House. But the Constitution specifies (please see p. 5) that the House of Representatives "shall be composed of Members chosen every second Year by the People of the several States, and the Electors in each State shall have the Qualifications requisite for Electors of the most numerous Branch of the State Legislature." So if the District is to have a full

member in the House, the Supreme Court may require a constitutional amendment.

Some proponents of District of Columbia voting rights respond that Congress derives its constitutional authority to pass the bill from the District clause of the Constitution. But a recent Congressional Research Service report suggests that giving the District a vote in the House would be an overreach of congressional authority: "While the existing practice of allowing District of Columbia residents to vote for a non-voting Delegate would appear to fall comfortably within its authority under the District Clause, giving such Delegate a vote in the House would arguably have an effect that went beyond the District of Columbia. Such a change would not just affect the residents of the District of Columbia, but would also directly affect the structure of and the exercise of power by Congress. More significantly, if the Delegate were to cast the decisive vote on an issue of national import, then the instant legislation could have a significant effect nationwide."

Advocates for the District of Columbia have been reluctant to focus their efforts on an amendment due to the low probability of its enactment. Congressional Democrats made an attempt in 1978, submitting an amendment for ratification that would have given the District the voting power of a state, including two senators. The effort was resisted by Republicans. There were also concerns about whether the District of Columbia, which was more populous than a number of states but has been losing residents, was entitled to two senators. The amendment effort expired in 1985 with the support of just sixteen states.

AMENDMENT XXIV.

[Proposed 1962; Ratified 1964]

1. The right of citizens of the United States to vote in any primary or other election for President or Vice President, for electors for President or Vice President, or for Senator or Representative in Congress, shall not be denied or abridged by the United States or any State by reason of failure to pay any poll tax or other tax.[313]

2. The Congress shall have power to enforce this article by appropriate legislation.

---

313. What exactly did the states and the Congress intend the phrase "any poll tax or other tax" to comprehend? The general purpose of the amendment is clear by its history. Before its passage, poll taxes were among the last surviving legal loopholes states could use to disenfranchise African American citizens, who, though everyone would be taxed at the same rate to cast a vote, tended to be poorer and more easily discouraged from voting by the prospect of a tax. The Supreme Court in 1937 upheld the constitutionality of poll taxes in a case from Georgia, *Breedlove v. Suttles*. The opinion, by Justice Pierce Butler, was one of memorable vapidity. Georgia's poll tax was a dollar a year, but it grew cumulatively, and Georgians who wished to vote had to be paid up. Women were exempt. The plaintiff in *Breedlove* was white, and Butler's opinion offered no glimpse of any consideration of the prideful racial bigotry that lay behind the use of the poll tax in Georgia. The justice merely asserted that "to make payment of poll taxes a prerequisite of voting is not to deny any privilege or immunity protected by the Fourteenth Amendment. Privilege of voting is not derived from the United States, but is conferred by the state and, save as restrained by the Fifteenth and Nineteenth Amendments and other provisions of the Federal Constitution, the state may condition suffrage as it deems appropriate." By the time the Twenty-fourth Amendment was passed, only five

states—Alabama, Arkansas, Mississippi, Texas, and Virginia—were employing a poll tax.

Shortly after ratification, the Supreme Court, relying on the Fourteenth Amendment, ruled that poll taxes were also unconstitutional in state elections. More recently, the question of what is involved in a poll tax, and what is to be comprehended by the phrase "any poll tax or other tax," has been raised in connection with requirements that would-be voters produce photo identification. As the 2008 presidential election approached, the Indiana voter ID law was challenged. The high court, in an opinion by Justice Stevens, noted that "under *Harper*, even rational restrictions on the right to vote are invidious if they are unrelated to voter qualifications." But the Court ruled, to quote its summary, that each of the interests Indiana had asserted in its voter ID law "is unquestionably relevant to its interest in protecting the integrity and reliability of the electoral process."

Professor Bruce Ackerman and student Jennifer Nou of Yale Law School responded with an opinion piece in Slate.com arguing that the Court should have struck down the law via the Twenty-fourth Amendment. The photo ID requirement, they said, is tantamount to a poll tax: "Americans have long fought hard to protect the right to vote and a generation ago emphatically rejected the idea of paying for the ballot. As the civil rights revolution reached its peak, Congress and the states in 1964 enacted the 24th Amendment, forbidding any 'poll-tax or other tax' in federal elections. Yet, remarkably enough, this basic text went unmentioned by the Supreme Court when it upheld Indiana's photo-ID law."

AMENDMENT XXV.

[Proposed 1965; Ratified 1967]

1. In case of the removal of the President from office or of his death or resignation, the Vice President shall become President.

2. Whenever there is a vacancy in the office of the Vice President, the President shall nominate a Vice President who shall take office upon confirmation by a majority vote of both Houses of Congress.

3. Whenever the President transmits to the President pro tempore of the Senate and the Speaker of the House of Representatives his written declaration that he is unable to discharge the powers and duties of his office, and until he transmits to them a written declaration to the contrary, such powers and duties shall be discharged by the Vice President as Acting President.

4. Whenever the Vice President and a majority of either the principal officers of the executive departments or of such other body as Congress may by law provide, transmit to the President pro tempore of the Senate and the Speaker of the House of Representatives their written declaration that the President is unable to discharge the powers and duties of his office, the Vice President shall immediately assume the powers and duties of the office as Acting President.

Thereafter, when the President transmits to the President pro tempore of the Senate and the Speaker of the House of Representatives his written declaration that no inability exists, he shall resume the powers and duties of his office unless the Vice President and a majority of either the principal officers of the executive department or of such other body as Congress may by law provide, transmit within four days to the President pro tempore of the Senate and the Speaker of the House of Representatives their written declaration that the President is unable to discharge the powers and duties of his office. Thereupon Congress shall decide the issue, assembling within forty eight hours for that purpose if not in session. If the Congress, within twenty one days after receipt of the latter written declaration, or, if Congress is not in session, within twenty one days after Congress is required to assemble, determines by two thirds vote of both Houses that the President is unable to discharge the powers and duties of his office, the Vice President shall continue to discharge the same as Acting President; otherwise, the President shall resume the powers and duties of his office.[314]

314. This amendment, ratified in 1967 in the wake of the assassination of President John F. Kennedy, resolves critical uncertainties that plagued the original presidential succession clause (please see footnote 170) for Article 2, Section 1. The vice presidential appointment clause was exercised following the Watergate crisis in 1973, when President Richard Nixon chose the minority leader in the House, Representative Gerald Ford, to replace Vice President Spiro Agnew after Agnew resigned in disgrace. It was exercised again in 1974, when Ford succeeded Nixon and appointed Governor Nelson Rockefeller to be vice president.

President Ronald Reagan did not invoke the Twenty-fifth Amendment's clause concerning the president's temporary inability after he was shot by a would-be assassin in 1981. This was when Secretary of State Haig, as the president's life hung in the balance, uttered his immortal gaffe during remarks to reporters at the White House: "Constitutionally, gentlemen, you have the President, the Vice President, and the Secretary of State in that order, and should the President decide he wants to transfer the helm to the Vice President, he will do so. He has not done that. As of now, I am in control here, in the White House, pending return of the Vice President and in close touch with him. If something came up, I would check with him, of course." In the line of succession, two offices were between the vice president and the secretary of state—the Speaker of the House and the president pro tempore of the Senate. Haig defended his blunder by explaining that he was asked not about the line of succession but about who was running the government.

In 1985, when Reagan underwent surgery for colon cancer, he wrote a letter transferring power to Vice President George Bush. But he intentionally declined to invoke the Twenty-fifth Amendment specifically—the vice president was not even immediately notified of the power transfer. In part, Reagan chose this approach because he wanted to avoid imposing a precedent on his successors. Nevertheless, President George W. Bush did invoke the Twenty-fifth when he transferred power to Vice President Cheney during two colonoscopies, in 2002 and 2007.

Some, including a self-appointed panel of medical experts, historians, and former White House doctors, have advocated putting a protocol in place that would give physicians a greater say in determining when a president is impaired and when the impairment has ended. When Reagan reclaimed power in 1985, eight hours after he surrendered it, he was so groggy that he could barely sign the letter to make it official. The decision was made by his chief of staff without the authorization of the White House doctor, who later said they should have waited at a least a day.

AMENDMENT XXVI.

[Proposed 1971; Ratified 1971]

The right of citizens of the United States, who are eighteen years of age or older, to vote shall not be denied or abridged by the United States or by any State on account of age.[315]

The Congress shall have power to enforce this article by appropriate legislation.

315. The distinction of fastest approval for an amendment goes to this one from 1971, seven months after it was introduced in the Sen-

ate. "Never had a constitutional amendment been proposed, passed, and ratified so quickly." The movement to lower the voting age to eighteen began during World War II. President Eisenhower called for this constitutional amendment in his 1954 State of the Union address. During the Vietnam conflict, lawmakers became uncomfortable that some draftees were too young to vote. These concerns gave rise to the slogan, "Old enough to fight, old enough to vote." Congress altered the Voting Rights Act of 1965, lowering the voting age to eighteen for all elections on the federal, state, and local levels. This law was regarded as unconstitutional by many, including President Nixon, though he signed it anyway because he "strongly favored the 18 year old vote" and anticipated a court challenge, according to Thomas Neale of the Congressional Research Service.

In 1970 the Supreme Court, in a 5 to 4 decision, held that while Congress could set the voting age for federal elections, it did not have the power to do the same for state and local races. It ruled that under Article I, Section 2 of the Constitution, "the States have the power to set qualifications to vote in state and local elections, and the whole Constitution reserves that power to the States except as it has been curtailed by specific constitutional amendments. No amendment (including the Equal Protection Clause of the Fourteenth Amendment and the other Civil War Amendments) authorizes Congress' attempt to lower the voting age in state and local elections." The case was brought by the state against Nixon's attorney general, John Mitchell.

The Court's decision worried about the states having to maintain two voter registration lists, one for federal elections and another for state and local elections. Hence the speed with which the amendment cleared not only the Congress but three-quarters of the states. Despite the alacrity of the states on their behalf, those between ages eighteen and twenty-four have been the least likely to exercise their right to vote. Yet support obtains for lowering the voting age further. Some who support youth voting rights note how important they can be in promoting a progressive agenda. In Iran, according to one author, "enfranchised sixteen- and seventeen-year-olds may have made the difference in the 2000 electoral victory of reformist, prodemocracy forces."

In 2007 Iran raised the country's voting age to eighteen from fifteen—a rare action for a country to take.

AMENDMENT XXVII.

[Proposed 1789; Ratified 1992]

No law, varying the compensation for the services of the Senators and Representatives, shall take effect, until an election of Representatives shall have intervened.[316]

---

316. In 1982, more than two hundred years after the ratification of the Constitution, Gregory Watson, an undergraduate at the University of Texas, was "digging through books" at the public library at Austin "when he stumbled across a list of amendments that Congress sent out to the states to be ratified and which were never returned for lack of sufficient endorsement," the *Pittsburgh Post-Gazette*, in recounting the story, reported in 2002. One of them was the amendment on congressional pay. "This one immediately stood out and captured my attention," Watson said. He had been researching another measure, the Equal Rights Amendment, which had failed in ratification, but was intrigued that the amendment on congressional pay had no built-in expiration date and could still be ratified. He decided to write a paper on this, and his professor gave him a C because "I had not convinced her the amendment was still pending." So he "began writing to legislators around the nation" and, as the *Post-Gazette* put it, the amendment came back ratified.

The Twenty-seventh is not the most consequential of amendments. Congressional pay is now raised automatically by a cost of living increase that lags the consumer price index and was adjudged, after the amendment was passed, to be something other than a Congress raising its own pay. But was the America that enacted the Twenty-seventh Amendment in 1992 the same country that proposed it more than two centuries earlier? Six states ratified when it was first proposed, followed by Ohio in 1873, which did so simply to protest a congressional pay increase. The rest of the ratifications came more than a century later. Did this amendment really pass the strict test the founders envisioned? The Supreme Court offered some guidance in *Coleman v. Miller*, when it stated that it was up to Congress to decide whether an amendment on child labor—proposed in 1924—had been legitimately ratified by the Kansas legislature thirteen years later. "The Congress, in controlling the promulgation of the adoption of a constitutional amendment, has the final determination of the question whether, by lapse of time, its proposal of the amendment had lost its vitality before being adopted by the requisite number of legislatures," the Court said. The judges' reasoning was not part of the Court's holding, leading the Department of Justice to conclude in 1992 that the time taken to ratify the Twenty-seventh Amendment had no bearing on its legality, regardless of Congress's opinion.

Concerns about the long-term consequences of the Twenty-seventh's ratification were drowned out by election-year politics. "The pay-raise amendment's long delay in ratification had at first raised questions, among scholars and legislators alike, as to whether the measure was indeed a legitimate change to the Constitution," Richard Berke of the *New York Times* reported in 1992. "But among the lawmakers, at least, those questions quickly yielded to the election-year pressure of avoiding any appearance that they were resisting a curb on their privileges." Berke also reported that at the time the Twenty-seventh was passed, other partly ratified amendments included one that would prohibit Congress from banning slavery and another that could increase the size of Congress to more than five thousand members.

What can be said conclusively about the ratification of the Twenty-seventh Amendment is that it attests to one of the great truths of this most remarkable of parchments—that it is accessible and inspiring, beckoning the learned and the student alike to sit down with it and start thinking: Where does our government come from? What were the founders intending? And what might be done to improve on a document that, while it has proven a sturdier vessel of liberty than any other, contains no limit on the number of times it can be amended and establishes no bar as to what Americans may join the debate over its future.

Notes

〰️

1 *"I confess, as I enter the Building"*: Harry Alonzo Cushing, ed., *The Writings of Samuel Adams* (New York: Putnam, 1908), 4:324.

1 *"Who authorized them to speak the language"*: Jonathan Elliott, *The Debates in the Several State Conventions on the Adoption of the Federal Constitution* (Philadelphia: Lippincott, 1861), 3:22.

1 *"We appeared totally to have forgot the business"*: Cited in Philip B. Kurland and Ralph Lerner, eds., *The Founders' Constitution* (Chicago: University of Chicago Press, 1987), 1:282–283. Available online at http://press-pubs.uchicago.edu/founders.

2 *"I know very well all the common-place rant of State sovereignties"*: *Founders' Constitution*, 2:3–4.

2 *"Nothing can exceed the wickedness and folly"*: *Letters and Other Writings of James Madison, Fourth President of the United States, 1816–1828* (1865), 1:268; Henry D. Gilpin, ed., *The Papers of James Madison*, 2:630; cited in Edward Field, ed., *The State of Rhode Island and Providence Plantations*, 2 vols. (1902).

2 *"We have, probably, had too good an opinion of human nature"*: Gordon S. Wood, *The Creation of the American Republic, 1776 to 1787* (New York: Norton, 1972). The letter was dated August 15, 1786.

2 *"We may indeed with propriety be said to have reached"*: Jacob Ernest Cooke, ed., *The Federalist* (Middletown: Wesleyan University Press: 1961), p. 91. The subtitle of 15 *Federalist* about the "insufficiency of the present confederation" is in Alexander Hamilton, James Madison, John Jay, *The Federalist Papers, Federalist no. 15*, available at http://thomas.loc.gov/home/histdox/fed_15.html.

3 *"Here, in strictness, the people surrender nothing"*: Cooke, ed., *Federalist*, p. 578.

4 *Abruptly in mid-July . . . subsequently dropped*: Max Farrand, *The Fathers of the Constitution* (New Haven, CT: Yale University Press, 1921), pp. 120–121.

4 *"direct taxation should follow"*: Ibid.

4 *"This body alone forecast the continued existence of the states"*: Jackson Turner Main, *The Anti-Federalists: Critics of the Constitution, 1781–1788* (Chapel Hill: University of North Carolina Press, 2004), p. 137.

5 *"Who are to be the electors of the federal representatives?"*: Cooke, ed., *Federalist*, p. 385.

5   *Requirements . . . were applied differently to black voters and white voters:* See Section 4 of the Voting Rights Act (1965), http://tinyurl.com/4wf6nx.

6   *"Where the Constitution is silent about the exercise of a particular power":* U.S. *Term Limits, Inc. v. Thornton,* 514 U.S. 779 (1995).

7   *"Indians not taxed" meant "Indians living on reservations":* http://tinyurl .com/mah9k6.

7   *In 1940 the government did away with the category "Indians not taxed":* http://tinyurl.com/37te6a.

7   *"The numbers of people were taken by this article":* Thomas Jefferson, *The Writings of Thomas Jefferson* (Washington, DC: Taylor & Maury, 1853), pp. 28–29. An earlier edition of Jefferson's autobiography is cited in *Founders' Constitution,* 2:87.

7   *Benjamin Harrison . . . "proposed as a compromise":* Jefferson, *Writings.*

8   *William Davie . . . "saw that it was meant by some gentlemen":* Founders' Constitution, 2:106.

8   *"The admission of slaves into the Representation":* Founders' Constitution, 2:111.

9   *"the absurdity of increasing the power of a State in making laws":* Founders' Constitution, 2:120.

9   *had been dislocated temporarily by World War I:* For this and more information on the 1920 census, see Margo J. Anderson and Stephen E. Feinberg, *Who Counts? The Politics of Census-Taking in Contemporary America* (New York: Russell Sage Foundation, 2001), p. 27; M. L. Balinski and H. Peyton Young, *Fair Representation: Meeting the Ideal of One Man, One Vote* (Washington, DC: Brookings Institution, 2001), p. 51. Both volumes are available online at Google Books, books.google.com/books.

9   *"the breadth of congressional methodological authority":* Utah et al. v. Evans, Secretary of Commerce, et al., 536 U.S. 452 (2001).

9   *"Despite their awareness that estimation techniques":* Ibid.

9   *as much information as possible:* A discussion of this issue is included at the website of the Electronic Privacy Information Center, http://epic.org/ privacy/census.

9   *"Congress has repeatedly directed an enumeration":* Knox v. Lee [Legal Tender Cases], 79 U.S. 457 (1870).

10   *"a measure of discretion":* United States Department of Commerce et al. v. Montana et al., 503 U.S. 442, 443 (1992).

10   *but was adjusted back to 435:* http://tinyurl.com/37te6a.

10   *"number of inhabitants":* Max Farrand, ed., *The Records of the Federal Convention of 1787* (New Haven, CT: Yale University Press, 1911), 1:561.

11   *Madison urged . . . "fit men to undertake the service":* Founders' Constitution, 2:100–102.

11 *the House was expanded to 105 seats: Congressional Digest,* 1921–1922, p. 21. Available online at Google Books, http://books.google.com/books.

12 *there is no requirement that the Speaker actually be a member of the House:* Samuel McCall, *The Business of Congress* (New York: Columbia University Press, 1911), p. 121.

13 *"was only consenting, after they had struggled":* See "The Genuine Information," in Herbert J. Storing, ed., *The Complete Anti-Federalist,* 7 vols. (Chicago: University of Chicago Press, 1981). Cited in *Founders' Constitution,* 2:212–213.

13 *"It is true, that if all the States . . . refuse to elect Senators":* Cohens v. Virginia, 19 U.S. 264 (1821).

13 *"If he has a family, he will take his family with him":* Max Farrand, ed., *The Records of the Federal Convention of 1787* (New Haven, CT: Yale University Press, 1911), 3:194.

14 *"If one third new members are introduced":* Founders' Constitution, 2:214.

14 *Hiram Fong drew the longer term, Oren Long the shorter:* http://tinyurl .com/mexh70.

15 *This age requirement mimics that of the Roman senate:* Joseph Story, *Commentaries on the Constitution of the United States,* 3 vols. (Boston: Hilliard, Gray, 1833), 2:205. James Kent, *Commentaries on American Law* (Boston: Little, Brown, 1901), 3:228. Cited in *Founders' Constitution,* 2:243.

15 *"could not think of excluding those foreigners . . . ," "meritorious aliens from emigrating to this Country":* Founders' Constitution, 2:240–241.

15 *ended the brief Senate career of Geneva-born Albert Gallatin:* See "Cases of Contested Elections in Congress," http://tinyurl.com/md6awy.

16 *Madison's notes show that Elbridge Gerry . . . "he would be without employment":* Founders' Constitution, 2:244.

16 *Cheney himself cited Article I:* Congressional Oversight Committee, http://oversight.house.gov/story.asp?id=1371.

16 *"Perhaps the best thing that can be said":* Barton Gellman, "The Power of Vice," *Slate,* October 6, 2008, http://tinyurl.com/m7j28q.

17 *his duties included buying firewood and tending to the Senate's horses:* Senate Historical Office, *James Mathers, Doorkeeper and Sergeant at Arms, 1789–1811,* www.senate.gov. http://tinyurl.com/nkw5qa.

17 *fifty cents for admission to the chamber:* Charles Neider, ed., *Punch, Brothers, Punch: The Comic Mark Twain Reader* (Lanham, MD: Rowman & Littlefield, 2004), p. 347ff.

17 *after the vice president and the Speaker of the House:* Senate Historical Office, *President Pro Tempore,* http://tinyurl.com/mvle2q.

18 *Seventeen persons have been impeached since America's founding:* Eric Foner and John Arthur Garraty, eds., *The Reader's Companion to American History*

(New York: Houghton Mifflin Harcourt, 1991), p. 539; Michael Gerhardt, *The Federal Impeachment Process* (Chicago: University of Chicago Press, 2000), p. 201, nn. 3–7.

18   *but before the House voted:* Mark Grossman, *Political Corruption in America: An Encyclopedia of Scandals, Power, and Greed,* 2nd ed. (Boulder: ABC-Clio, 2003), p. 405.

19   *"There are known denominations of men":* Story, *Commentaries,* 3:689.

19   *"The Supreme Court of the United States shall consist":* U.S. Code, Title 28, Section 1, http://tinyurl.com/quyj7p.

20   *"Will it be pretended, for I have heard such a suggestion":* Founders' Constitution, 2:167.

20   *Impeachment convictions do not necessarily disqualify a person:* Matthew Franck, posting, November 20, 2006, *National Review* online, weblog "Bench Memos." Available at http://tinyurl.com/srfke.

21   *"The Senate's practice":* Michael Gerhardt, *The Federal Impeachment Process* (Chicago: University of Chicago Press, 2000), p. 35.

21   *disqualified the former judges:* Ibid., p. 60.

21   *"detailed judicial supervision of the election process":* Crawford et al. v. Marion County Election Board et al., 553 U. S. ___ (2008).

21   *"With uncommon zeal and virulence":* Story, *Commentaries,* 2:280.

22   *"Those illumined genii may see":* Elliott, *Debates,* 3:175.

22   *"There is intended to be a general election":* Cooke, ed., *Federalist,* pp. 401–402.

23   *"Notorious . . . exaggerated and unreasonable influence":* "The General Election Day," *New York Times,* November 3, 1878, http://tinyurl.com/oryn5s.

23   *the justices cited this clause in upholding the conviction of several members of the Ku Klux Klan:* Michael Anthony Ross, *Justice of Shattered Dreams: Samuel Freeman Miller and the Supreme Court During the Civil War Era* (Baton Rouge: Louisiana State University Press, 2003), p. 247.

24   *"It would not be either necessary, or becoming in congress to prescribe the place, where it should sit":* Story, *Commentaries,* 2:292.

24   *"A great vice in our system was that of legislating too much":* Cited in Founders' Constitution, 2:283.

25   *until after the next Congress had been elected:* Bruce Ackerman, *The Failure of the Founding Fathers: Jefferson, Marshall, and the Rise of Presidential Democracy* (Cambridge: Belnap, 2007), p. 118.

26   *in 1890 in one of those cases:* Details from *United States v. Ballin,* 144 U.S. 1 (1892).

26   *"a majority of the Senators present":* Rules of the Senate, http://tinyurl.com/nerory.

26　*a majority of those present . . . can order the sergeant at arms to make arrests:* Office of the Clerk, Rules of the House of Representatives of the United States, http://tinyurl.com/q8f6vm.

26　*"We had a hurried caucus among the Republicans in the cloakroom":* Irvin Molensky, "A Senator Is Captured, but Not His Mind," *New York Times,* February 25, 1988, http://tinyurl.com/ras87s.

27　*"The Sergeant at Arms was a little fellow":* Congressional Record, June 12, 2006, http://tinyurl.com/qloexn. Aspects of Specter's retelling, which came nearly twenty years after the fact, are contradicted by earlier press reports. For instance, the *Times* article states that Giugni got into Packwood's door with a skeleton key.

27　*"possibilities for filibustering exist because":* Richard S. Beth and Stanley Bach, *Filibusters and Cloture in the Senate,* March 28, 2003, http://tinyurl.com/8cx8k.

28　*generally limited to a single hour of debate:* James V. Saturno, *Considering Measures in the House Under the One-Hour Rule,* http://tinyurl.com/myk98o.

28　*"a mistress . . . who, though ugly to others":* Walter Gaston Shotwell, *Life of Charles Sumner* (New York: Crowell, 1910), p. 317.

28　*one senator . . . and two representatives . . . have been expelled by a two-thirds vote:* Congressional Quarterly website, http://tinyurl.com/mo2zvj.

29　*it refused to seat Brigham H. Roberts:* For the vote tally, see note 1 in the Supreme Court case *Barry v. United States ex Rel. Cunningham,* 279 U.S. 597 (1929), http://tinyurl.com/kwm4gu.

29　*fanned by an anti-Mormon agitator:* The role of the anti-Mormon agitator is discussed in Ferenc Morton Szasz, *The Protestant Clergy in the Great Plains and Mountain West, 1865–1915* (Lincoln: University of Nebraska Press, 2004), pp. 157–158.

29　*"Does the House of Representatives indorse":* Brigham H. Roberts, "The Roberts Case in Congress," *New York Times,* November 19, 1899, http://tinyurl.com/ltjat8.

29　*"martyr to a spasm of prejudice":* "Roberts Excluded: Vote 268 to 50," *New York Times,* January 26, 1900, http://tinyurl.com/r6h25j.

29　*"Unquestionably, Congress has an interest in preserving":* Powell v. McCormack, 395 U.S. 486, 548 (1969).

30　*"It was assumed in argument . . . those matters entered on the journal we need not inquire":* Field v. Clark, 143 U.S. 649, 670–671 (1892).

31　*"While the principles and designs of the individual members":* The Debates and Proceedings in the Congress of the United States (Gales & Seaton, 1853), February 19, 1794.

31　*"after the end of the present session of Congress":* Ibid., February 20, 1794.

31　*"an unprincipled newspaper letter writer":* Allan Nevins, *Polk: The Diary of a President, 1845–1849* (London: Longmans, Green, 1952), 3:354.

31   *He continued to file stories, under the dateline: "Custody of the Sergeant at Arms":* Senate Historical Office, *The Senate Arrests a Reporter,* http://tinyurl.com/njezqg.

32   *There have been several secret sessions:* The information in the above paragraph comes from a CRS report titled *Secret Sessions of Congress: A Brief Historical Overview,* http://tinyurl.com/n38828.

32   *"It is clear that, in respect to the particular mode in which, or with what fullness, shall be kept the proceedings": Field v. Clark,* 143 U.S. 649, 671 (1892).

32   *"had rather strike out the yeas & nays," "in stuffing the journals": Founders' Constitution,* 2:290.

33   *the Senate requires only eleven senators to force a roll call:* Betsy Palmer and Stanley Bach, "Ordering a Rollcall Vote in the Senate," http://tinyurl.com/kmtgk9.

33   *"They will never agree":* All preceding quotes in footnote cited in *Founders' Constitution,* 2:291.

34   *"meets both the language and the spirit of the 27th amendment": Boehner v. Anderson,* 809 F.Supp. 138 (D.D.C. 1992).

34   *"would be unjust as the Legislature was to be a national Assembly":* Preceding quotes in footnote cited in *Founders' Constitution,* 2:325–326.

35   *"Without the privilege, a single private civil litigant":* Akhil Reed Amar, *America's Constitution: A Biography* (New York: Random House, 2005), p. 101.

35   *"When a Representative is withdrawn from his seat by summons":* Aaron Clark, *Manual of Parliamentary Procedure* (New York: Child & Wells, 1826), 88, http://tinyurl.com/labfpg.

35   *"the 30,000 people":* Some editions of Jefferson's *Manual* say 47,400.

36   *"to withdraw himself from the criminal law of the land": Williamson v. United States,* 207 U.S. 425 (1908).

36   *"is practically obsolete": The Constitution of the United States of America, Analysis and Interpretation: 2002 Edition and Supplement,* http://tinyurl.com/6nz822.

36   *Roger Jepsen:* "The Senate: Embattled Heartland Republicans," *Time,* October 8, 1984; Anthony Lewis, "Abroad at Home, How to Celebrate," *New York Times,* January 17, 1985.

36   Chicago Tribune *sprang upon the Treaty of Versailles:* Versions of this story can be found in Lloyd Wendt, *Chicago Tribune: The Rise of a Great American Newspaper* (Chicago: Rand McNally, 1979), p. 442; John Bach McMaster, *The United States in the World War* (New York: D. Appleton, 1920), pp. 379–380.

37   *confirmed Saxbe:* "Handing the Ball to Bill Saxbe," *Time,* November 12, 1973, http://tinyurl.com/m6yvxo.

37 *Harvard professor Steven Breyer:* John F. O'Connor, "The Emoluments Clause: An Anti-Federalist Intruder in a Federalist Constitution," *Hofstra Law Review* 24 (1995), http://tinyurl.com/lntbkc.

37 *"we should not delude the American people":* Mary Russell, "Robert Byrd Sees Saxbe Job Illegal," *Washington Post*, November 20, 1973, http://tinyurl.com/r4z5ac.

37 *the Black appointment:* "Judiciary: Nominee no. 93," *Time*, August 23, 1937, http://tinyurl.com/kox9he; O'Connor, pp. 111–112.

37 *Van Ness: The History of Congress*, January 1803, p. 395; available on Google Books, http://books.google.com/books.

37 *Edward Baker of Illinois and Representative Archibald Yell of Arkansas:* David P. Currie, *The Constitution in Congress: The Federalist Period, 1789–1801* (Chicago: University of Chicago Press, 1997), p. 248.

38 *"by a Member of Congress performing independent judicial functions":* United States v. Lane, 60 M.J. 781, 15 (A.F. Ct. Crim. App. 2004).

38 *"taxation & representation are strongly associated":* Founders' Constitution, 2:380.

39 *"The house of representatives can not only refuse":* Cooke, ed., Federalist, p. 394.

39 *"whatever taxes are imposed are but means to the purposes provided by the act":* Millard v. Roberts, 202 U.S. 429 (1906).

39 *"A learned commentator supposes that every bill":* Story, Commentaries, 2:343.

40 *"The whole of the very able and ingenious argument . . . ," "nor that he shall date it":* Gardner v. The Collector, 73 U.S. 499 (1867).

41 *"I have maturely considered the Act passed by the two Houses":* The text of the veto is available online at http://tinyurl.com/lodsmg.

41 *"most famous veto message":* Karlyn Kohrs Campbell and Kathleen Hall Jamieson, *Presidents Creating the Presidency: Deeds Done in Words* (Chicago: University of Chicago Press, 2008), p. 85.

41 *"as much the duty . . . to decide upon the constitutionality":* Campbell and Jamieson, *Presidents*, p. 198.

41 *"This bill spends too much . . . This bill has too many earmarks":* George W. Bush, veto message (H. DOC. NO. 110-76), http://tinyurl.com/q8e29h.

41 *there had been 1,484 vetoes:* http://tinyurl.com/mw3arm. The report considers only vetoes that were returned to Congress, not vetoes in which the president has pocketed the bill while, or until, Congress has adjourned.

41 *the rate is about one in five:* Ibid.

42 *"expectation that the president would likely observe the Christian Sabbath":* Levinson, "So Many Origins," *The New Republic*, February 22, 2010, www.tnr.com/book/review/so-many-origins.

42   *"By withholding the bill, the President took upon himself"*: Henry Clay, "Veto of the Land Bill," December 5, 1833, http://tinyurl.com/m95lsv.

43   *"The fact that the President has ten days"*: Edward S. Corwin, The Constitution and What It Means Today (Princeton: Princeton University Press, 1978), p. 35.

43   *"The latitude of the general words here used"*: Albert Ellery Bergh, ed., *The Writings of Thomas Jefferson* (Washington, DC: Thomas Jefferson Memorial Association, 1907), 3:63.

43   *four forms of congressional action:* Guide to Legislative Process in the House, http://tinyurl.com/nnewdb.

44   *"that if the negative of the President was confined to bills"*: Founders' Constitution, 2:396.

44   *1941 Lend Lease Act:* Edward S. Corwin, *The Constitution and What It Means Today* (Princeton: Princeton University Press, 1978), p. 37.

45   *"contain a concise and definite statemen"*: Enumerated Powers Act, H.R. 1359, introduced in the House on March 6, 2007, http://tinyurl.com/q8eqf3.

45   *"Rarely has so much rested on so small a point"*: Philip Hamburger, "Getting Permission," *Northwestern University Law Review* 101, no. 405 (2007): 442–443.

45   *Hamilton described duties, imposts, and excises:* Cooke, ed., Federalist, pp. 133–134.

46   *"A tax, in the general understanding of the term"*: United States v. Butler, 297 U.S. 1 (1936).

46   *slaughterhouses, spinners of cotton, tobacco:* Agricultural Adjustment Act, Section 9, www.nationalaglawcenter.org/assets/farmbills/1933.pdf.

46   *"The only qualification of the generality of the phrase in question"*: Alexander Hamilton, *Report on Manufactures*, 1913 ed., p. 40, http://tinyurl.com/lc67eo.

47   *"There was need of help from the nation if the people were not to starve"*: Chas. C. Steward Mach. Co. v. Collector, 301 U.S. 548, 586–587 (1937).

47   *"Congress may spend money in aid of the 'general welfare'"*: Helvering v. Davis, 301 U.S. 619 (1937).

48   *"My idea is that Congress have an unlimited power to raise money"*: The Writings of James Monroe, vol. 6, *1817–1823* (New York: Putnam's, 1902), pp. 265–266, http://tinyurl.com/ny62qq.

48   *"Is the tax on tobacco void"*: Head Money Cases, 112 U.S. 580, 594–595 (1884).

48   *"The one issue that has been raised repeatedly is whether the requirement"*: United States v. Ptasynski, 462 U.S. 74, 82–84 (1983).

49   *"to borrow money, or emit bills on the credit of the United States":* The Articles of Confederation, http://tinyurl.com/np6l8y.

49   *a signal of the founders' intention to deny the Congress the power to issue paper money:* Edwin Vieira Jr., "The Forgotten Role of the Constitution in Monetary Law," *Texas Review of Law and Politics,* 1997.

49   *"Under this authority, the Congress may mortgage":* Brutus no. 8, cited in *Founders' Constitution,* 2:472. Most scholars believe that Brutus was the nom de plume of New York delegate Robert Yates.

50   *"The most important of the particular non-military powers of Congress":* William Winslow Crosskey, *Politics and the Constitution in the History of the United States* (Chicago: University of Chicago Press, 1980), p. 17.

50   *"the commercial intercourse between nations":* Gibbons v. Ogden, 22 U.S. 1 (1824). 51 *"What if the chickens are all at one end?":* Peter H. Irons, *The New Deal Lawyers* (Princeton: Princeton University Press, 1982), p. 99.

51   *the justices began to laugh:* Hadley Arkes, *The Return of George Sutherland* (Princeton: Princeton University Press, 1997), p. 85.

51   *"how far the federal government may go":* A. L. A. Schechter Poultry Corp. v. United States, 295 U.S. 495, 546 (1935).

51   *"The possession of a gun in a local school zone":* United States v. Lopez, 514 U.S. 549 (1995).

52   *the law "cannot be upheld under the Commerce Clause":* http://tinyurl.com/Florida-v-U-S-complaint.

52   *a "direct and substantial effect on the interstate health care market":* http://tinyurl.com/USReplyFlorida-v-US.

52   *"a free white person":* The Naturalization Act of 1790, http://tinyurl.com/92jb8n.

53   *three times that decade:* The Harvard University Library maintains an excellent timeline online at http://ocp.hul.harvard.edu/immigration/dates.html.

54   *was death:* The Coinage Act of April 2, 1972, www.constitution.org/uslaw/coinage1792.txt.

54   *"If anybody has any idea of hoarding our silver coins":* The American Presidency Project, http://tinyurl.com/msgxpp.

54   *"The states are expressly prohibited":* H. W. Richardson, *The National Banks* (New York: Harper, 1880), p. 25, http://tinyurl.com/nvktwd.

55   *"the intention and declared meaning of the constitution":* Thomas Hart Benton, *Thirty Years' View; or, A History of the American Government for Thirty Years, from 1820–1850,* 2 vols. (1854–1856; reprint, Westport, CT: Greenwood, 1968), http://tinyurl.com/nsrqtf.

55   *1.5 percent: Reports of Committees,* 5 vols. (Washington, DC: Government Printing Office, 1877), p. 190, http://tinyurl.com/ld65fo.

55 *authorized use of the metric system nationwide in 1866:* The Metric Conversion Act, December 23, 1975, http://tinyurl.com/2d2q14.

56 *overriding President Wilson's veto:* Heidi G. Yacker, "Daylight Savings Time," Congressional Research Service, 1998, http://tinyurl.com/novxnf.

56 *"We will notice briefly an argument presented in support":* Knox v. Lee, 79 U.S. 457, 552–553 (1870).

57 *"restrain the circulation of notes":* CRS Annotated Constitution, p. 305, http://www.gpoaccess.gov/constitution/pdf2002/001-Title.pdf.

57 *"The king may also, by his proclamation":* Cited in *Founders' Constitution*, 3:2.

57 *"If the word* current *had been omitted":* Ibid., 3:10.

58 *"All former acts authorizing the currency":* Act Relating to Foreign Coins, February 21, 1857, http://tinyurl.com/qd8dsk.

59 *"I view it as a source of boundless patronage":* Founders' Constitution, 3:28.

59 *"Such a view of the Constitution":* Elliott, *Debates*, 4:469.

60 *"In case of an atomic attack . . . within hours of an attack":* "President Eisenhower: Build America's Roads," *Executive Intelligence Review*, February 3, 2006, http://tinyurl.com/qs4n8j.

60 *"The United States may give up the post office":* Milwaukee Social Democratic Pub. Co. v. Burleson, 255 U.S. 407 (1921).

61 *"The economic effect of this 20-year extension":* Eldred v. Ashcroft, 537 U.S. 186, 58 (2003).

62 *"The only reason why photographs":* Burrow-Giles Lithographic Co. v. Sarony, 111 U.S. 53 (1884).

62 *"His claim is not to a hitherto unknown natural phenomenon":* Diamond v. Chakrabarty, 447 U.S. 303 (1980).

62 *"It would be a dangerous undertaking":* Bleistein v. Donaldson Lithographing Co., 188 U.S. 239 (1903).

63 *"to identify the essential characteristics of a trademark":* Trademark Cases, 100 U.S. 82 (1879).

64 *"To have inferior courts appointed":* From Luther Martin, "Genuine Information," in Storing, ed., *Complete Anti-Federalist*, 2.4.58. Cited by the *Founders' Constitution*, 3:62.

65 *"And singular as it may appear":* United States v. Palmer, 16 U.S. 610 (1818).

65 *piracy on the high seas:* Jacob D. Wheeler, *Reports of Criminal Law Cases* (New York: Gould, Banks, 1851), 2:xxxi, http://tinyurl.com/qy2tf3.

65 *"not only the waters of the ocean":* Story, *Commentaries*, 3:56–57.

66 *"By this law we are to understand":* James Kent, John Melville Gould, and Oliver Wendell Holmes, *Commentaries on American Law*, 12th ed. (Boston: Little, Brown, 1896), p. 1, http://tinyurl.com/rajckk.

66 *"the most prominent subjects under this head":* William Rawle, *View of the Constitution of the United States,* 2nd ed., Carolina Academic Press Historical Reprint Series (2009). Available on *The Founders' Constitution* online at http://press-pubs.uchicago.edu/founders.

66 *The law declared:* American Presidency Project, http://tinyurl.com/m2f3xa.

66 *"However abhorrent this traffic may be":* *The Antelope,* 23 U.S. 66 (1825).

67 *Five formal declarations of war:* A chart is available on Wikipedia at http://tinyurl.com/8y4dn. It also lists twelve instances in which the United States has undertaken "extended military engagements that were explicitly authorized by Congress, short of a formal declaration of war." They involved France in 1798; the Barbary States in 1801 and 1815; Paraguay in 1859; Bolshevist Russia in 1918; Lebanese rebels in 1958; Vietnamese communists in 1964; Syria and certain militias in Lebanon in 1973; Iraq in 1991; the Taliban regime in Afghanistan and al Qaeda globally in 2001; and Iraq in 2002. Wikipedia's list notes that in Korea President Truman cited authority under United Nations resolutions. Congress and the president have been in what might be called a constitutional tug-of-war-powers for centuries; additional citations are at page 133.

67 *street corner and arrested:* Susan Dudley Gold, *Korematsu v. United States* (Tarrytown, NY: Marshall Cavendish Benchmark, 2006), pp. 53–54.

67 *"unable to conclude that":* *Korematsu v. United States,* 323 U.S. 214, 217–218 (1944).

67 *has been used to suggest that the founders:* For example, John Hart Ely, *War and Responsibility: Constitutional Lessons of Vietnam and Its Aftermath* (Princeton: Princeton University Press, 1995), p. 74.

68 *Jefferson Davis issued a proclamation:* An account is included in the *Official Records of the Union and Confederate Navies in the War of the Rebellion,* published under the direction of the secretary of the Navy in 1921. Available online at http://tinyurl.com/qx3lo2.

68 *"What real objection can be urged":* William Salter, *The Life of James W. Grimes* (New York: D. Appleton. 1876), p. 221ff., http://tinyurl .com/mr3k4g.

68 *"privately armed and equipped persons and entities":* September 11 Marque and Reprisal Act of 2001, http://tinyurl.com/mfer59.

69 *"letter of marque with a fancy title":* Seth Gitell, "We're Bombarding Our Enemies—With Legal Briefs," *Wall Street Journal,* August 10, 1998.

69 *Senator John McCain:* Senate debate transcript, http://tinyurl.com/lgs5vf.

69 *recounts a conversation at the White House:* The quotes are from Barton Gellman, *Angler: The Cheney Vice Presidency* (New York: Penguin, 2008), p. 172.

70 *in a legal opinion not made public during the Civil War:* Charles E. Hughes, "War Powers Under the Constitution," *Massachusetts Law Quarterly,* August 1917, http://tinyurl.com/o3vblz.

71   *"And as further evidence that the conclusion we reach"*: Selective Draft Law *Cases*, 245 U.S. 366 (1918).

71   *"America would never be more than two years away from presumptive demilitarization"*: Amar, *America's Constitution*, p. 116.

71   *"In 1904, the question arose whether"*: See the CRS Annotated Constitution, available online at http://tinyurl.com/po4rdf.

72   *"no legal objection to a request"*: Ibid.

72   *"All the vessels of the intended fleet"*: The Grayson quote is from *Founders' Constitution*, 3:169.

72   *Norfolk:* http://tinyurl.com/m8qz73.

72   *prohibition against standing appropriations:* Amar, *America's Constitution*, p. 116.

73   *"Arbiter of Europe in America"*: Cooke, ed., *Federalist*, p. 68.

73   *there was at least a proposal to amend the Constitution:* Corwin, *Constitution*, p. 111.

73   *"For the reasons which differentiate military society"*: Parker v. Levy, 417 U.S. 733 (1974).

74   *"The power to make the necessary laws"*: Hamdan v. Rumsfeld, 548 U.S. 557 (2006).

74   *"deliberately pledge the whole national force"*: From Phillips's introduction to *The Constitution a Pro-Slavery Compact* (New York: American Anti-Slavery Society, 1845), pp. 6–7.

74   *Congress quickly transferred . . . its authority:* Militia Act of 1792, 2nd Congress, sess. 1, chap. 28. Passed May 2, 1792; http://tinyurl.com/lq5f98.

74   *the Whiskey Rebellion:* James Andrew Cutchfield, *George Washington: First in War, First in Peace* (New York: Macmillan, 2005), p. 186, http://tinyurl .com/lyx99c.

75   *"argued that, internal disorders aside"*: Donald R. Hickey, *The War of 1812: A Forgotten Conflict* (Champaign-Urbana: University of Illinois Press, 1990), p. 260, http://tinyurl.com/nydrjy.

75   *"The power itself is to be exercised"*: Martin v. Mott, 25 U.S. 19 (1827).

76   *summoning the state's National Guard:* "The National Guard could not be ready soon enough to defuse the crisis, and Ike was uncertain of the Arkansas guard's loyalty." Daniel Levitas, *The Terrorist Next Door: The Militia Movement and the Radical Right* (New York: Macmillan, 2002), pp. 47–49, http://tinyurl.com/m7kc9e.

76   *to follow federal orders:* David Allen Nichols, *A Matter of Justice: Eisenhower and the Beginning of the Civil Rights Revolution* (New York: Simon & Schuster, 2007), p. 195, http://tinyurl.com/nphs4j.

76 *28 of them would be shot:* CNN.com, "Mississippi and Meredith Remember," October 1, 2002, http://tinyurl.com/l7cs79.

76 *would quell the rebellion:* William Doyle, "Forgotten Soldiers of the Integration Fight," *New York Times,* 2002.

76 *"'Organizing' meant proportioning": Preparedness for National Defense: Hearings Before the Committee on Military Affairs United States, Sixty-fourth Congress,* pt. 13 (Washington, DC: Government Printing Office, 1916), http://tinyurl.com/nxrmmm.

77 *"Those of us who are male": Silveira v. Lockyer,* 328 F.3d 567 (9th Cir. 2003).

77 *"The militia of the United States consists":* U.S. Code, Title 10, Section 311, http://tinyurl.com/4d6rf8.

77 *"Until 1952, the statutory authority": Perpich v. DOD,* 496 U.S. 334 (1990).

78 *invasion of neighboring Nicaragua:* Richard Halloran, "U.S. Reservists Build Key Road in Honduras," *New York Times,* April 5, 1987.

78 *"send approximately 450 National Guardsmen":* Monte M. F. Cooper, "*Perpich v. Department of Defense:* Federalism Values and the Militia Clause," *University of Colorado Law Review,* 1991, p. 637.

78 *"The consent of a Governor":* U.S. Code, Title 10, Section 12301, http://tinyurl.com/nvjcep.

78 *The opinion, written by Justice Stevens: Perpich v. DOD,* 496 U.S. 334 (1990).

79 *In 1973 Congress granted home rule:* From the Council of the District of Columbia website, http://tinyurl.com/l7psu5.

79 *"I do hereby declare":* From his proclamation on the founding of the city, http://tinyurl.com/pszool.

80 *one of the issues affecting the decision:* Clayton E. Jewett and John O. Allen, *Slavery in the South: A State-by-State History* (Westport, CT: Greenwood, 2004), p. 56.

80 *61.4 square miles:* http://quickfacts.census.gov/qfd/states/11000.html.

80 *would remain in effect:* Law of February 27, 1801, 2 U.S. Stat. at Large, p. 103, chap. 15, sec. 1, held "that the laws of Virginia and Maryland respectively shall continue in force in the portions of the District ceded by them." John Codman Hurd, *The Law of Freedom and Bondage in the United States* (New York: Little, Brown, 1862), pp. 25–26.

80 *"a mutinous group of soldiers":* Mark Noll, *Princeton and the Republic, 1768–1822* (Vancouver: Regent College Publishing, 2004), p. 82.

80 *"Without it, not only the public authority":* Cooke, ed., *Federalist,* p. 289.

81 *"Mr. Gouverneur Morris did not dislike the idea":* Elliott, *Debates,* 5:374.

81 *"a novel kind of provision":* Cited in *Founders' Constitution,* 3:220.

81 *"where men are to live":* Ibid., 3:225.

81   *"become the sanctuary of the blackest crimes":* Ibid., 3:222.

81   *"The public money expended on such places":* Cooke, ed., *Federalist,* pp. 289–290.

82   *"has not been strictly construed":* Collins v. Yosemite Park & Curry Co., 304 U.S. 518, 528 (1938).

82   A *1956 report: Report of the Interdepartmental Committee for the Study of Juris-diction over Federal Areas Within the States,* April 1956, http://tinyurl.com/ nh49ep.

82   *cede Los Alamos: Federal Areas Within States Committee Report,* http://tinyurl .com/m7z5pf; Jon Hunner, *Inventing Los Alamos: The Growth of an Atomic Community* (Norman: University of Oklahoma Press, 2007), p. 151. Avail-able online at http://tinyurl.com/lewwyo.

83   *"to cede to the United States jurisdiction":* Louis Henkin, *Foreign Affairs and the United States Constitution* (New York: Oxford University Press, 1996), p. 466 n. 72.

83   *"Under such a clause as this":* Cited in *Founders' Constitution,* 3:239.

83   *"Congress are authorized to defend the nation":* Bergh, 10:165.

84   *"What is a power":* Cooke, ed., *Federalist,* pp. 204–205.

84   *"The result of the most careful and attentive":* McCulloch v. Maryland, 17 U.S. 316, 412–421 (1819).

85   *"In assessing damages":* Cited in *Legal Tender Cases,* 79 U.S. 457, 458 (1870).

85   *"whether a law is a necessary and proper means":* Ibid., pp. 571–772.

86   *"it is sustainable as a 'necessary and proper' implementation of the power of Con-gress over interstate commerce":* Wickard v. Filburn, 317 U.S. 111, 119 (1942).

86   *"That the compact which exists between the North and the South":* Garrison of-fered these words as a resolution at a meeting of the Massachusetts Anti-Slavery Society in 1843. Shortly afterward, his newspaper began carrying that message on its masthead; Frank Luther Moot, *A History of American Magazines* (Cambridge: Harvard University Press, 1938), 2:228.

87   *"Twenty years will produce all the mischief ":* W.E.B. Du Bois, *The Suppression of the African Slave Trade to the United States of America* (New York: Long-mans, Green, 1904), p. 60.

87   *"It ought to be considered as a great point":* Cooke, ed., *Federalist,* pp. 281–282.

87   *"I consider this as laying the foundation":* Du Bois, *Suppression,* p. 66.

88   *"approved of the object of the motion":* Thomas Hart Benton, *Abridgment of the Debates of Congress, from 1789 to 1856* (New York: Appleton, 1857), 1:73.

88   *"whirled into a discussion":* Du Bois, *Suppression,* p. 75.

88 *"the most celebrated writ in the English law":* William Blackstone, *Blackstone's Commentaries,* 9th ed. (Chicago: Callaghan, 1915), p. 328. Available online at http://tinyurl.com/qfvqec.

88 *"simply assumes . . . it will be a part of the law of the land":* Corwin, *Constitution,* p. 124.

89 *"If the privilege of habeas corpus":* Boumediene v. Bush, 553 U.S. ___ (2008).

89 *Jonathan Adler of Case Western Reserve Law School:* The Volokh Conspiracy, http://volokh.com/posts/1213319118.shtml.

89 *"game of bait-and-switch":* Boumediene v. Bush, 553 U.S. ___ (2008).

89 *suspended habeas corpus in parts of that state:* Jerrold M. Packard, *The Lincolns in the White House* (New York: Macmillan, 2005), pp. 44–45.

90 *"not the slightest reference to the executive department":* Ex parte Merryman, 17 F. Cas. 144 (1861).

90 *Lambdin Milligan: Indiana: A Guide to the Hoosier State* (New York: Oxford University Press, 1947), p. 315.

90 *"Martial law cannot arise from a* threatened *invasion":* Ex parte Milligan, 71 U.S. 2, 127 (1866).

91 *"most notorious bill of attainder in American history":* Leonard Williams Levy, *Origins of the Bill of Rights* (New Haven: Yale University Press, 2001), p. 72.

91 *"that from and after the passing of this act":* The bill can be viewed at http://tinyurl.com/nuom89.

91 *"I cannot contemplate it without horror":* Founders' Constitution, 3:396.

91 *"We do not hold today that Congress cannot weed":* United States v. Brown, 381 U.S. 437, 461 (1965).

92 *"I see no escape, therefore, from the conclusion":* Nixon v. Administrator of General Services, 433 U.S. 425, 540–541 (1977).

93 *sentenced to pay $500:* These details are from William B. Faherty, "Cummings, John A. (1840–1873)," in Lawrence O. Christensen et al., eds., *Dictionary of Missouri Biography* (Columbia: University of Missouri Press, 1999), pp. 224–225.

93 *"impose additional punishment to that prescribed when the act was committed":* Cummings v. Missouri, 71 U.S. 277, 328 (1867).

93 *"Congress has never enacted a capitation tax":* Erik Jensen, *The Taxing Power: A Reference Guide to the United States Constitution* (Westport, CT: Greenwood, 2005), pp. 121–122.

93 *"What was the precise meaning of* direct *taxation?":* James Madison, *Notes of Debates in the Federal Convention of 1787,* ed. Adrienne Koch (New York: Norton, 1987), p. 494, http://tinyurl.com/m2dnrt.

94 *"Whether direct taxes, in the sense of the Constitution":* Hylton v. United States, 3 U.S. 171, 177 (1796).

94   *"Founders usually used the term 'direct tax'":* Calvin H. Johnson, "Apportionment of Direct Taxes: The Foul-up in the Core of the Constitution," *William and Mary Bill of Rights Journal,* 1998, p. 9, http://tinyurl.com/p5baoh.

94   *"Apportioning an income tax":* Jensen, *Taxing Power,* p. 7.

95   *"The provision was made in favor of the southern states":* Hylton v. United States, 3 U.S. 171, 177 (1796).

95   *"a glitch, or foul-up, in the core of the Constitution":* Johnson, "Apportionment of Direct Taxes," p. 3.

95   *"To illustrate the absurdity of apportionment":* Johnson, "Apportionment of Direct Taxes," p. 8.

96   *"was new in the late eighteenth century":* Jensen, *Taxing Power,* pp. 6–7.

96   *during debate on this clause:* Following quotes cited in *Founders' Constitution,* 3:366–367.

97   *"not mean that exporters are exempt":* United States v. United States Shoe Corp., 523 U.S. 360, 361–62 (1998).

97   *"To 'clear' is to obtain":* Israel Ward Andrews, *Manual of the Constitution of the United States* (Cincinnati: Van Antwerp, Bragg, 1874), p. 151.

98   *"It is a mistake to assume that Congress is forbidden":* Pennsylvania v. Wheeling & Belmont Bridge Company, 59 U.S. 421, 433–435 (1855).

98   *two delegates from Maryland:* Israel Ward Andrews, *Manual of the Constitution of the United States* (Cincinnati: Van Antwerp, Bragg, 1874), pp. 151–152.

98   *"They in a word hold the purse":* Cooke, ed., *Federalist,* p. 394.

98   *"The purse & the sword":* Cited in *Report of Congressional Committees Investigating the Iran/Contra Affair,* November 17, 1987, p. 412.

99   *"While the Boland Amendment had some ambiguities":* David Abshire and Richard Neustadt, *Saving the Reagan Presidency* (Texas A&M University Press, 2005), p. 5.

99   *"Until otherwise ordered":* Hart v. United States, 118 U.S. 62, 65 (1886).

99   *"No pardon could have had":* Ibid., p. 67.

100   *His affidavit:* The Fisher affidavit is available at www.fas.org/sgp/foia/1947/fisher.pdf.

101   *"may truly be denominated the corner stone":* Cooke, ed., *Federalist,* p. 578.

101   *the House's idea:* According to *Congressional Digest* (1922), 1:23. Available online at Google Books, http://books.google.com/books.

101   *"Would it add to his fame":* Thomas Hart Benton, *Abridgment of the Debates of Congress, from 1789 to 1856* (New York: Appleton, 1857), 1:68.

101   *"What, sir, is the intention of this business":* Ibid., p. 66.

101   *1784 letter to his daughter: Founders' Constitution,* 3:381.

102   *"When an emissary of the French Republic":* See Brian Palmer, "The Executive Gift Exchange," Slate.com, April 2, 2009.

102   *less than $335:* See the Justice Department website at www.usdoj.gov/jmd/ethics/gifte.htm.

102   *according to the relevant law:* 5 U.S. Code Section 7342; available online at www.usdoj.gov/jmd/ethics/docs/5usc7342.htm.

104   *cited by Justice Hugo Black: United States v. California,* 332 U.S. 19 (1947).

104   *"resolving Holocaust-era insurance claims": American Ins. Assn. v. Garamendi,* 539 U.S. 396 (2003).

105   *"provisions in the Constitution prohibiting the States":* From oral arguments in *Crosby v. National Foreign Trade Council,* 530 U.S. 363 (2000).

105   *Canada, Germany, Mexico, and South Korea:* For details on Wisconsin, see Brief 98-5 from the Wisconsin Legislative Reference Bureau. The brief was prepared in June 1998. Available online at http://tinyurl.com/mdf4ge.

106   *twenty-five sister-state relationships:* California State Senate website, http://tinyurl.com/n2thzr.

106   *"By the Constitution of the United States all foreign affairs":* Marty D. Matthews, *Forgotten Founder: The Life and Times of Charles Pinkney* (Columbia: University of South Carolina Press, 2004), p. 78, http://tinyurl.com/nzw28y.

106   *Pinckney warned:* Matthews, *Forgotten Founder,* p. 78; Tim Matthewson, *A Proslavery Foreign Policy: Haitian-American Relations During the Early Republic* (Westport, CT: Greenwood, 2003), p. 22, http://tinyurl.com/mgvypl.

107   *"unconstitutionally and unlawfully confederated":* Charles Sumner, *The Works of Charles Sumner* (Boston: Lee & Shepard, 1874), 6:301.

107   *"The Constitution of the United States prohibits": Williams v. Bruffy,* 96 U.S. 176 (1877).

107   *"[For states] to grant letters": Barron v. Mayor & City Council of Baltimore,* 32 U.S. 243, 249 (1833).

107   *"What is a bill of credit?":* Following quotes are from *Craig v. Missouri,* 29 U.S. 410, 431–432 (1830).

108   *"Surely, as he admitted, the state":* David P. Currie, *The Constitution in the Supreme Court: The First Hundred Years, 1789–1888* (Chicago: University of Chicago Press, 1992), p. 188, http://tinyurl.com/ovbkoe.

109   *"The extension of the prohibition to bills of credit":* Cooke, ed., *Federalist,* p. 300.

109   *"South Carolina led the van in 1703":* William L. Snyder, *Great Speeches by Great Lawyers* (New York: Baker, Voohis, 1901), p. 428.

109   *above recitation:* The case was about the constitutionality of the Legal Tender Act.

109   *"The Constitution, by prohibiting the States": Reports of the Silver Commission of 1876* (Washington, D.C.: Government Printing Office, 1887), p. 182, http://tinyurl.com/r6raz4.

109   *One such bill:* www.in.gov/legislative/bills/2009/IN/IN0453.1.html.

110   *Luther Martin told Marylanders:* Cited in *Founders' Constitution*, 3:394.

110   *"The policy of protecting contracts against impairment": Home Building & Loan Assn. v. Blaisdell,* 290 U.S. 398 (1934).

111   *"American aversion to aristocracy": Zobel v. Williams,* 457 U.S. 55, 71 (1982).

111   *Camps Newfound/Owatonna, Inc. v. Town of Harrison et al.:* 520 U.S. 564 (1997).

112   *the commerce clause:* Article I, Section 8, Clause 3.

112   *"unearthed numerous Founding era examples": Camps Newfound/Owatonna, Inc. v. Town of Harrison,* 520 U.S. 564 (1997).

113   *"protecting its people against the evils of intemperance": Bowman v. Chicago & Northwestern Ry. Co.,* 125 U.S. 465 (1888).

113   *"criminals, or pauper lunatics": People v. Compagnie Generale Transatlantique,* 107 U.S. 59 (1883).

113   *"to prevent evasion under colour":* William Rawle, *A View of the Constitution of the United States of America,* 2nd ed. (Philadelphia: Philip H. Nicklin, 1829), p. 116.

114   *"interpose, if at any time any statute": Turner v. Maryland,* 107 U.S. 38, 54 (1883).

114   *"A charge upon a vessel": Huse v. Glover,* 119 U.S. 543 (1886).

114   *"It is a tax or a duty that is prohibited": Packet Company v. Keokuk,* 95 U.S. 80, 85 (1877).

114   *Republic of Texas agreed to bow: Texas State Historical Association Quarterly* 13, July 1909 to April 1910, p. 124, http://tinyurl.com/nt3sv2.

116   *"If Massachusetts, in forwarding its exhibits": Virginia v. Tennessee,* 148 U.S. 503, 518 (1893).

116   *"In expounding the Constitution of the United States": Holmes v. Jennison,* 39 U.S. 540, 571 (1840).

117   *"shall have received certain advice":* Articles of Confederation, Article 6.

117   *"In 1812, Georgia was dissatisfied":* Henry Cabot Lodge, *The Life and Letters of George Cabot,* 2nd ed. (Cambridge: John Wilson, 1877), p. 522, http://tinyurl.com/nterxn.

118   *"An embargo, though not an act of war": Louisiana v. Texas,* 176 U.S. 1 (1900).

118 *"A considerable pause"*: Max Farrand, ed., *The Records of the Federal Convention of 1787*, rev. ed., 4 vols. (New Haven, CT: Yale University Press, 1937). Cited in *Founders' Constitution*, 3:491.

118 *"government policy would thereby be less changeable"*: Richard J. Ellis, *Founding the American Presidency* (Lanham, MD: Rowman & Littlefield, 1999), p. 32, http://tinyurl.com/lhpnxu.

119 *"If there was going to be a national executive"*: Richard Brookhiser, *Founding Father* (New York: Simon & Schuster, 1997), p. 60, http://tinyurl.com/msczy3.

119 *Alexander Hamilton noted this:* Alexander Hamilton, "Pacificus, no. 1" (1793). Cited in *Founders' Constitution*, 4:65.

120 *"I have no illusion that any decision by this Court"*: *Youngstown Sheet & Tube Co. v. Sawyer*, 343 U.S. 579, 654 (1952).

121 *"tended to destroy the great motive to good behavior"*: Farrand, ed., *Records of the Federal Convention*. Cited in *Founders' Constitution*, 3:495.

121 *"If it be essential to the preservation of liberty"*: Ibid.

121 *"considered an Executive during good behavior"*: Ibid., 3:495–496.

123 *"No one faithful to our history can deny"*: *Ray v. Blair*, 343 U.S. 214, 232 (1952).

125 *"swell, diminish, or be influenced by a candidate's victories"*: William C. Kimberling, *The Electoral College*, p. 7, www.fec.gov/pdf/eleccoll.pdf.

125 *Christian Sabbath:* Neale's Congressional Research Service report. These explanations come from the Election Assistance Commission's website: www.eac.gov/voter/faq. "Lawmakers wanted to prevent Election Day from falling on the first of November for two reasons: November 1 is All Saints Day, a holy day of obligation for Roman Catholics. In addition, most merchants were in the habit of doing their books from the preceding month on the first of the month. Congress was apparently worried that the economic success or failure of the previous month might influence the vote of the merchants."

125 *"to avoid the necessity of changing the laws"*: Mr. Duncan on December 9, 1844, House of Representatives, 28th Congress, 2nd sess.; "A Century of Lawmaking for a New Nation: U.S. Congressional Documents and Debate, 1774–1875," *Congressional Globe*, http://tinyurl.com/l2xfom.

125 *"History teaches that the electors"*: *Ray v. Blair*, 343 U.S. 214, 228–230 (1952).

126 *"the children of citizens of the United States"*: Act of March 26, 1790, 1 Stat. 104.

127 *"It's preposterous that a technicality"*: Adam Liptak, "A Hint of New Life to a McCain Birth Issue," *New York Times*, July 11, 2008.

127 *rumors that he was born in Canada:* Carl Huse, "McCain's Canal Zone Birth Prompts Queries About Whether That Rules Him Out," *New York Times*,

February 28, 2008; Michael Dobbs, "McCain's Birth Abroad Stirs Legal Debate," *Washington Post*, May 2, 2008.

127   *"It cuts off all chances for ambitious foreigners":* Story, *Commentaries*, 3:333.

128   *"seems to have felt the need of such a clause":* Corwin is quoted in Alexander Heard and Michael Nelson, *Presidential Selection* (Chapel Hill, NC: Duke University Press, 1987), p. 123.

128   *This age requirement:* Amar, *America's Constitution*, p. 161; *Documentary History of the Ratification of the Constitution* (Madison: Wisconsin Historical Society, 2003), 9:655, 679. Amar's note 79 also cites how newspapers advocated Jefferson over Adams because the former had no legitimate sons.

129   *"I have no child for whom I could wish":* Amar, *America's Constitution*, p. 162; Dorothy Twohig, ed., *The Papers of George Washington* (Charlottesville: University of Virginia Press, 1987), 2:162–163.

129   *"When a man shall get the chair": Founders' Constitution*, 3:505.

131   *"It is evident . . . that without proper attention to this article":* Cooke, ed., *Federalist*, pp. 492–493.

131   *a written opinion:* Cited in Walter Evans, *For the Independence of the Federal Judiciary Under Article Three, Section One of the Constitution of the United States* (Louisville, KY: Westerfield-Bonte, 1920), p. 17.

131   *"had enacted legislation under which the President":* Cited in *The Northwestern Reporter*, vol. 153, July 9–October 15, 1915 (St. Paul: West, 1915), p. 372.

132   *"The House committee had proposed":* Currie, *Constitution in Congress*, pp. 33–34.

132   *"The Gipper is a dipper":* This quote comes from Sid Taylor, the director of research at the NTU.

132   *asserted that the pension violated the ban:* "Constitution Is Cited as Bar to Pension for Reagan," *New York Times*, August 29, 1987.

132   *"Given that President Reagan's retirement benefits":* Robert Delahunty on the compensation clause. In Edwin Meese, Matthew Spalding, and David Forte, eds., *The Heritage Guide to the Constitution* (New York: Regnery, 2005), p. 193.

133   *"On Tuesday his inner copy editor":* Steven Pinker, "Oaf of Office," *New York Times*, January 21, 2009.

133   *"out of an abundance of caution":* Michael D. Shear, "Obama Sworn In Again, with Right Words," *Washington Post*, January 22, 2009.

133   *Coolidge retook the oath:* David Greenberg, *Calvin Coolidge* (New York: Macmillan, 2007), p. 44.

133   *President Arthur also took the oath a second time:* Robert Brent Mosher, comp., *Executive Register of the United States, 1789–1902* (Baltimore: Lord Baltimore Press, 1903), p. 240.

134 *a letter to his friend James Conkling:* The text of the letter can be found online at http://tinyurl.com/rdj9rt.

134 *"Whether the President, in fulfilling his duties":* Prize Cases, 67 U.S. 635, 670 (1862).

135 *only five times:* Ryan Hendrickson, *The Clinton Wars* (Nashville, TN: Vanderbilt University Press, 2002), p. 1.

135 *"The constitutional powers of the President":* The War Powers Act of 1973, Public Law 93-148, 93rd Congress, H. J. Res. 542, November 7, 1973.

135 *"War Powers Consultation Act":* Peter Baker, "Obama to Hear Panel on Changes to War Powers Act," *New York Times,* December 11, 2008.

136 *"Their opinion is to be given him in writing":* Founders' Constitution, 4:12.

136 *"a court in the last resort":* Melvin Urofsky and Paul Finkelman, *Documents of American Constitutional and Legal History* (New York: Oxford University Press, 2002).

137 *"A pardon is a deed to the validity":* United States v. Wilson, 32 U.S. 150, 161 (1833).

137 *Neither would talk:* "Journalists Ignore President's Pardon; Tribune Employees Decline to Tell Source of Their Information as to Grand Jury," *New York Times,* February 20, 1914.

137 *"the grace of a pardon":* Burdick v. United States, 236 U.S. 79, 90–91 (1915).

138 *"unilateral policy decisions made by politically accountable executives":* Brian C. Kalt, "Once Pardoned, Always Pardoned," *Washington Post,* January 26, 2009.

138 *"The words 'for offenses against the United States'":* Ex parte Grossman, 267 U.S. 87, 113 (1925).

139 *"It will be the office of the President to nominate":* Alexander Hamilton, "The Federalist no. 66," *Independent Journal,* March 8, 1788.

139 *"They debated it and proposed alterations":* John Quincy Adams and Charles Francis Adams, *Memoirs of John Quincy Adams* (New York: Lippincott, 1875), 6:427, http://tinyurl.com/mfw4kn.

140 *"sent Jay to London":* "Treaties," http://tinyurl.com/2yb8vz.

140 Goldwater v. Carter: 444 U.S. 996 (1979).

140 *"The Supreme Court's dismissal of the case":* John Yoo, *The Powers of War and Peace* (Chicago: University of Chicago Press, 2005), p. 190, http://tinyurl.com/nwqjuz.

140 *"If President Bush is allowed to terminate the ABM treaty":* Bruce Ackerman, "Treaties Don't Belong to Presidents Alone," *New York Times,* August 29, 2001.

141 *"Your authority in all matters touching the relations":* Edmund James Carpenter, *America in Hawaii: A History of United States Influence in the Hawaiian*

Islands (New York: Small, Maynard, 1899), p. 202, http://tinyurl.com/ko3q65.

142 *"executive agents are also useful":* Alecander DeConde, Richard Dean Burns, and Fredrik Longevall, *Encyclopedia of American Foreign Policy* (New York: Simon & Schuster, 2002), p. 38, http://tinyurl.com/nbfmev.

142 *"We're going to bork him. We're going to kill him politically":* John Fund, "The Borking Begins," *Wall Street Journal,* January 8, 2001.

142 *The nomination hearings for Thomas:* This summary is drawn from "A History of Conflict in High Court Appointments," NPR, June 6, 2005.

143 *some 30 of 145 nominations:* One count is at http://tinyurl.com/nd4jeb.

143 *"The foremost danger":* Freytag v. Commissioner, 501 U.S. 868, 904 (1991).

143 *"The person who nominates or makes appointments to offices":* Lectures on Law, *Founders' Constitution,* 4:110.

144 *"poised to undo thousands of patent decisions":* Adam Liptak, "In One Flaw, Questions on Validity of 46 Judges," *New York Times,* May 6, 2008.

145 *"felt like a hollow man":* Louis Harlan, *Booker T. Washington: The Wizard of Tuskegee* (New York: Oxford University Press, 1986), p. 22.

145 *"is not wholly consistent with the best interests":* T. J. Halstead, *Recess Appointments: A Legal Overview* (Washington, DC: Congressional Research Service, 2005), p. 20.

145 *"under unusual circumstances":* Linda Greenhouse, "Dole Suggests a Way for President to Seat Bork Before Senate Vote," *New York Times,* July 28, 1987.

145 *said he would refrain from recess appointments:* David E. Rosenbaum, "Clinton Vow to Congress Ends a Threat to His Nominations," *New York Times,* June 17, 1999.

145 *a series of thirty-second meetings:* "Senate Stays in Session to Block Bush Recess Appointments," CNN.com, November 19, 2007.

146 *State of the Union messages:* American Presidency Project, www.presidency.ucsb.edu/sou.php.

146 *"A bill was passed to complete and man three new frigates":* Samuel Eagle Forman, *Our Republic: A Brief History of the American People* (New York: Century, 1922), p. 176, http://tinyurl.com/nqaapm.

147 *"In accepting the Democratic presidential nomination":* Andrew Glass, "Truman Convenes Special Session of Congress, July 26, 1948," Politico.com, July 26, 2007.

147 *No president has exercised the adjournment power:* Edward Francis Cooke, *A Detailed Analysis of the Constitution* (Lanham, MD: Rowman & Littlefield, 2002), p. 73, http://tinyurl.com/nuwdwz.

148 *"The right of the Executive to receive ambassadors":* Alexander Hamilton, "Pacificus, no. 1" (1793). Available in *Founders' Constitution,* 4:65.

149 *"The president's proclamation, and especially Hamilton's interpretation of it":* James Roger Sharp, *American Politics in the Early Republic* (New Haven, CT: Yale University Press, 1995), pp. 75–78.

149 *"It is evident, therefore, that if the executive":* James Madison, "The Letters of Helvidius, no. III." Mr. Hamilton, Mr. Madison, and Mr. Jay, *"The Federalist," on the New Constitution* (Hallowell, ME: Glazier, Masters, & Smith, 1842), pp. 491–492, http://tinyurl.com/ljw66x; http://tinyurl.com/l8rgcw.

149 *"The Constitution, section 3, Article 2":* In re Neagle, 135 U.S. 1, 63–64 (1890).

150 *"A marshal of the United States":* 6 U.S. Op. Atty. Gen. 466 (1854). Cited in C. C. Andrews, *Digest of the Opinions of the Attorneys General of the United States* (Washington, DC: R. Farnham, 1857), p. 312.

151 *"Whoever, except in cases and under circumstances expressly authorized":* U.S. Code Title 18, Section 1385.

152 *"What, then, is an impeachable offense?":* J. Y. Smith and Lou Cannon, "Gerald R. Ford, 93, Dies; Led in Watergate's Wake," *Washington Post,* December 27, 2006.

152 *"is the right to determine actual controversies arising between adverse litigants":* Muskrat v. United States, 219 U.S. 346, 361 (1911).

152 *"Whoever attentively considers the different departments of power":* Cooke, ed., *Federalist,* pp. 522–523.

153 *more than 850 Article III judgeships:* http://tinyurl.com/ln656n; further information on the number of district judgeships can be obtained at http://tinyurl.com/kjcvke.

154 *as Madison noted: Founders' Constitution,* 3:61.

154 *"very extensive; their jurisdiction comprehends":* Founders' Constitution, 1:261. 154 *"The constitution of New-York, to avoid investigations":* Cooke, ed., *Federalist,* pp. 533–534.

155 *"The Constitution makes the same mistake":* Jeremy L. Fisher, "My Boss, Justice Stevens," *New York Times,* August 9, 2010, http://tinyurl.com/Yes-Judge.

156 *Writing in the Wall Street Journal, two law professors:* Steven G. Calabresi and James Lindgren, "Justice for Life?" *Wall Street Journal,* April 10, 2005.

156 *"Neither of America's first two chief justices":* Amar, *America's Constitution,* p. 223.

157 *"I regard an act of Congress retaining in the Treasury":* Cited in *Evans v. Gore,* 253 U.S. 245, 258 (1920).

157 *objected to a provision in the 1919 tax law:* Evans, *For the Independence of the Federal Judiciary,* p. 5.

157 *"Here, the plaintiff was paid the full compensation":* Evans v. Gore, 253 U.S. 245, 254 (1920).

157   *"To suggest that it makes inroads upon the independence of judges"*: O'Malley v.
      Woodrough, 307 U.S. 277, 282 (1939).

158   *at the age of 104: Federal Judicial History*, http://tinyurl.com/mfzz38.

158   *"As I entered my vote in the docket book"*: www.supremecourthistory.org/
      04_library/subs_volumes/04_c12_j.html; G. Edward White, *American Judi-
      cial Tradition: Profiles of Leading American Judges* (New York: Oxford Uni-
      versity Press, 1988), p. 387.

158   *salary of $217,400:* Duties of the Chief Justice, http://tinyurl.com/kv9dzp.

158   *"now reached the level of constitutional crisis"*: Chief Justice John Roberts, *2006
      Year-End Report on the Federal Judiciary*, http://tinyurl.com/n9rjcq.

159   *"In one description of cases, the jurisdiction of the Court is founded"*: Cohens v.
      Virginia, 19 U.S. 264, 393 (1821).

161   *Chief Justice Jay wrote in 1793:* Chisholm v. Georgia, 2 U.S. 419, 475 (1793).

162   *handed down an opinion in 1930:* Ohio ex Rel. Popovici v. Agler, 280 U.S. 379,
      383–384 (1930).

162   *"The judicial power of federal courts is constitutionally restricted"*: Flast v. Cohen,
      392 U.S. 83, 94–95 (1968).

164   *"had located great trees that once grew there"*: Mississippi v. Arkansas, 415 U.S.
      289, 295 (1974).

164   *"There is nothing which can be detected by the unassisted senses"*: Missouri v. Illi-
      nois, 200 U.S. 496, 517 (1906).

165   Scott v. Sandford: For further details, see Paul Finkelman, *Dred Scott v.
      Sandford: A Brief History with Documents* (New York: St. Martin's, 1997).

165   *"Can a negro, whose ancestors were imported into this country"*: Scott v. Sandford,
      60 U.S. 393, 403–406 (1856).

166   *tried for trespass and whipped:* Michael Bellesiles, *Revolutionary Outlaws:
      Ethan Allen and the Struggle for Independence on the Early American Frontier*
      (Charlottesville: University of Virginia Press, 1995), pp. 93–94.

166   *"The decision, which was the only one rendered"*: Hampton Lawrence Carson,
      The History of the Supreme Court of the United States (Philadelphia: Ziegler,
      1902), 1:70–75.

167   *Justice Henry Baldwin wrote:* Henry Baldwin, *A General View of the Origin
      and Nature of the Constitution and Government of the United States* (Philadel-
      phia: John C. Clark, 1837), p. 174.

167   *"It appears that the court of France"*: Farrand, *Fathers of the Constitution*, p. 5.

168   *The courts also objected to the fact:* See *American Historical Review*, 13: 281.
      Farrand's article is mentioned on page 58 n. 1 in William Henry Glasson,
      Federal Military Pensions in the United States (Washington, DC: Byron
      Adams, 1918), http://tinyurl.com/kuc3yz.

168 *"The most celebrated constitutional-law case":* Amar, *America's Constitution*, p. 229.

169 *William Marbury:* The facts in this paragraph derive from David Forte, "Marbury's Travail: Federalist Politics and William Marbury's Appointment as Justice of the Peace," *Catholic University Law Review,* Winter 1996, http://tinyurl.com/mw6035.

170 *"The constitution is either a superior, paramount law":* Marbury v. Madison, 5 U.S. 137, 177 (1803).

170 *"The scariest chase I ever saw since* The French Connection*":* From the oral arguments for *Scott v. Harris,* 550 U.S. ___ (2007).

170 *"entering the YouTube Era":* Adam Liptak, "Supreme Court Enters the YouTube Era," *New York Times,* March 2, 2009.

170 *"Relying on a* de novo *review of a videotape":* Scott v. Harris, 550 U.S. ___ (2007).

171 *"that divesting the Supreme Court of jurisdiction":* "Memorandum: Proposals to Divest the Supreme Court of Appellate Jurisdiction: An Analysis in Light of Recent Developments by John Roberts, Special Assistant to the Attorney General," http://tinyurl.com/meuy6b.

172 *"No court, justice, or judge shall have jurisdiction to hear":* U.S. Code, Title 28, Section 2241, http://tinyurl.com/r5rods.

172 *"an unreconstructed Mississippi newspaper editor":* "Memorandum: Proposals to Divest the Supreme Court of Appellate Jurisdiction," p. 8.

172 *"We are not at liberty to inquire into the motives":* Ex parte McCardle, 74 U.S. 506, 514 (1868).

173 *1996 Defense of Marriage Act:* www.govtrack.us/congress/billtext.xpd?bill =h110-724.

173 *"any matter that relates to the alleged establishment of religion":* www.govtrack .us/congress/billtext.xpd?bill=h110-2104.

173 *"Had Article III imposed a rigid mandate":* Amar, *America's Constitution,* p. 234.

173 *State House Speech of October 6, 1787: Founders' Constitution,* 4:392.

174 *74,226 . . . pleaded out:* www.ojp.usdoj.gov/bjs/fed.htm#Prosecution.

174 *"that the word 'jury' and the words 'trial by jury' were placed":* Thompson v. Utah, 170 U.S. 343, 350 (1898).

175 *"Lord Coke's explanation": Williams v. Florida,* 399 U.S. 78 (1970).

176 *Two editors of the* Indianapolis News*:* The story is told in John Langdon Heaton, *The Story of a Page: Thirty Years of Public Service and Public Discussion in the Editorial Columns of the New York World* (New York: Harper, 1913), pp. 263–284. Available online at http://tinyurl.com/ltq9jk.

176   *"If the history of liberty means anything"*: "Court Throws Out Canal Libel Case," *New York Times*, October 13, 1909, http://tinyurl.com/lavuss.

177   *"a trip that caused major hardship"*: Philip Shriver Klein and Ari Hoogenboom, *A History of Pennsylvania* (University Park: Penn State Press, 1973), p. 116.

177   *"may be defined to be offenses committed in the District of Columbia"*: George W. Paschal, *The Constitution of the United States Defined and Carefully Annotated* (Washington, D.C.: Morrison, 1868), p. 211.

178   *"conspicuously omitted the phrase defining as treason"*: CRS Annotated Constitution, http://tinyurl.com/mu45la.

178   *"To conspire to levy war and actually to levy war"*: *Ex parte Bollman and Swartwout*, 8 U.S. 75, 126 (1807).

179   *Tomoyo Kawakita: Kawakita v. United States*, 343 U.S. 717 (1952).

179   *"difficulties created by the Burr case have been obviated"*: CRS Annotated Constitution, http://tinyurl.com/modp9v.

179   *"Crimes so atrocious as those"*: *Ex parte Bollman and Swartwout*, 8 U.S. 75, 126–127 (1807).

180   *no more than seven years:* Excerpts of this are available in *Founders' Constitution*, 4:436.

180   *"The punishment of high treason by the common law"*: Story, *Commentaries*, 3:170.

181   *between five years in prison to death:* http://tinyurl.com/5m8bp6.

181   *"Attainder means, in its original application, the staining or corruption"*: William Whiting, *War Powers of the President, Military Arrests, and Reconstruction of the Union* (Boston: John Shorey, 1864), p. 100. The final words of his quotation here are taken from Blackstone.

181   *"It is well known, that corruption of blood, and forfeiture of the estate"*: Story, *Commentaries*, 3:170–171.

181   *"As treason may be committed against the United States"*: Cooke, ed., *Federalist*, p. 290.

182   *According to Whiting:* A copy of Lincoln's message is contained on page 408 of Whiting, *War Powers*, http://tinyurl.com/lr2aow.

183   *"The very purpose of the full-faith and credit clause"*: The quotation comes from Justice Stone's opinion in *Milwaukee County v. M. E. White Co.*, 296 U.S. 268 (1935), involving a suit by Milwaukee County against an Illinois business over unpaid taxes on income that the company earned at Wisconsin.

183   *has called the clause a detour:* Lawrence Meir Friedman, *Private Lives: Families, Individuals, and the Law* (Cambridge: Harvard University Press, 2004), pp. 36–38.

184   *"respecting a relationship between persons of the same sex":* U.S. Code, Title 28, Section 1738C.

184   *"I have long opposed governmental recognition":* President Clinton's statement on same-gender marriage, http://tinyurl.com/nvzmo6.

184   *"The Constitution delegates to the United States no power":* Laurence Tribe, "Toward a Less Perfect Union," *New York Times,* May 25, 1996.

184   *"rigid and literal interpretation of the Full Faith and Credit Clause":* Wilson v. Ake.

185   *"The inquiry is, what are the privileges and immunities of citizens":* Corfield v. Coryell, 6 Fed. Cas. 546, no. 3,230 C.C.E.D.Pa. 1823.

187   *has described the Taney memo:* Andrew Kull, *The Color-Blind Constitution* (Cambridge: Harvard University Press, 1994), chap. 1; the characterizations of prequel and dress rehearsal come from an email exchange with the author.

188   *In 1859 Willis Lago, a free black man living in Ohio:* The description of *Kentucky v. Dennison* is from Justice Thurgood Marshall's opinion in *Puerto Rico v. Branstad,* 483 U.S. 219 (1987).

188   *"Though the decision gave considerable dissatisfaction":* Charles Warren, *The Supreme Court in United States History, 1856–1918* (Beard Books, 1999), 3:89.

189   *Morgan had lived her whole life free:* Paul Finkelman, "Upholding the Fugitive Slave Law of 1793," in John Johnson, ed., *Historic U.S. Court Cases* (New York: Routledge, 2001), p. 591.

189   *testifying on their own behalf:* Fugitive Slave Act of 1850, http://tinyurl.com/nour39.

190   *"In the Sherman Booth affair the long string of failures":* Robert Cover, *Justice Accused* (New Haven, CT: Yale University Press, 1975), p. 185.

191   *"We've got a great union. There's absolutely no reason to dissolve it":* W. Gardner Selby and Jason Embry, "Perry Stands By Secession Comments," *Austin American-Statesman* website, April 17, 2009, http://tinyurl.com/c44sm7.

191   *John Breckenridge:* In more recent books his name is spelled Breckinridge.

191   *"The Constitution has made no provision":* John P. Foley, ed., *The Jefferson Cyclopedia* (New York: Funk & Wagnalls, 1900), p. 510.

191   *"The Constitution gave Congress the power to form new states":* Garry Wills, *Negro President: Jefferson and the Slave Power* (New York: Mariner, 2005), p. 119.

192   *prepared a memo:* His memo, reported by Sam Roberts for the *New York Times,* is available at http://tinyurl.com/kklawd. Panetta was erroneous in placing the relevant constitutional provision in Article III.

192   *West Virginia was created:* For the facts of West Virginia's founding, see Sheldon Winston, "Statehood for West Virginia: An Illegal Act?" *West*

Virginia History Journal 30, no. 3 (April 1969): 530–534, http://tinyurl.com/m5tl43.

192 *"It is said that the admission of West Virginia is secession":* Marion Mills Miller, ed., *Life and Works of Abraham Lincoln: Centenary Edition* (New York: Current Literature, 1907), 6:208.

192 *Joint Resolution of the Congress of Texas of June 23, 1845:* A copy of the resolution is available at http://tinyurl.com/nxnwfn.

193 *westward growth of slavery:* See Finkelman, *Dred Scott v. Sandford*, pp. 8–10.

194 *"An act of Congress which deprives a citizen":* Cited in Finkelman, *Dred Scott*, p. 40.

194 *"a territory of the United States or other place":* Cited in *Mormon Church v. United States*, 136 U.S. 1, 5 (1890).

195 *constitutionality of the Wild Free-Roaming Horses and Burros Act:* These excerpts are from the Supreme Court's decision in *Kleppe v. New Mexico*, 426 U.S. 529 (1976).

195 *civil strife in Rhode Island:* Edward Field, *State of Rhode Island and Providence Plantations at the End of the Century: A History* (Boston: Mason, 1902), 3:50.

196 *"This is the first occasion, so far as the government":* Alexander Gurdon Abell, *Life of John Tyler, President of the United States* (New York: Harper, 1843), pp. 239–240.

196 *an offer that Dorr declined:* Arthur May Mowry, *The Dorr War* (Providence: Preston & Rounds, 1901), pp. 170–180.

196 *"Under this article of the Constitution it rests with Congress":* Luther v. Borden, 48 U.S. 1, 42 (1849).

197 *"Whereas the 4th section of the Constitution":* Glenna Schroeder-Lein and Richard Zuczek, *Andrew Johnson: A Biographical Companion* (Boulder: ABC-Clio, 2001), p. 330.

198 *"Slaves, in the insurgent States":* Texas v. White, 74 U.S. 700, 727–778 (1869).

198 *"In a confederacy founded on republican principles":* Cooke, ed., *Federalist*, pp. 291–292.

198 *a 1999 hearing:* The transcript is available at http://tinyurl.com/m7dmb9.

198 *"A constitutional road to the decision":* Cooke, ed., *Federalist*, p. 339.

199 *"The plan now to be formed will certainly be defective":* Founders' Constitution, 4:576.

199 *"Congress has never approved":* Nelson Lund, Testimony before the House Judiciary Committee, Subcommittee on the Constitution, March 25, 1998. Transcript available at http://tinyurl.com/m7dmb9.

199 *"no amendments of the proper kind":* Founders' Constitution, 4:577.

199   *more than four hundred petitions:* David C. Huckabee, *Constitutional Conventions: Political and Legal Questions,* Congressional Research Service, http://tinyurl.com/klzlfl.

201   *four states . . . would later rescind:* Irwin Gertzog, *Congressional Women: Their Recruitment, Integration, and Behavior* (Westport, CT: Greenwood, 1995), p. 189.

201   *the ERA still failed to get the requisite votes:* John Vile, *Encyclopedia of Constitutional Amendments, Proposed Amendments and Amending Issues, 1789–2002* (Boulder: ABC-Clio, 2003), p. 179.

202   *"championed the cause of state rights":* Everett Somerville Brown, *Ratification of the Twenty-First Amendment to the Constitution of the United States: State Convention Records and Laws* (New Jersey: Lawbook Exchange, 2003), pp. 514–519.

203   *"never could agree to give a power": Founders' Constitution,* 4:577.

203   *"expressed his fears that three fourths":* Ibid.

204   *"Of historical interest only":* Corwin, p. 272.

204   *"was not paying the interest":* Charles Beard, *An Economic Interpretation of the Constitution of the United States* (New York: Macmillan, 1921), p. 32.

204   *"Continental paper bought at two and three shillings":* Ibid., pp. 263–264.

206   *"to execute the laws, not make them": Medellín v. Texas,* 552 U.S. ___ (2008).

206   *"The whole foundation of the State's rights": State of Missouri v. Holland,* 252 U.S. 416, 434 (1920).

206   *"The states have no power": McCulloch v. Maryland,* 17 U.S. 316 (1819).

206   *27 states were and 23 weren't:* Fox Butterfield, "Period of Confusion Expected After Ruling on Brady Law," *New York Times,* June 28, 1997.

207   *"The Federal Government may neither issue directives": Printz v. United States,* 521 U.S. 898 (1997).

208   *"There is, and can be, no dispute": Torcaso v. Watkins,* 367 U.S. 488 (1961).

211   *"restrain the rest from consulting their safety":* Preceding quotes cited in *Founders' Constitution,* 648–657.

211   *"To have required the unanimous ratification":* Cooke, ed., *Federalist,* pp. 296–297.

211   *"It is one of those cases which must be left":* Ibid., p. 298.

212   *"The members of the convention met without knowing":* Quoted in Jack Rakove, *Original Meanings* (New York: Vintage, 1997), p. 114.

212   *"Who would propose a suitable set of amendments?":* Ibid., p. 112.

213   *"Why declare that things shall not be done":* Cooke, ed., *Federalist,* p. 578.

213   *"that those who have been friendly": Founders' Constitution,* 4:480.

213   *"tangential" ways:* Andrew Kull, memo to the author, April 23, 2009.

214   *"feared, not only federal interference":* Joseph M. Snee, "Religious Disestablishment and the Fourteenth Amendment," *Washington University Law Quarterly,* 371 (December 1954).

215   *"Believing with you that religion is a matter":* Jefferson's letter can be found at http://tinyurl.com/8uox6.

215   *A posting on beliefnet.com:* http://tinyurl.com/6s2nl7.

215   *"typically had little to do with a separation of church and state":* Philip Hamburger, *Separation of Church and State* (Cambridge: Harvard University Press, 2002), p. 107.

215   *not disestablished until 1818:* A tabular summary of the disestablishment of churches in the states is available at http://en.wikipedia.org/wiki/State _religion.

216   *"entanglement with religion":* Preceding quotes are from *Lemon v. Kurtzman,* 403 U.S. 602, 612–614 (1971).

216   *"Like some ghoul in a late night horror movie":* *Lamb's Chapel v. Center Moriches Union Free School District,* 508 U.S. 384 (1993).

218   *"In our opinion, the statute immediately under consideration":* *Reynolds v. United States,* 98 U.S. 145, 166–167 (1878).

219   *"That the First Amendment speaks separately":* *Houchins v. KQED, Inc.,* 438 U.S. 1, 17 (1978).

220   *"We admit that in many places":* *Schenck v. United States,* 249 U.S. 47, 52 (1919).

221   *"a silent, passive expression of opinion," "which school disciplinary regulations are 'reasonable'":* *Tinker v. Des Moines Sch. Dist.,* 393 U.S. 503 (1969).

221   *"25 arrests":* Summary available at http://tinyurl.com/kudokh.

222   *"would not contest having printed":* Doug Linder, in *Historians on America,* U.S. State Department, p. 5, available at http://tinyurl.com/phf8ah.

222   *"The fact that for approximately one hundred and fifty years":* *Near v. Minnesota,* 283 U.S. 697 (1931).

223   *"I believe that every moment's continuance":* *New York Times Co. v. United States,* 403 U.S. 713 (1971).

224   *"rule compelling the critic of official conduct":* *New York Times Co. v. Sullivan,* 376 U.S. 254, 279–280 (1964).

226   *"Congress may not abridge the 'right to anonymous speech'":* *Citizens United v. Federal Election Commission,* 558 U.S. (January 2010).

226   *"The most alarming Process":* *Founders' Constitution,* 5:199.

226 *"'Petitioning'"* . . . *"has come to signify any nonviolent, legal means":* Adam Newton and Ronald K. L. Collins, First Amendment Center website, http://tinyurl.com/kwax5h.

227 *"Litigation may well be the sole practical avenue":* Cited in Adam Newton and Ronald K. L. Collins, First Amendment Center.

227 *"both Beauharnais and his group were making a genuine effort":* Beauharnais v. Illinois, 343 U.S. 250 (1952).

228 *a well-regulated militia* . . . *"necessary" to the security of a free state:* www.newswithviews.com/Vieira/edwin11.htm.

228 *"relic of the American Revolution":* Anne E. Kornblut, "Ashcroft Pushes New Gun Policy," *Boston Globe,* July 15, 2001, p. A1.

228 *"This declaration of rights":* Cited in *Founders' Constitution,* 5:210.

228 *"The Second Amendment is naturally divided":* District of Columbia v. Heller, 554 U.S. ___ (2008).

229 *"to pronounce the Second Amendment extinct":* Preceding quotes from *District of Columbia v. Heller,* 554 U.S. ___ (2008).

229 *"the palladium of the liberties of a republic":* Story, *Commentaries,* 3:746.

230 *"Various guarantees create zones of privacy":* Griswold v. Connecticut, 381 U.S. 479 (1965).

231 *"The billeting of soldiers upon the citizens":* St. George Tucker, *Blackstone's Commentaries: With Notes of Reference to the Constitution and Laws of the Federal Government of the United States and of the Commonwealth of Virginia,* 5 vols. (Union, NJ: Lawbook Exchange, 1996), 1:300–301.

231 *"plain object is to secure":* Story, *Commentaries,* 3:747.

231 *"willingness seriously to entertain":* Engblom v. Carey, 677 F.2d 957.

232 *"conspiracy of amazing magnitude":* Olmstead v. United States, 277 U.S. 438 (1928).

233 *"have been so eroded":* Katz v. United States, 389 U.S. 347, 353 (1967).

233 *"Despite the fact that the sniff":* United States v. Place, 462 U.S. 696, 707 (1983).

233 *"a firm line at the entrance":* Kyllo v. United States, 533 U.S. 27 (2001).

234 *"The grand jury may consist of any number":* Story, Commentaries, 3:657–658.

235 *"While, to many people's way of thinking":* Bruce T. Olson, preface to *The Grand Jury,* by George J. Edwards (New York: AMS Press, 1973).

235 *"Any prosecutor who wanted to, could indict a ham sandwich":* Sol Wachtler, *After the Madness* (eReads.com, 2003), p. 254.

236 *"We have here two sovereignties":* United States v. Lanza, 260 U.S. 377, 382 (1922).

237   *one of the most famous Supreme Court Cases of all time:* Miranda v. Arizona, 384 U.S. 436 (1966).

238   *1354 statutory reconfirmation:* Text available online at http://tinyurl.com/n6qgmt.

238   *"The use of the words 'due process'":* Bernard H. Siegan, Property Rights: From Magna Carta to the Fourteenth Amendment (New Brunswick, NJ: Transaction, 2001), pp. 105–107.

238   *"And an act of Congress which deprives":* Scott v. Sandford, 60 U.S. 393, 403–406 (1856).

239   *"Of course, the plaintiff's position":* Moyer v. Peabody, 212 U.S. 78, 84–85 (2001).

239   *"In all" . . . "the nine petitioners own 15 properties":* Kelo v. City of New London, 545 U.S. 469 (2005).

241   *the center of a famous case:* Penn Central Transportation Co. v. New York City, 438 U.S. 104 (1978).

241   *"the perceived social and economic evils":* Hawaii Housing Auth. v. Midkiff, 467 U.S. 229 (1984).

241   *twenty-five states:* Jonathan V. Last, "The Kelo Backlash," Weekly Standard, August 21, 2006, http://tinyurl.com/ktcz58.

243   *"Then call them to our presence":* Coy v. Iowa, 487 U.S. 1012, 1016 (1988).

243   *upheld a Maryland conviction:* Maryland v. Craig, 497 U.S. 836 (1990).

243   *the following colloquy:* Gideon v. Wainwright, 372 U.S. 335 (1963).

243   *"that, in the great majority of the States":* Betts v. Brady, 316 U.S. 455, 471 (1942).

244   *Gideon . . . was found to have been not guilty:* For the classic account of Gideon v. Wainwright, see Anthony Lewis, Gideon's Trumpet (New York: Random House, 1964).

245   *$1 million to friends and family:* CBSNews.com, "Madoff to Remain Free on Bail in Penthouse," January 12, 2009.

245   *Judiciary Act of 1789:* A copy of the law can be found at http://tinyurl.com/ko736w.

245   *"federal law has unequivocally provided":* Stack v. Boyle, 342 U.S. 1, 4 (1951).

246   *"evolving standards of decency":* Kennedy v. Louisiana, 544 U.S. _____ (2008).

247   *"I am voting against the petition":* Kennedy v. Louisiana, on Petition for Rehearing (2008).

248   *"The great residuum":* Gailland Hunt, ed., The Writings of James Madison (New York: G. P. Putnam's Sons, 1904), 5:383.

248   *"some specific constitutional provision":* Preceding quotes from Griswold v. Connecticut, 381 U.S. 479 (1965).

249 *"mostly a source of intermittent curiosity":* Russell L. Caplan, "The History and Meaning of the Ninth Amendment," 69 *Virginia Law Review* 223–225, as quoted by Kyle Alexander Casazza, "Inkblots: How the Ninth Amendment and the Privileges or Immunities Clause Protect Unenumerated Constitutional Rights," 80 *S. Cal. L. Rev.* 1983.

249 *"This right of privacy, whether it be founded":* Roe v. Wade, 410 U.S. 113 (1973).

249 *"an amendment that says 'Congress shall make no'":* Cited in Casazza, "Inkblots." Available online at http://tinyurl.com/nu4t42.

250 *"added nothing to the instrument as originally ratified":* United States v. Sprague, 282 U.S. 716, 733 (1931).

250 *"but a truism":* United States v. Darby, 312 U.S. 100, 124 (1941).

250 *"States are not mere political subdivisions":* New York v. United States, 488 U.S. 1041 (1992).

251 *"The power of the Federal Government":* Printz v. United States, 521 U.S. 898 (1997).

251 *"far from being prepared to say":* Chisholm v. Georgia, 2 U.S. 475 (1793).

254 *"failed to demonstrate a specific":* Jones v. Bush, 122 F. Supp. 2d 713 (N.D. Tex. 2000).

254 *"changed the fundamental structure":* Alexander Tsesis, *The Thirteenth Amendment and American Freedom: A Legal History* (New York: NYU Press, 2004), p. 2, http://tinyurl.com/lhp5n7.

255 *"did not outright disagree with Sumner's perspective":* Ibid., p. 47.

255 *"It is true that slavery cannot exist without law":* Civil Rights Cases, 109 U.S. 3 (1883).

256 *"authorized Congress to do more than merely dissolve":* Jones v. Alfred H. Mayer Co., 392 U.S. 409 (1968).

256 *until 1995:* James Edward Bond, *No Easy Walk to Freedom: Reconstruction and the Ratification of the Fourteenth Amendment* (Westport, CT: Greenwood, 1997), p. 47, http://tinyurl.com/n2ex49.

256 *"distrust of the will and capacity of the Supreme Court":* Jack Rakove, ed., *The Annotated U.S. Constitution and Declaration of Independence* (Cambridge: Belknap Press/Harvard University Press, 2009). Cited in Adam Liptak, "More Perfect," *New York Times,* January 8, 2010.

257 *"No questions so far-reaching and pervading":* Slaughterhouse Cases, 83 U.S. 36, 67 (1872).

258 *"whether an Indian":* Elk v. Wilkins, 112 U.S. 94 (1884).

259 *"shut down the fight for the rights of Indians":* Valerie Sherer Mathes and Richard Lowitt, *The Standing Bear Controversy* (Champaign-Urbana: University of Illinois Press, 2003), p. 169.

259 *the Supreme Court has demurred:* The complexity and subtlety of the incorporation process can be glimpsed in a chart of the process as it relates to just the elements of the First Amendment. It is published online by Professor Adam Samaha and the University of Minnesota Law School and can be found at http://tinyurl.com/mv6yzc.

259 *"This right of privacy, whether it be founded":* Roe v. Wade, 410 U.S. 113, 153 (1973).

260 *"Constitutional protection of the woman's decision":* Planned Parenthood v. Casey, 505 U.S. 833 (1992).

260 *"To reach its result, the Court necessarily has had to find":* Roe v. Wade, 410 U.S. 113, 153 (1973).

261 *"The general right to make a contract":* Lochner v. New York, 198 U.S. 45, 53 (1905).

262 *"We think the enforced separation of the races":* Plessy v. Ferguson, 163 U.S. 537, 548 (1896).

262 *"The plaintiffs contend that segregated public schools":* Brown v. Board of Education of Topeka, 347 U.S. 483, 488–495 (1954).

263 *"In my view, there is no basis for a right":* Grutter v. Bollinger, 539 U.S. 306 (2003).

264 *"We think that this contention presents a question":* Saunders v. Wilkins, http://tinyurl.com/m43x2l.

265 *"to barter our birthright":* Joseph Bliss James, *The Ratification of the Fourteenth Amendment* (Atlanta, GA: Mercer University Press, 1984). p. 59, http://tinyurl.com/lh3y2m.

265 *"singled out for punishment":* "Restoration of Citizenship Rights to Jefferson F. Davis Statement on Signing S. J. Res. 16 into Law," October 17, 1978. John T. Woolley and Gerhard Peters, American Presidency Project, americanpresidency.org.

265 *"slavery having been recognized as lawful":* Osborn v. Nicholson, 80 U.S. 654, 654–655 (1871).

266 *the Court asserted the supremacy of its own authority over that of the Congress:* 521 U.S. 507 (1997).

267 *"out of politics and reconstruction completed":* Xi Wang, *The Trial of Democracy: Black Suffrage and Northern Republicans, 1860–1910* (Athens: University of Georgia Press, 1997), p. 52, http://tinyurl.com/nbyv8a.

267 *"a measure of grander importance":* George Washington Williams, *History of the Negro Race in America from 1619 to 1880* (New York: Putnam's, 1883), p. 420, http://tinyurl.com/n97paa.

267 *"the period between 1867 and the early 1870s":* Richard Zuczek, *Encyclopedia of the Reconstruction Era: A–L* (Westport, CT: Greenwood, 2006), p. 83, http://tinyurl.com/mp7pen.

268   *"The language and purpose of the Fifteenth Amendment":* South Carolina v. Katzenbach, 383 U.S. 301, 324–337 (1966).

269   *"put most of the taxable wealth":* Corwin, *Constitution,* p. 26.

269   *"in imposing a tax on the income or rents":* Pollock v. Farmers' Loan & Trust Co., 157 U.S. 429 (1895).

272   *determined the legislatures' choices:* Summary drawn from "Direct Election of Senators," http://tinyurl.com/6qvxh.

272   *"has become to this generation of leaders":* http://tinyurl.com/mdxe9q.

272   *"a truth that no senator except a retiring one would dare say":* Bruce Bartlett, "Repeal the 17 Amendment," National Review Online, May 12, 2004, http://tinyurl.com/lkugja.

272   *joint resolution submitted to the Montana house and senate:* Text of the resolution is available at http://tinyurl.com/mvttjx.

274   *Burris has denied any wrongdoing:* http://tinyurl.com/mlmoz9.

274   *"thus far and in general, followed":* Doug Kendall and Hannah McCrea, "Drinking to the Progressive Constitution," Huffington Post, December 5, 2008, http://tinyurl.com/5mmpev.

275   *"with the same spirit that kept her out of the Union":* "Rhode Island's Single Handed Fight for Liquor," *New York Times,* January 25, 1920.

275   *the* National Prohibition Cases: 253 U.S. 350 (1920).

275   *"invaded the sovereignty of Rhode Island":* David E. Kyvig, *Repealing National Prohibition* (Kent, OH: Kent State University Press, 2000), pp. 17–18.

276   *"male inhabitants" over the age of twenty-one:* Amendment 14, Section 2.

276   *"From the outset of the Revolutionary War":* D. Grier Stephenson, *The Right to Vote: Rights and Liberties Under the Law* (Boulder: ABC-Clio, 2004), pp. 117–118, http://tinyurl.com/koymkt.

276   *same one that had been introduced in 1878:* "The Constitution: The 19th Amendment." National Archives and Records Administration, http://tinyurl.com/5vjqsy.

277   *politically palatable to lawmakers:* Stephenson, *Right to Vote,* pp. 174–177.

277   *five minutes into his presidency:* www.msnbc.msn.com/id/28753348.

279   *"If it should happen that in a general election":* Excerpts of the Judiciary Committee report are at www.gpoaccess.gov/constitution/html/amdt20.html.

280   *"What the plaintiffs complain of is the refusal":* State Board of Equalization v. Young's Market Co., 299 U.S. 59, 62 (1936).

281   *"The tax exemption is not saved":* Bacchus Imports, Ltd. v. Dias, 468 U.S. 263, 264 (1984).

281   *"invalidated by the spending power limitation":* South Dakota v. Dole, 483 U.S. 203, 203–204 (1987).

282 *rendering them more conservative:* James A. Morone, *Hellfire Nation: The Politics of Sin in American History* (New Haven: Yale University Press, 2004), p. 342.

282 *"It is obvious that the only method":* Brown, *Ratification of the Twenty-First Amendment,* p. 4.

283 *despite the near certainty that he would be reelected:* Ethan M. Fishman, William D. Pederson, and Mark J. Rozell, *George Washington: Foundation of Presidential Leadership and Character* (Westport, CT: Greenwood, 2001), p. 73, http://tinyurl.com/ltyec7.

283 *"second termitis":* This and subsequent quotes from James MacGregor Burns and Susan Dunn, "No More Second-Term Blues," *New York Times,* January 5, 2006.

283 *"Nothing appears more plausible at first sight":* Alexander Hamilton, *"The Federalist no. 72," Independent Journal,* March 19, 1788.

284 *"shall be composed of Members":* Article I, Section 2, Clause 1

285 *District clause of the Constitution*: Article 1, Section 8, Clause 17.

285 *"While the existing practice of allowing":* Kenneth R. Thomas, "The Constitutionality of Awarding the Delegate for the District of Columbia a Vote in the House of Representatives or the Committee of the Whole," p. 9.

285 *just sixteen states:* Stephenson, *Right to Vote,* p. 294.

286 *"to make payment of poll taxes a prerequisite":* Breedlove v. Suttles, 302 U.S. 277, 283 (1937).

286 *only five states . . . were employing a poll tax:* Time, "The 24th Amendment," January 31, 1964, http://tinyurl.com/l5mch7.

287 *the Supreme Court . . . ruled that poll taxes:* Harper v. Virginia Bd. of Elections, 383 U. S. 663 (1966).

287 *"under Harper, even rational restrictions":* Crawford et al. v. Marion County Election Board et al., no. 07-21 (2008).

287 *"Americans have long fought hard":* Bruce Ackerman and Jennifer Nou, "Hey, What About the 24th?" Slate.com, May 2, 2008.

289 *"Constitutionally, gentlemen, you have the President":* John D. Feerick, *The Twenty-Fifth Amendment* (New York: Fordham University Press, 1992), pp. xii–xiii.

290 *should have waited at least a day:* "Committee Offers Rules for the Transfer of Presidential Power," *New York Times,* December 4, 1996.

290 *"Never had a constitutional amendment":* Jody C. Baumgartner and Peter L. Francia, *Conventional Wisdom and American Elections: Exploding Myths, Exploring Misconceptions* (Lanham, MD: Rowman & Littlefield, 2007), p. 5.

291 *1954 State of the Union:* Available at http://www.vlib.us/amdocs/texts/dde1954.htm.

291 *"strongly favored the 18 year old vote":* Thomas H. Neal, *The Eighteen Year Old Vote: the Twenty-Sixth Amendment and Subsequent Voting Rates of Newly Enfranchised Age Groups,* Congressional Research Service (1983), Northern Kentucky University Library, 16.

291 *"the States have the power to set qualifications":* Oregon v. Mitchell, 400 U.S. 112 (1970).

291 *least likely to exercise their right to vote:* Pam Beluck, "Sixteen Candles, but Few Blazing a Trail to the Ballot Box," *New York Times,* August 26, 2007.

291 *"enfranchised sixteen- and seventeen-year-olds":* Michael S. Cummings, *Beyond Political Correctness: Social Transformation in the United States* (Boulder: Lynne Rienner, 2001), p. 188, http://tinyurl.com/llnmp4.

292 *the amendment came back ratified:* Dennis Roddy, "The Constitution's 27 Amendments: The Ways We Embrace Their Spirit Every Day," *Pittsburgh Post-Gazette,* November 27, 2002, http://tinyurl.com/m9co2f.

293 *"The Congress, in controlling the promulgation":* Coleman v. Miller, 307 U.S. 433, 434 (1939).

293 *regardless of Congress's opinion:* Congressional Pay Amendment, www.usdoj .gov/olc/congress.17.htm.

293 *"The pay-raise amendment's long delay":* Richard L. Berke, "Congress Backs 27th Amendment," *New York Times,* May 21, 1992.

293 *"But among the lawmakers, at least, those questions":* Richard L. Berke, "More Amendments Lurk in the Mists of History," *New York Times,* May 24, 1992.

Acknowledgments

This book grew out of work over more than forty years on five news-papers—the *Anniston Star, Pacific Stars and Stripes*, the *Wall Street Journal*, the *Forward*, and the *New York Sun*—and I am grateful to many colleagues who, in the course of thousands of editorial meet-ings, helped me think through the news in countless conversations that, in one way or another, touched on the Constitution. Ira Stoll, the managing editor of the *Sun*, was a brilliant partner in crafting an editorial stance that gave deference to the Constitution. I am grate-ful, as well, to myriad news sources—lawyers, plaintiffs, defendants, academics, government offcials, business men and women, and labor leaders—who took the time to educate a newspaperman who was al-most always on deadline.

Joseph Goldstein, formerly the court reporter of the *New York Sun*, was chief researcher of *The Citizen's Constitution*. He was joined in that work by two other former staff members of the paper, Ross Goldberg, a reporter, and Gary Shapiro, a lawyer and longtime associ-ate editor of the newspaper. They provided me memoranda on nearly every clause of the Constitution. Additional research and fact check-ing was done by Keith Staskiewicz. John Seeley, a former deputy managing editor of the *Sun*, read the manuscript for style. Without their collective effort this book would not have been possible.

Financial support for the research effort was provided by Roger and Susan Hertog and, via the Hudson Institute, by the Robert and Ardis James Foundation and is gratefully acknowledged.

All or portions of the manuscript were read by a number of indi-viduals: Andrew Kull, professor of law at Boston University and au-thor of *The Color-Blind Constitution*; Jack Fuller, who, after serving as special assistant to Attorney General Edward Levi, made his career as a journalist and was editor of *Chicago Tribune*; Michael Rips, a former clerk to Justice William Brennan who went on to practice law and to write, including for the *New York Sun*; Robert D. Goldstein, professor of law at the University of California–Los Angeles; Philip Hamburger, professor of law at Columbia University and author of *Separation of Church and State*; and Aziz Huq, a former clerk to Justice Ruth Bader Ginsberg and assistant professor of law at the University of Chicago. Each made a number of valuable suggestions, which I very much appreciate, though the opinions and any errors herein are my own.

My own enthusiasm for the Constitution has been stoked over the years by a number of friends. They did not participate in the production of this book. But they inspired me a great deal more than I might have mentioned to them along the way. They include Judge Jose Cabranes of the 2nd United States Circuit Court of Appeals; Judge Robert D. Sack, who, when he was counsel to Dow Jones & Company, gave me and many other of its editors a minicourse in First Amendment law and is now on the 2nd United States Circuit; Bernard Nussbaum, a former White House counsel; and Robert Morgenthau, the district attorney of New York County.

May I also express my appreciation of four individuals now deceased: Herbert Prashker, who was a former clerk to Justice Harlan Stone and over many dinners shared his love of the law; Charles Morgan, the great civil rights lawyer who welcomed me to his office in Atlanta; Robert L. Bartley, the editor of the *Wall Street Journal* who brought me onto its editorial board; and the chief judge of the United States District Court for the Middle District of Alabama, Frank Johnson, who, when I was a young newspaperman, received me in his chambers, shared some of his Home Run brand cigarettes, and gave me an early appreciation of the Constitution as a road to freedom.

Finally, I thank my wife and friend, Amity Shlaes, who taught me, among many other things, what a joy writing a book can be and who gave me, in addition to all else, our four children, Eli, Theo, Flora, and Helen. There have been no happier hours in my study—or anywhere else in my life—than the ones when they have stopped by.

INDEX